ISBN 978-1-331-90779-4
PIBN 10252517

This book is a reproduction of an important historical work. Forgotten Books uses state-of-the-art technology to digitally reconstruct the work, preserving the original format whilst repairing imperfections present in the aged copy. In rare cases, an imperfection in the original, such as a blemish or missing page, may be replicated in our edition. We do, however, repair the vast majority of imperfections successfully; any imperfections that remain are intentionally left to preserve the state of such historical works.

1 MONTH OF
FREE
READING

at

www.ForgottenBooks.com

By purchasing this book you are eligible for one month membership to ForgottenBooks.com, giving you unlimited access to our entire collection of over 700,000 titles via our web site and mobile apps.

To claim your free month visit:

www.forgottenbooks.com/free252517

Similar Books Are Available from
www.forgottenbooks.com

A

MEMORANDUM OF EXTRACTS

FROM

PAPERS ON THE PERMANENT SETTLEMENT OF BENGAL.

Printed under the superintendence of a Sub-Committee of the British Indian Association to take into consideration and report on the proposed Income Tax.

CALCUTTA:

PRINTED BY C. H. MANUEL, CALCUTTA PRINTING AND PUBLISHING COMPANY (LIMITED) NO. 1, WESTON'S LANE, COSSITOLLAH.

1860.

THE Revenue levied upon the zemindar under the Mahomedan rule was "a tax upon the rent of land." The British Government have also regarded it as such, as the discussions contained in the Land Revenue Papers, both ante-and-post Settlement Papers, abundantly testify. In fact, it could not be otherwise, inasmuch as nine-tenths of the gross rental constituted the revenue to the State, which was equivalent to a tax of 90 per cent. on the income of the landholders. This tax has been pronounced repeatedly to be exorbitant, so much so that strong doubts were entertained at the time of the Settlement as to the zemindars being able to bear this heavy burden. Mr. Shore in a minute, dated the 21st December 1789, wrote :—

4. " It will, I believe, be admitted that equality in taxation is of great importance ; and, in justice, all the subjects of a State should contribute, as nearly as possible, in proportion to the income which they enjoy under its protection. On the other hand, it is allowed that a considerable degree of inequality is a less evil than a very great degree of uncertainty ; and that annual assessments of the land tax give rise to more inconveniences than they pretend to rectify.

5. " That the contributions of the zemindars are disproportioned to their respective incomes, we know with certainty ; we also profess to take from them nine-tenths of their receipts. The proportion paid by the cultivators of the soil may be reckoned at a half, or it may be nearer, perhaps, to three-fifths of the gross produce. Taking this at 100 parts, the claims of Government may be estimated at 45. The zemindars and under-renters may be supposed to have 15, and 40 remains with the cultivators of the soil. In the two last classes, some enjoy considerably more than the assigned proportion ; others, again, less."

Lord Cornwallis, admitting the fact of the exorbitant valuation, maintained that the permanency of the settlement will induce immovements which will greatly indemnify the landholders for the heavy amount of assessment :—

" Mr. Shore observes, that we profess to take from the zemindars nine-tenths of their receipts ; and, under these circumstances, allowing for the common variations in the state of society, in the improvement, and in the decline of agriculture, and admitting the probable alterations in the value of silver, it is certain that the constancy of the assessment may be of great inconvenience, and even ruinous to many of the contributors ; and, in this case, that there will be a necessity of some future alteration, which must always take place to the disadvantage of Government, if the assessment be now declared fixed for ever.

" Were there any grounds for supposing that a system which secures to the landholder the possession of his lands, and the profits arising from the improvement of them will occasion a decline in agriculture, then might we apprehend that a permanent assessment would, in progress of time, bear hard upon the contributors ; but reason and experience justify the contrary supposition : in which case, a fixed assessment must be favourable to the con-tributors, because their resources will gradually increase, whereas the demand of Government will continue the same."—*Minute of Lord Cornwallis, dated February 3rd, 1790.*

Again :

" But let us suppose that hereafter it should be found necessary to grant remissions in districts which may suffer from drought or inundation, this is no argument against a permanent assessment ; for, under the present system of variable assessment, we are frequently obliged to grant considerable deduc-tions on these accounts, and there is no prospect of our being able to dis-continue them, so long as the country is assessed at its full value, and no more is left to the landholder than is barely sufficient for his subsistence, and for defraying the charges of collecting the rents from his lands.

" There is this further advantage to be expected from a fixed assessment, in a country subject to drought and inundation, that it affords a strong inducement to the landholder to exert himself to repair as speedily as possi-ble the damages which his lands may have sustained from these calamities ;

for it is to be expected that when the public demand upon his lands is limited to a specific sum, he will employ every means in his power to render them capable of again paying that sum, and as large a surplus as possible for his own use. His ability to raise money to make these exertions will be proportionably increased by the additional value which the limitation of the public demand will stamp upon his landed property : the reverse of this is to be expected when the public assessment is subject to unlimited increase.

" I am of opinion, therefore, that there is no reason to apprehend a greater deficiency in the public revenues from drought and inundation, when the assessment is fixed, than we have hitherto sustained under the system of variable assessments ; on the contrary, that we have very sufficient grounds for supposing that the necessity for granting remissions on these accounts will become gradually less. It further appears to me, that the practice of heaping up the public revenue, by charging occasionally the improved estate of one landholder with deficiencies in the public revenue assessed upon the land of his neighbour, is both unjust and impolitic ; and that, until this practice is discontinued, both the landholders and their under-tenants and ryots will in general remain in a state of impoverishment, and that landed property will continue at its present depreciated value."

        *   *   *

" Now, if Mr. Shore's calculation of the proportion which the zemindars in general receive of the produce of their lands be accurate, it is obvious that every temporary loss must fall upon Government ; for so long as we profess to leave the zemindars no more than that proportion, and claim a right to appropriate the excess to the public use, from what funds are they to make these losses good ? But when the demand of Government is fixed, an opportunity is afforded to the landholder of increasing his profits, by the improvement of his lands ; and we may reasonably expect that he will provide for occasional losses, from the profits of favourable seasons."—*Ibid.*

Such being the nature of the tax levied upon the land, every care was taken to inspire confidence in the landholders that the tax then imposed would never be enhanced for any State exigencies whatever, and that they would never be called upon to pay any additional tax on account of the land under any circumstances, however emergent the necessities of the State may be. Mr. Law, the Collector of Shahabad, having pointed out the desirableness or good policy of an exceptional provision for extraordinary levies for extraordinary occasions, such as war, following the English precedent in such cases, Mr. Shore held that not only would such a clause be nugatory of the principle of the proposed Settlement, but that it would be extremely pernicious and arbitrary, inasmuch as "the land tax in England did not bear a proportion of nine-tenths to the income of the proprietor" as was proposed for Bengal. He thus wrote :—

" 29. But the perpetuity of assessment is qualified by Mr. Law, by the intro-duction of a clause, that the proprietors of mookururee tenures shall be subject to a proportion of a general addition, when required by the exigencies of Government. This qualification is, in fact, a subversion of the fundamental principle ; for, the exigencies not being defined, a Government may interpret the conditions according to its own sense of them ; and the same reasons which suggest an addition to the assessment, may perpetuate the enhance-ment. The explanation given by Mr. Law to this objection is, that temporary extraordinaries must have temporary resources, and even the land at home is liable to a general tax during war ; but the land tax in England does not bear a proportion of nine-tenths to the income of the proprietor.

" 30. Notwithstanding the explanation, I shall consider the qualifying clause as either nugatory or pernicious, and as standing in direct contradic-tion to the principle of a mookururee settlement. The very term implies an unalterable assessment ; and, if the explanation be founded on necessity, it is decisive against the perpetuity of it.

" 31. It is certainly a question of some curiosity, as well as of importance, to inquire what ideas the people themselves entertain of this clause, in a deed which professes to confer upon them estates subject to a fixed land tax. Is it possi-ble to conceive that they understand the consequences of it, and their extent ? The Zemindars of Bengal would reason very accurately upon them, and con-clude that the proposal to fix the assessment upon their estates unalterably, and, at the same time, to connect that proposal with a clause authorising enhancement at the discretion of the Government, was irreconcileable in its terms, and they would probably indulge suspicions unfavourable to the in-tentions of the Government. Is it unfair to conclude, that a reliance upon the personal qualities of Mr. Law, his honour, his probity, and his zeal, so successfully displayed to the advantage of the Company, and for the happiness of those placed under his authority, has disarmed suspicion, and gained consent to a proposition which has never been well considered or understood? Let this be as it may, I deem the proposition of mookururee settlement, subject to an increase upon exigency, a solecism ; and that permanency must be given up, or the clause be withdrawn."—*Minute of Mr. Shore, dated December 8th, 1789.*

In the same spirit is the announcement in Regulation I. of 1793 :—

" VI. ART. V.—In the event of the proprietary right in lands that are, or may become, the property of Government, being transferred to individuals, such individuals, and their heirs, and lawful successors shall be permitted to hold the lands at the assessment at which they may be transferred for ever.

" VII. ART. VI.—It is well known to the *zemindars*, independent *talookdars*, and other actual proprietors of land, as well as to the inhabitants of Bengal, Behar, and Orissa in general, that from the earliest times, until the present period, the public assessment upon the lands has never been fixed, but that, according to established usage and custom, the rulers of these provinces have, from time to time, demanded an increase of assessment from the proprietors of land ; and that, for the purpose of obtaining this increase, not only frequent investigations have been made to ascertain the actual produce of their estates, but that it has been the practice to deprive them of the management of their lands, and either to let them in farm, or to appoint Officers on the part of Government to collect the assessment immediately from the *ryots*. The Honourable Corut of Directors, considering these usages and measures to be detrimental to the prosperity of the country, have, with a view to promote the future ease and happiness of the people, authorised the foregoing declarations ; and the *zemindars*, independent *talookdars*, and other actual proprietors of land, with or on behalf of whom a settlement has been, or may be, concluded, are to consider these orders, fixing the amount of the assessment, as irrevocable, and not liable to alteration by any persons whom the.Court of Directors may hereafter appoint to the administration of their affairs in this country.

" The Governor General in Council trusts that the proprietors of land, sensible of the benefits conferred upon them by the public assessment being fixed for ever, will exert themselves in the cultivation of their lands, under the certainty that they will enjoy exclusively the fruits of their own good management and industry, and that no demand will ever be made upon them, or their heirs, or successors, by the present, or any future Government, for an augmentation of the public assessment, in consequence of the improvement of their respective estates."—*Regulation I. of* 1793.

The Land was considered as heavily taxed as it could possibly be, and with a view to provide against future contingencies, it was declared that any future augmentation to the resources of the State was to be looked for in the imposition of duties on commerce, and not in the enhancement of the land-tax ·—

" Although Government has an undoubted right to collect a portion of the produce of the lands to supply the public exigencies, it cannot, consistent with the principles of justice and policy, assume to itself a right of making annual or periodical valuations of the lands, and taking the whole produce, except such portion as it may think proper to relinquish to the proprietors for their maintenance, and for defraying the charges of managing their estates.

" The supreme power in every State must possess the right of taxing the subjects, agreeably to certain general rules ; but the practice which has prevailed in this country for some time past, of making frequent valuations of the lands, and where one person's estate has improved, and another's declined, of appropriating the increased produce of the former to supply the deficiencies in the latter, is not taxation, but in fact a declaration that the property of ' the landholder is at the absolute disposal of Government. Every man who is acquainted with the causes which operate to impoverish or enrich a country, must be sensible that our Indian territories must continue to decline as long as the practice is adhered to.

" The maxim, that equality in taxation is an object of the greatest importance, and that, in justice, all the subjects of a State should contribute, as nearly as possible, in proportion to the income which they enjoy under its protection, does not prove the expediency of varying the demand of Government upon the lands ; on the contrary, we shall find that, in countries in which this maxim is one of the leading principles in the imposition of taxes, the valuation of the land on which they are levied is never varied.

" In raising a revenue to answer the public exigencies, we ought to be careful to interfere as little as possible in those sources from which the wealth of the subject is derived.

" Agriculture is the principal source of the riches of Bengal ; the cultivator of the soil furnishes most of the materials for its numerous manufactures. In proportion as agriculture declines, the quantities of these materials must diminish, and the value of them increase, and consequently the manufactures must become dearer, and demand for them be gradually lessened. Improvement in agriculture will produce the opposite effects.

" The attention of Government ought therefore to be directed to render the assessment upon the lands as little burdensome as possible : this is to be accomplished only by fixing it. The proprietor will then have some inducement to improve his lands ; and as his profits will increase in proportion to his exertions, he will gradually become better able to discharge the public revenue.

" By reserving the collection of the internal duties on commerce, Government may at all times appropriate to itself a share of the accumulating wealth of its subjects, without their being sensible of it. The burden will also be more equally distributed ; at present, the whole weight rests upon the landholders and cultivators of the soil.

" Whereas the merchants and inhabitants of the cities and towns, the proprietors of rent-free lands, and, in general, all persons not employed in the cultivation of the lands, paying revenue to Government, contribute but little in proportion to their means, to the exigencies of the State. It is evident, therefore, that varying the assessment on the lands is not the mode of carrying into practice the maxim, that all the subjects of a State ought to contribute to the public exigencies in proportion to their incomes ; and that other means must be employed for effecting this object."—*Minute by Lord Cornwallis, dated February* 3rd, 1790.

To the same import is the following, which occurs in the Government letter to the Court of Directors, dated the 6th March 1793 :—

" If at any future period the public exigencies should require an addition to your resources, you must look for it in the increase of the general wealth and commerce of the country, and not in the augmentation of the tax upon the land, &c., &c."—*Letter of the Governor-General in Council to the Court of Directors, dated March 6th,* 1793.

As a step to that direction the Board of Revenue, in considering the practicability and limits of the Settlement, recommended in one of their Resolutions, the propriety of the Government resuming the right of levying sayer collections and internal duties on commerce, hitherto exclusively invested in the zemindars. Such a clause was, however, held as an invasion on the proprietary rights of the zemindars by Mr. Shore, who thus remarked :—

Resolution IV.—"That the gunges, bazaars, hauts, and other sayer collections be not included in any settlement with any zemindar, but that for the present they remain under the exclusive jurisdiction of an officer appointed by the collector, who is to propose such regulations as he may think best calculated for regulating and collecting the duties.

" Amongst the objections urged to this proposition, I find one only stated against it, as an invasion of the zemindaree rights ; and this is very pointedly made by the acting collector of Bhaugulpore, who observes that, on asking the sentiments of a zemindar upon the separation proposed, he replied with sullen emphasis, that " *Government, if it pleased, might take from him his whole zemindaree.*"

" If the same objection existed in the other parts of Behar, I conclude it would have been stated. The reason why it is not, may possibly be this, that the system of management adopted in Behar for so many years, having been calculated to destroy all ideas of right in the proprietors of the soil, beyond their admitted claims to a tithe of their proprietary rights, they consider all besides this at the discretion of Government ; whereas in Bhaugulpore the management has partaken more of the nature of that established in Bengal, and the zemindars will urge their claims with a confidence proportioned to it.

"If this were not the case, I should conclude that the principle recom-mended ought to be extended to the gunges and sayer held and collected by the proprietors and tenants of the altumgha and jaghire lands; for, as right is concerned, I see no reason why that of the zemindars should be invaded, whilst men of another description are left unmolested; nor, if public utility only be consulted, why the inconvenience resulting from variable rates in one instance, and the number of managers, should not operate equally to prove the neces-sity of a reform in another, and the propriety of undertaking it.

"In Bengal, I conceive, most of the zemindars would argue in the manner pointed out by the acting collector of Bhaugulpore; nor do I think the observation of the Board of Revenue a sufficient reply to it: that con-sidering the actual practice of the Government they were subject to, long before the administration of their present rulers, the adoption of the set-tlement would leave them no ground of complaint; and that in general, they would agree to relinquish the sayer collections, to obtain a perma-nent assessment of their lands, is a doubtful opinion—they ought and must submit, but that the submission would be voluntary cannot be affirmed; but a Government should consider what is right in itself, and not merely to be influenced by the opinions of its subjects.

"In the propositions for the settlement of Bengal, I extended the re-gulations regarding the gunges as far as I could, without a declared violation of proprietary right; but the arguments against the measure in Bengal are much stronger than in Behar, to which the present discussion applies; and I shall hereafter state them."—*Minute of Mr. Shore, dated September* 18*th*, 1789.

Lord Cornwallis, on the other hand, while acknowledging the rights of the zemindars contended for by Mr. Shore and the force of the latter's reasoning, maintained that individual rights and immunities should give way to considerations of Imperial interests and necessities :—

"Mr. Shore's propositions for the settlement of Bengal will point out his sen-timents regarding the collection of the internal duties; and I believe it was principally at my instance, that he acquiesced in the resolution for taking the collection of these duties into the hands of Government, in Behar, as entered on our proceedings of the 12th September last.

2

" It was by my desire, also, that similar instructions were issued to the collector of Midnapore.

" To those who have adopted the idea, that the zemindars have no property in the soil, and that Government is the actual landlord, and that the zemindars are officers of Government removable at pleasure; the question regarding the right of the zemindars to collect the internal duties on commerce would appear unnecessary. The committing the charge of the land revenues to an officer, and the collection of the internal duties to another, would to them appear only a deviation from the practice of the Mogul Government, and not an infringement of the rights of individuals ; but what I have already said will be sufficient to show that these are not grounds upon which I have recommended the adoption of the measure.

" I admit the proprietary rights of the zemindars, and that they have hitherto held the collection of the internal duties ; but this privilege appears to me so incompatible with the general prosperity of the country, that however it may be sanctioned by long usage, I conceive there are few who will not think us justifiable in resuming it.

*   *   *   *   *

" The inefficacy of the power of Government to restrain zemindars from these oppressive exactions, whilst they are allowed to possess the right of levying taxes of any kind upon commerce, has been long experienced in many shapes. It is only by the total resumption of this right, that such abuses can be prevented ; and as the general interests of the community require that a regular system of taxation upon the internal trade of the country should be established, we are justified by the constant practice of our own country, and that of other nations, in demanding from individuals, upon granting them full compensation of their present value, a surrender of privileges which counteract so beneficial a measure.

" Further benefits are to be derived from this arrangement, when the amount of the internal duties, the rates by which they are levied, and the articles subject to the payment of them, are ascertained. Some may be increased, and others diminished or struck off, according as may be judged advisable ; and in course of time, as commerce and wealth increase, such resolutions may be made in the duties on the internal trade, and the foreign imports and exports as will afford a large addition to the income of the public, whenever its necessities may require it, without discouraging trade or manufactures, or imposing any additional rent on the lands."—*Minute of Lord Cornwallis, dated February 3rd, 1790.*

The principle enunciated above received effect in Regulation XXVII. of 1793, by which the Government resumed the right of levying internal duties on commerce. The preamble to the said Regulation has the following :—

" Experience having at length proved that prohibitory orders for preventing oppression were not attended with the desired effect, it was determined, on the 11th June 1790, to take from the landholders the power of imposing and collecting duties altogether, and to exercise this privilege immediately and exclusively on the part of Government. The consequences of this measure were expected to be the effectual abolition of many vexatious duties on articles of internal manufacture and consumption, as well as on exports and imports ; the suppression of many petty monopolies and exclusive privileges, which had been secretly continued to the great prejudice of the lower orders of people ; and, as the natural effects of the reform of these abuses, benefit to trade, and ease to inhabitants of the country in general. *A further consequence expected from the exercise of this privilege, was a future opportunity of augmenting the public revenue in case the exigencies of Government should render it indispensably necessary, without increasing the assessment on the land.*"

As a further corroboration to the fact that the Government having already exorbitantly taxed the landholders, had set apart the Commercial and Mercantile classes for future taxation, the following extract from the preamble to Regulation XXIII. of 1793, though in some respects rescinded by Regulation VI. of 1793, abundantly testifies to the course and spirit of subsequent legislation in matters of taxation :—

" Upon the introduction of a general system of police on the 7th December 1792, the Governor-General in Council determined that the expense of the establishments should be defrayed by the merchants, traders, and shop-keepers residing in the several cities, towns, bazaars, and gunges. He considered it equitable that this expense should be charged upon the commercial part of the community : *first,* because they are particularly interested in the establish- ment of an efficient police, from having at all times a large property moving about the country, and consequently being liable to suffer more than any other descriptions of individuals from the depredations of robbers ; *secondly, because they carried on the whole internal trade of the country free of duty, in consequence of the late abolition of the inland customs, and, although one of the most opulent classes of the people, paid no immediate tax to the State.*

It has been often contended that the zemindars of Bengal had possessed no proprietary rights in the soil, until the grant of the same by the Go- vernment in 1793, but the authors of the Permanent Settlement, who it must be conceded had ample opportunities of investigation, and, perhaps, better sources of information, held a quite contrary opinion. Mr. Shore, while proving in the clearest language possible the proprietary rights of the zemindars, maintained on the other hand, that without permanency of assessment the recognition of such rights would be a " cruel mockery." In concurring with Mr. Shore on this head, Lord Cornwallis not only repudi- ated the claims of Government to proprietary rights in the soil, but also declared that the assumption of such a title on the part of Government would be prejudicial to the public interests, as the following extract will show :—

" Mr. Shore has most ably and, in my opinion, most successfully, in his minute delivered in June last, argued in favour of the rights of zemindars to the pro- perty of the soil. But if the value of permanency is to be withdrawn from the settlement now in agitation, of what avail will the power of his arguments be to the zemindars for whose rights he has contended ? They are now to have their property in farm for a lease of ten years, provided they will pay as good rent for it ; and this property is then to be again assessed, at whatever rent the Government of this country may, at that time, think proper to impose. In any part of the world, where the value of property is known, would not such a concession of a right of property in the soil be called a cruel mockery ?

" In a country where the landlord has a permanent property in the soil, it will be worth his while to encourage his tenants, who hold his farm in lease, to improve that property ; at any rate, he will make such an agreement with them, as will prevent their destroying it. But when the lord of the soil him-self, the rightful owner of the land,. is only to become the farmer for a lease of ten years, and if he is then to be exposed to the demand of a new rent, which may perhaps be dictated by ignorance or rapacity, what hopes can there be—I will not say of improvement, but of preventing desolation ? Will it not be his interest, during the early part of that term, to extract from the estate every possible advantage for himself; and, if any future hopes of a Permanent Settlement are then held out, to exhibit his lands at the end of it in a state of ruin ?

" Although, however, I am not only of opinion that the zemindars have the best right, but from being persuaded that nothing could be so ruinous to the public interest, as that the land should be retained as the property of Govern-ment, I am also convinced that, failing the claim of right of the zemindars, it would .be necessary for the public good to grant a right of property in the soil to them, or to persons .of other descriptions. I think it unnecessary to enter into any discussion of the grounds upon which their right appears to be founded."—*Minute of Lord Cornwallis, dated September* 18*th*, 1789.

Doubts have often been expressed that the Permanent Settlement was a hasty measure, based upon crude information and a wrong and false estimate of the interests of Government. But the following account of the Settlement from the pen of Lord Cornwallis shows the contrary to have been the fact :—

" The history of this settlement may be traced upon the public proceed-ings ; and I trust that the state to which it has reduced many of the land-holders will suggest to the Court of Directors very strong arguments in favour of a permanent assessment, and prove to them the justness of Mr. Shore's own observation :—" That the mere admission of the rights ' of the zemindars, unless followed by the measures that will give value to it, will operate but little towards the improvement of the country ; that the demands of a foreign dominion, like ours, ought certainly to be more moderate than the impositions of the native rulers, and that, to render the value of what we possess permanent, our demands ought to . be fixed ; that, removed from the controul of our Government the distance of half the globe, every prac-ticable restriction should be imposed upon the administration in India with.

out circumscribing its necessary power, and the property of the inhabitants be secured against the fluctuations of caprice, or the license of unrestrained controul."

*   *   *   *

" I trust, however, that it cannot be imagined that I would recommend that the proposed settlement should be made with a blind precipitation ; or without our having obtained all the useful information that, in my opinion, can be expected of the real state and value of the different districts.

"Twenty years have been employed in collecting information. In 1769, supervisors were appointed ; in 1770, provincial councils were established ; in 1772, a committee of circuit was deputed to make the settlement, armed with all the powers of the presidency ; in 1776, ameens were appointed to make a hustabood of the country ; in 1781, the provincial councils of revenue were abolished, and collectors were sent into the several districts, and the general council and management of the revenues were lodged in a committee of revenue at Calcutta, under the immediate inspection of Government. Like our predecessors, we set out with seeking for new information ; and we have now been three years in collecting it. Voluminous reports have been transmitted by the several collectors on every point which was deemed of importance. The object of these various arrangements has been to obtain an accurate knowledge of the value of the lands, and of the rules by which the zemindars collect the rents from the ryots."—*Minute of Lord Cornwallis, dated February 3rd*, 1790.

It is thus clear that the Permanent Settlement was a long-discussed and deliberate measure, that it was effected from a consideration of the then urgent necessities of the State and a wholesome regard for the public interests, that the assessment established by it was a tax of 90 per cent. on the income of the zemindars derived from the land, their proprietary rights in the soil being acknowledged and confirmed by the authors of the Settlement after a most searching and patient investigation, extending over a period of twenty years, that with a view to provide against future exigencies of the State the right of levying internal duties on trade hitherto enjoyed by the zemindars was wrested by the Government, and the commercial and mercantile classes, who had been all along exempt from taxation, were held the legitimate objects of contribution to meet the future demands of the State, and that the same obligation was acknowledged in subsequent legislation. The fresh imposition of a further tax on the income of the zemindars derived from the land therefore cannot but have the effect of the violation of the Permanent Settlement, and necessarily of the faith of Government.

APPENDIX.

Minute by Rajah Suttshurn Ghosal Bahadoor.

I HAVE read with due attention and intense interest that portion of the speech of the Right Honourable James Wilson, delivered in the Legislative Council of India on the 18th February last, which discusses the imposition of a tax on income derived from the real property in the permanently-settled districts of Bengal. The speaker very ingeniously attempted to show that Lord Cornwallis, in proclaiming the Decennial Settlement fixed for ever, never intended to exempt the zemindars from the burden of a general income tax. But express provisions in the enactment declaring the permanency of the Settlement prove to the contrary: Section 7, Reg. I. of 1793 declares, that " the Governor General in Council trusts that the proprietors of land, sensible of the benefits conferred upon them by the public assessment being fixed for ever, will exert themselves in the cultivation of their lands under the certainty that they will enjoy exclusively the fruits of their own good management and industry, and that *no demands will ever be made upon them or their heirs or successors by the present or any future Government, &c.*" It is expressly stated in the Preamble to Regulation XXVII. of 1793 that the Legislature in resuming and abolishing the sayer or internal duties and taxes had three objects in view ; 1*st*, the promotion of commerce ; 2*nd*, general relief of the inhabitants from oppressive taxes ; 3*rd*, the augmentation of income "*in case the exigencies of Government should render it indispensably necessary to augment the public revenue without increasing the assessment on the lands.*" On these legislative enactments rests the zemindars' claim to exemption, and not, as the speaker emphatically pronounced, on any "incidental expression of the Court of Directors," or on any unknown intention which Lord Cornwallis "had at heart" in making the Perpetual Settlement. These legislative enactments clearly prove that Government have waived their right to tax the zemindars, with whom a perpetual settlement was concluded, and their heirs and lawful successors. It may be a matter of controversy that the tax proposed is not on land, but on income derived from land. Such an argument may be easily rebutted by the admission of the speaker, that it is an " indirect" charge upon the land. But Government have pledged themselves not to demand any further contribution in reference to land the tax of which has been fixed in perpetuity. Whether the Perpetual Settlement was a measure indiscreet or unstatesmanlike, that is another question, and foreign to our present purpose. Its projectors, observed Lord Hastings in his minute of the 31st December 1819, conceived this measure in a pure spirit of generous humanity and disinterested justice. As Land Revenue cannot be increased without reversing the Perpetual Settlement, income from land cannot be reasonably taxed without infringing the indefeasible rights of zemindars of estates the revenues of which have been permanently settled.

C. H. MANUEL, Calcutta Printing and Publishing Company (Limited,) No. 1, Weston's Lane, Cossitollah.

REMARKS

AND

EXTRACTS FROM OFFICIAL REPORTS

ON THE

BENGAL TENANCY BILL.

BY

J. DACOSTA.

LONDON:

W. H. ALLEN & CO., 13 WATERLOO PLACE. S.W

1884.

PRICE ONE SHILLING.

THE

BENGAL TENANCY BILL.

London, February 1884.

Great excitement and alarm have been occasioned in Bengal by the introduction, in the Legislative Council of India, of a measure bearing the above title, which deals with the rights of property, proposes to abolish the freedom of contract, and would deprive a large class of the people of the protection they now receive from the law courts.

The avowed objects of the Bill are—

" (1) to give reasonable security to the tenant in the occupation " and enjoyment of his land ; and

" (2) to give reasonable facilities to the landlord for the settlement " and recovery of his rent " ;

but an examination of its provisions renders it clear that these objects are unattainable under their operation, and that the Bill is calculated to produce effects exactly opposed to them. Such is the view taken by the Bengal officials (Commissioners, District Judges, and Collectors) whom the Government consulted on the subject last summer, and extracts from whose reports will be found in the Appendix to this paper.

The weight due to the opinions of these officials, who are members of the Covenanted Civil Service of India, may be gathered from the fact that they form the principal and most trusted channel by which the Government receives its information on the state of the country, the condition and feelings of the people, and the details of the administration ; they have, indeed, not inaptly been called " the eyes and ears of the Government." It is, moreover, by them that the new Bill would have to be administered ; and their strong condemnation of it is the more significant, that their feelings and training would incline them, one would think, rather to support than to oppose the Government whom they serve, and on whose

1 *

good-will in no small degree depend their advancement and welfare.

For such a body of men to condemn the main provisions of the Bill as unjust, iniquitous, unnecessary, calculated to set class against class, to incite to strife and litigation, and to result in grievous injury to both the landowners and the cultivators, would argue a very strong conviction against the proposed legislation; and when their administrative experience and their daily intercourse with the people are taken into consideration, can any doubt exist as to their opinion, expressed under official responsibility, being entitled to greater confidence than the views of the author or originator of the Bengal Tenancy Bill, whose very name is unknown to the public, and who is, therefore, but an irresponsible adviser of the Government?

The promoters of the measure have said that legislation was undertaken on this occasion at the instance of the zemindars, and that the necessity of introducing the clauses which relate to the position of the tenants arose from the pledge which the Government gave to the ryots in 1793. How far these pleas can be accepted as a justification of the Bill will appear from the following statement.

To begin with the pledge alluded to, it is inferred from the following passage in Regulation I. of 1793 :—

" It being the duty of the ruling power to protect all classes of " people, and more particularly those who, from their situation, are " most helpless, the Governor-General in Council will, whenever he " may deem it proper, enact such regulations as he may think neces- " sary for the protection and welfare of the dependent talookdars, " ryots, and other cultivators of the soil."

The pledge, it will be seen—if there be one in the above passage —is to protect the talookdars and cultivators, while the Bill would despoil those very talookdars and the zemindars in order to create a new class of middlemen; and would take away from the cultivators, whom it professes to protect, the protection they now enjoy against the undue enhancement of their rents. In other words, the measure has been put forward under a delusive plea which has gained for it the sympathy and support of many in this country; while few have studied its clauses and ascertained its real tendency and scope.

The ryots or cultivating tenants in Bengal may be classed under two distinct heads, viz. those who have and those who have not occu- pancy rights. The former are entitled, from prolonged residence, to hold their land so long as they pay their rents punctually, and they are protected by existing laws from the undue enhancement of their rents: the bulk of the ryots belong to this class, and their number has been increasing steadily. The other class consists of yearly tenants, or tenants who hold their land under a lease.

Now, the Bill proposes to cancel every lease, and confer on the lessee, and generally on every ryot, a permanent right of occupancy, provided he has held his land for twelve years, or tenanted any plot, however small, in the same estate for that period, or even held various plots in it for shorter periods amounting to twelve years : it proposes, moreover, to do away with the payment of rent as a necessary condition for the preservation of an occupancy right, and to render occupancy rights transferable by sale without the consent of the landlord ; also to confer such rights, permanently and at once, in respect of all lands of which the new occupancy ryot may become the tenant in the same estate, although he may have held them only for a few days. At the same time elaborate provisions are made for preventing that the landlord should demand a full rent from the new occupancy ryot, the maximum being fixed at less than half the rate sanctioned by custom and general usage, and, indeed, of the rate which the Government itself continues to claim in the Crown estates of Bengal and in the other provinces where the Government is the landlord. Protected by these conditions, the new occupancy ryot is to be allowed to sublet all the land over which he may acquire the newly-invented occupancy right, free from the restrictions as to rent which are to be imposed on the landlord.

The inevitable result of these provisions must be to enrich the new middleman (misnamed occupancy ryot, since neither residence nor cultivation is required for his qualification) at the expense of the zemindars and talookdars on the one hand, and of the ryots or cultivating tenants on the other, regardless of the faith we have pledged to the former, and of our bounden duty, irrespective of all pledges, to protect the latter.

The effect of the Bill would, in short, be to despoil the zemindar of proprietary rights solemnly guaranteed to him in 1793 ; to take from the cultivator (for whose benefit the measure has professedly been framed) the protection he now has against excessive rents, and to call in a new class of middlemen, under the fictitious name of occupancy ryots, to share in the profit from land, vesting them with the power of absorbing the lion's share, although they would have to contribute neither labour nor capital for its production.

The marvellous equanimity and complacency with which a result so deplorable and so contrary to the avowed objects of the Bill, is viewed by its promoters at Section 41 of the *Statement of Objects and Reasons*, would betray the fact that such is actually the end for which the measure has been prepared, and that it represents its real object. The passage in the *Statement* runs thus :—

" That the powers of transferring and subletting which the Bill

" recognises, may in time lead to a state of things in which the bulk
" of the cultivators would not be occupancy ryots, but under-ryots
" with but little protection from the law, is, indeed, within the range
" of possibility; but if such a state of things should arise, we may
" rest assured that the Government of the day will know how to deal
" with it."

Unjustifiable and disastrous as a similar result might be, it would
not be difficult to point to the motives which may have rendered it
desirable in the estimation of the author of the measure.

Bengal, under the permanent settlement of 1793, has attained a
degree of prosperity unknown in the other provinces of our Indian
Empire, and the official reports on the condition of the country have,
for years, represented its peasantry in a thriving and progressive
state. Before 1793 one-third of the land was jungle, the bulk of the
ryots lived on the verge of starvation, and the land-tax, which formed
the only source of State revenue, could never be recovered in its
entirety. At the same time there was no prospect of improvement in
the existing state of things, as capitalists stood aloof from agricultural
enterprise, owing to the prevailing system of periodically re-assessing
the land-tax; a system under which the fruit of the capital invested
in the clearance, improvement, and cultivation of land was exposed
to be absorbed in the Government demand at the next assessment of
the tax.

At present not only is the land revenue collected in Bengal with
an ease and regularity never attained in the other provinces of India,
but new and growing sources of revenue have been opened out,
which already yield almost three times as much as the land-tax. In
short—

" The Bengal of to-day offers a startling contrast to the Bengal
" of 1793; the wealth and prosperity of the country have marvellously
" increased—increased beyond all precedent under the permanent
" settlement . . . A great portion of this increase is due to the zemin-
" dari body as a whole, and they have been very active and powerful
" factors in the development of this prosperity."—Report of the
Commissioner of Burdwan, Gazette of India, 20th October 1883.

This growing prosperity has, for many years, excited the cupidity
of a certain class of financiers. The salt duty was raised in Bengal
to fifteen hundred per cent. of the value of the salt when shipped at
Liverpool. Direct taxation, Excise, Stamp, and Customs duties were
greatly increased, and cesses were imposed on the landholding and
agricultural classes under the colour of local taxation.

All this, however, did not satisfy financiers whose mind seemed
bent upon intercepting the profit from land before it could reach the
hands of those who had produced it. These financiers were not contented to wait until such profit should accumulate in the form of

national wealth; as then a portion of it only could be obtained through taxation. They resolved, therefore, on increasing the land-tax under some disguised form that would conceal its violation of the public faith pledged in 1793; and their first attempt took the shape of local and provincial cesses. The disguise, however, deceived neither the people nor the official class, a majority of whom strongly protested against the step; and a member of the Secretary of State's Council recorded his opinion on its character in the following remarkable but apposite terms :—" *We have no standing ground in* " *India except brute force, if we forfeit our character for truth.*"

A different scheme had, therefore, to be devised for attaining the object in view, and the Bengal Tenancy Bill would appear to be the form under which the new scheme is to be inaugurated.

At present the wealth produced by the labour of the cultivator, from the land supplied by the zemindar, and with the aid of the funds advanced by the capitalist, after satisfying the legitimate claim of the State, is distributed among those three agents or factors; and a residue, left in the hands of each, goes yearly to increase the national wealth in one form or another, whence the people and the Government both derive substantial benefit.

Under the Bill the landowner would scarcely receive enough to discharge the revenue, and the cultivator would be ground down by the [new middleman; while the latter, who is to be vested with unrestricted power to rack-rent the land, would absorb all the surplus profit yielded by it. This surplus could then be diverted into the coffers of the State, simply by the necessary taxation being imposed on the middleman; a process against which he could claim no protection under the permanent settlement, seeing that he was not a party to that compact.

There seems little room to doubt that such is the actual scheme in furtherance of which the Bengal Tenancy Bill has been introduced. The avowed objects of that Bill, at all events, are unattainable under its provisions, and common-sense will not permit us to believe that the ultimate object can be limited to enriching the money-lenders and other outsiders who are invited to acquire the extraordinary rights which it proposes to create.

Corroborative evidence of the intentions of the Government being at variance with the avowed objects of the Bill, is also supplied by the fact that, while so much stress is laid on the importance of restoring to the ryots the rights they are alleged to have possessed at the time of the permanent settlement, the Bill specially provides that no such rights shall be recognised in the Crown estates; and the Commissioner of the Presidency Division remarks in his report of the 31st December 1880 :—

" So far as the practice of the Government is concerned, I fail to

" find in their dealings with the ryots upon Crown lands any indica-
" tions of the recognition of a living tenant-right among any class of
" ryots save those known as *khudkash* and *kudeemi*."

While the policy inaugurated by this Bill appears to be regulated
by no fixed principle, it is, at the same time, a very short-sighted
policy, seeing that, for the sake of a temporary accretion of revenue,
to be obtained through breach of faith and spoliation, it would
arrest the whole course of prosperity which has flowed from the
permanent settlement, and reduce the agricultural population of
Bengal to the destitute and precarious condition of the Madras
and Bombay ryots, among whom millions drag a miserable existence on insufficient food, and a deficient harvest brings famine
with its many sufferings and horrors. Capital, in obedience to the
same laws which controlled its application before the introduction of
the permanent settlement, would once more stand aloof from agricultural enterprise in Bengal, and auction sales of estates for arrears of
revenue, fields abandoned by the cultivators and increasing difficulty
in the collection of the land-tax would mark in the official reports of
Bengal, as similar results have marked in those of Madras and
Bombay, the decline in the prosperity of the province.

That this is not the first time that the plea of protecting the ryot
would be used for supporting schemes of spoliation, may be seen
from the following passage in a Minute written by Sir Phillip Francis
in 1776 :—

" It is proposed to secure to the ryots the perpetual and undis-
" turbed possession of their lands. This language, I know, is popular,
" and has often been used to give countenance and colour to acts of
" violence and injustice against the zemindars and others of superior
" rank of the natives. Before we give perpetual possession we ought
" to determine the property. The State does not consist of nothing
" but the ruler and the ryot, nor is it true that the ryot is the pro-
" prietor of the land . . . . but it does not follow that because the
" ryot has no direct permanent property in the land, he should there-
" fore have no right, or that no care should be taken to protect him.
" Without his assistance, the land is useless to the zemindar. If
" they are left to themselves, they will soon come to an agreement in
" which each party will find his advantage. . . . . To dictate the
" specific terms of any lease is an invasion of the rights of property
" . . . . the intervention of the Government between the zemindar
" and the ryot should have no object but to enforce the execution of
" their respective engagements."

Having now seen how delusive is the professed object of securing
the ryot or cultivating tenant in the occupation and enjoyment of
his land, let us see what the Bill proposes for attaining its other

avowed object, *i.e.* to give acilities to the landlord for the recovery of his rent.

The promoters of the measure tell us that legislation on this occasion was undertaken at the instance of the zemindars. The facts to which this interpretation has been given, are as follows :—

In 1871, when the Government imposed an additional burden on land in Bengal, in the shape of a Road Cess payable partly by the zemindars, partly by their tenants, and requested the former to collect the tenant's portion free of charge and at their risk (a risk which involved the attachment and sale of their estates in case the full amount of the Cess was not paid into the treasury on the due date), the zemindars observed that they already experienced much trouble, delay, and expense in the collection of their rents, owing to the defective state of the law on the subject; that in order to save their estates from attachment, they had often to make good from other sources the deficiency which occurred in their rent collections, and that their difficulties would increase if they undertook the collection of the Government Cess on the conditions proposed. Finally, however, they accepted the duty and the risk, upon a promise which the Government then made to simplify the law for the recovery of rent.

The zemindars have, ever since, punctually fulfilled that duty which, in following years, was rendered more onerous, in consequence of new Cesses having been imposed in addition to the Cess of 1871 ; but the promise of the Government has not been redeemed to this day, while the opportunity it afforded for legislation has been turned to account for making the present attempt to despoil those very zemindars from whom a valuable consideration had been accepted and to whom assistance had been promised in return.

The course pursued in this instance is so extraordinary, so derogatory to the dignity of the ruling power, so repugnant to all sense of fairness, that it seems advisable, in stating it, to cite authentic testimony in support of the statement.

The District Judge of Tipperah in his report on the Bill, dated 12th May 1883, says :—

" I admit the difficulty of conceding to the zemindar his demand " for greater facility in the realisation of his dues ; but I am not " prepared to say that it could not be satisfied to a certain extent. " There is not, however, any attempt made to do so in the Bill. " This is one of the points where the zemindar, asking for bread, " has been given a stone."

The Commissioner of the Presidency Division, in his report of the 2nd July 1883, observes :—

" As to the recovery of rents, which was the beginning of the " legislation which has found its outcome in the present Bill, the

" landlords will hardly be satisfied with the relief given them. *On*
" *the principles on which the Bill is drawn* * the zemindars could not
" expect further relief. I suspect, however, that they expected, and
" 1 am not prepared to say that they have not a good right to expect,
" very much more substantial relief, as the outcome of their applica-
" tion for a summary method of realising rents, preferred during the
" last twelve years."

Reverting now to the promise which the Government made in
1871, we find that no step whatever was taken for redeeming it until
1873, when a Bill was sketched for the purpose, but was not proceeded with for reasons which have remained unknown to the public.
The next apparent step was taken in 1877, when Sir Ashley Eden,
on assuming the Government of Bengal, said :—

" The landlords have not such facility as they should have for the
" ready and prompt realisation of their rent and the Government
" cesses. My predecessor recorded a Minute expressing the intention
" of at once applying for the sanction of the Government of India to
" pass a short Bill to provide a system for the realisation of rent by
" a somewhat more summary and prompt process than that which
" now exists. I hope it will not be long before I shall be in a posi-
" tion to ask the Council to pass a Bill of the sort."

In 1878 a Bill was at last introduced by the Government of
Bengal ; and the following remarks made on the occasion by the
officer in charge of the Bill, will show how great was the necessity
for a measure of the kind :—

" Notwithstanding the fact that, in about seventy-five per cent. of
" the suits for arrears of rent, the claim is really not contested, the
" zemindars and other rent-receivers have often found themselves
" unable to recover their just dues without submitting to a process
" which entails costs that may possibly never be recovered, and
" delays that are frequently embarrassing and ruinous ; and even
" when the zemindar has got his decree, it by no means follows that
" he has got his rent. The Road Cess and Public Works Cess Acts
" have thrown upon the zemindars the responsibility of collecting,
" with their rents, and paying into the treasuries, all that portion of
" the fresh local and provincial taxation which falls upon tenants
" of every degree. If they cannot recover this easily and effectually
" from their tenants, they must, under penalty, pay the amount.
" themselves—a position which the State is obviously bound to
" render as little burdensome as possible."

Notwithstanding the above encouraging statement, this Bill also
was dropped after a time, upon the vague and inconclusive plea that,
as the law on rent seemed to require revision, it was advisable to

---

* These words were underlined obviously for the purpose of drawing attention to the
unprincipled character of the Bill.

deal with both subjects in one measure. A Rent Commission was thereupon appointed, consisting almost exclusively of Government servants, which held numerous meetings, but took no evidence and abstained even from examining the parties concerned; and it ultimately submitted in 1880 a draft Bill of a most complicated and revolutionary character. The following extracts from the official reports made on the Rent Commission's Bill will give a clearer idea of its nature.

The Commissioner of the Presidency Division said, on the 31st of December 1880:—

" The proposed Bill seems to me to contemplate grave infringe-
" ments on the rights of zemindars as hitherto recognised; to destroy
" such rights, and to give the holders no compensation for such
" damage done to their interests. It seems to me, moreover,
" peculiarly unjust to contemplate such restrictive legislation with
" reference to the rights of zemindars, when the whole tendency of
" recent legislation on the part of the Government has been to
" throw more responsibility on the landholders in the way of
" providing funds for improvements connected with the land."

The Commissioner of the Cooch Behar and Rajshahya Division, observed in his report, dated the 1st of February 1881:—

" Such important changes deeply affecting the rights and pecu-
" niary interests of a large and important class should only be made
" on very strong grounds, such as, for instance, the grounds advanced
" by Mr. Gladstone when introducing a somewhat similar measure
" for Ireland in 1870. He then urged that, as good general laws had
" failed to dispel the serious ill-feeling of the mass of the population,
" it was necessary to take an extreme step in a direction specially
" acceptable to that population, in the hope that it would put an end
" to what was always a serious political danger. No strong and
" special grounds, political or other, exist in the present case, nor are
" they asserted by the Rent Commission, who, indeed, seem to be
" unanimous in holding what is a nearly unanimous opinion, viz.
" that the ryots of Bengal are stronger than the zemindars."

The Commissioner of the Burdwan Division wrote on the 26th of April 1881:—

" From the experience I have had of the very great difficulty
" which officers of the Government feel in managing wards and
" attached estates in the Chittagong and Dacca Divisions, I am con-
" vinced that the position of the zemindar (landlord) in those parts
" is a precarious one. As far as I am able to judge, it will be
" rendered more so if the present Bill becomes law. . . . I am not
" aware that any section of the community in Bengal has suggested
" or manifested any desire for new legislation on the rent question."

The Bill of 1880 was the first indication that the Government had really no intention of keeping its promise of 1871, but only songut an opportunity for passing a confiscatory measure, in violation of the engagement entered into in 1793. The Bill, however, not having gone sufficiently far in the direction desired by the Government, another Bill was drawn on its lines with new and still more objectionable provisions. The new Bill was published under the title of the Bengal Rent Bill, and discussion on it was ostentatiously invited ; but it was afterwards twice materially altered before being submitted to the Secretary of State, without the public being allowed to know what were the changes made in it. This tortuous course evoked the following remarks from the Chief Justice of Bengal, when the Bill, in its original form, showing none of the alterations which had already been introduced into it, was submitted for the opinion of the High Court of Calcutta :—

" The Bill as it was first drafted by the Rent Commission differed " in many respects from that which has since been prepared by Mr. " Reynolds ; and we are now in still greater uncertainty as to what " is really proposed, because we learn that Mr. Reynolds' draft was " again materially altered before it was sent to the Government of " India, and that it has now been submitted with still further altera- " tions for the consideration of the Secretary of State.

" This method of dealing with important legislative measures is " inconvenient, and seems hardly fair to those classes of the com " munity whose interests may be most seriously threatened.

" The Bill, for aught we know, may be submitted to the Secretary " of State in a form which the Bengal public has never seen, and " upon which they had no opportunity of making a single comment. " In this form it will be discussed, and probably approved, at the " India Office ; and if it is then to be sent back to this country to be " dealt with in accordance with the views of the Secretary of State, it " is clear that those classes whose interests it is calculated to injure " may be placed at very great disadvantage."

The course apprehended by the Chief Justice was precisely the one followed in this instance ; and its unfairness and danger will become apparent when it is considered that the constitution of the Legislative Council is such as to enable the Government, at all times, to secure in it an official majority ; its ordinary members being made to understand that it is their duty to give their vote to the Government, irrespective of their personal opinion. The deliberations of the Legislative Council are thus reduced to a sham, and its functions are made to consist simply in the enactment of measures which have received the sanction of the Secretary of State ; a sanction neces- sarily granted upon a one-sided representation of the case, without the aid of the light which public and free discussion alone can throw upon all sides of a question. This dangerous course is now being followed, as far as the Government of India is concerned, in a matter affecting the rights and interests of fifty millions of our Indian fellow-subjects.

The Bengal Tenancy Bill consists of no less than 230 sections; but as the greater number refer to details which it would be useless to examine while the provisions they are intended to carry out are condemned, it might suffice here to point to the unsound principle on which many of the details have been framed, namely, on the principle of superseding the jurisdiction of the Law Courts by the intervention of Executive officers. Considering how large a portion of the produce of the land is claimed by the State as revenue, and how often the fiscal regulations have led to the acquirement of private estates by the Government at a nominal price, the Government is by no means a disinterested party in the differences which arise between its officers and the landowners, and between the latter and their tenants. By appointing, therefore, its own servants to adjudicate on such differences, the Government assumes the right of being the judge in its own case, and often of its own acts, seeing that the differences in question frequently arise from the action of the Revenue officers themselves.

This proposed supercession of the Law Courts by Executive officers has accordingly been condemned by officials, and strongly protested against by the landed classes, not only as conflicting with the Regulations of 1793, and likely, therefore, to lead to confusion and litigation, but as calculated to prevent a complete and impartial inquiry into the circumstances connected with the matter in dispute. The District Judge of Hoogly remarks :—

" It re-introduces a state of things which the preamble of Regu "lation II. of 1793 states was then found unsatisfactory."

The Commissioner of Burdwan says :—

" This (the preamble) is not forgotten by the zemindars in the " present day, and Chapter XI. is looked upon as an infringement of " the principle laid down in the above Regulation, which has, nearly " for a century, been one of the fundamental principles of British " rule."

The injustice which would be perpetrated if the provisions in Chapter XI. became law will appear more clearly on a perusal of the preamble in question, in which the following passage occurs :—

" All questions between the Government and the landholders " respecting the assessment and collection of the public revenue, and " disputed claims between the latter and their ryots (tenants), have " hitherto been cognisable in the Courts of Maal Adawlut, or " Revenue Courts. The collectors of revenue preside in these Courts " as judges, and an appeal lies from their decision to the Board of

" Revenue, and from the decrees of that Board to the Governor-
" General in Council in the department of revenue. The proprietors
" can never consider the privileges which have been conferred upon
" them as secure whilst the revenue officers are vested with these
" judicial powers. Exclusive of the objections arising to these
" Courts from their irregular, summary, and often *ex parte* pro-
" ceedings, and from the collectors being obliged to suspend the
" exercise of their judicial functions whenever they interfere with
" their financial duties, it is obvious that, if the regulations for
" assessing and collecting the public revenue are infringed, the
" revenue officers themselves must be the aggressors, and that indi-
" viduals who have been wronged by them in one capacity can
" never hope to obtain redress from them in another. Their financial
" occupations equally disqualify them for administering the laws
" between the proprietors of land and their tenants. Other security
" must be given to landed property, and to the rights attached to it,
" before the desired improvements in agriculture can be expected
" to be effected. Government must divest itself of the power of
" infringing, in its executive capacity, the rights and privileges which,
" as exercising the legislative authority, it has conferred on the land-
" holders. The revenue officers must be deprived of their judicial
" powers. All financial claims of the public, when disputed under
" the Regulations, must be subjected to the cognisance of courts of
" judicature, superintended by judges who, from their official situa-
" tions and the nature of their trusts, shall not only be wholly unin-
" terested in the result of their decisions, but bound to decide
" impartially between the public and the proprietors of land, and
" also between the latter and their tenants. The collectors of the
" revenue must not only be divested of the power of deciding upon
" their own acts, but rendered amenable for them to the Courts of
" Judicature, and collect the public dues, subject to a personal pro-
" secution for every exaction exceeding the amount which they are
" authorised to demand on behalf of the public, and for every
" deviation from the regulations prescribed for the collection of it.
" No power will then exist in the country by which the rights vested
" in the landholders by the Regulations can be infringed, or the
" value of landed property affected. Land must, in consequence,
" become the most desirable of all property, and the industry of
" the people will be directed to those improvements in agriculture
" which are as essential to their own welfare as to the prosperity of
" the State."

From the above passage it will be seen how justice was administered in Bengal before the introduction of the permanent settlement,
and the principle which has regulated its administration subsequently.
Under the former *régime* the condition and prospects of the country

were described in the following terms in a letter of the Governor-General to the Court of Directors, dated the 18th September 1783 ·—

"I may safely assert that one-third of the Company's territory in "Hindoostan is now a jungle inhabited only by wild beasts. Will "a ten years' lease induce any proprietor to clear away that jungle, "and encourage the ryots to come and cultivate his lands, when at "the end of that lease he must either submit to be taxed *ad libitum* "for the newly-cultivated lands, or lose all hopes of deriving any "benefit from his labours, for which, perhaps, by that time he will "hardly be repaid?"

The effect produced by the permanent settlement and improved administration of justice, inaugurated in 1793, will be seen from the following extract, already quoted at page 6 :—"*The Bengal of to-day* "*offers a startling contrast to the Bengal of* 1793; *the wealth and* "*prosperity of the country have marvellously increased—increased* "*beyond all precedent—under the permanent settlement. A great* "*portion of this increase is due to the zemindari body as a whole.*"

It is now proposed, under the Bengal Tenancy Bill, to set aside the permanent settlement as interpreted and carried out during the last ninety years, and to revert, in the administration of justice in Bengal, to the unsound principle and previously condemned system of vesting revenue officers with judicial powers. This proposal is the more startling that no urgent necessity has been pleaded for the change, nor any substantial advantage been shown as likely to accrue from it and from the Bill generally, to either of the two parties for whose benefit the measure has professedly been introduced. On the contrary, it is admitted that the Bill is calculated to deprive the landowners of valuable proprietary rights which they have hitherto possessed, and to leave the bulk of the cultivating tenants with but little protection from the law.

The principle and the main provisions of the proposed legislation, as will be seen from the extracts in the Appendix, have been condemned by every high official in Bengal, excepting the Lieutenant-Governor, who expressed his dissent from their opinions in a lengthy despatch covering twenty-five pages of the Government *Gazette* of 20th October 1883. It must be remembered, however, that the Lieutenant-Governor, having been a Member of the Viceroy's Council when the Bill was adopted, was committed to its support long before the district officials sent in the reports which condemn it. A perusal of his despatch, moreover, will show that his dissent is supported partly by declamatory arguments, and partly by groundless allegations. For instance, in order to prove the necessity of the proposed legislation, he says :—

"If there really be any persons who, in the face of the over-

" whelming accumulation of evidence afforded by the discussions of
" the past ten years, still question the necessity of legislation on the
" broad lines of the Bill, then it is quite hopeless that anything the
" Lieutenant-Governor could say would convince him,"

Hollow declamation of this sort, affording no ground whatever for
the formation of any opinion on the question at issue, seems out of
place in the discussion of a matter of literally vital importance.
Then, as regards alleged facts, the Lieutenant-Governor says :—

" In Bengal the demand for legislation came, in the first instance,
" from the landlords ; while in Behar the cry was from the ryots for
" protection from illegal enhancement and ejectment."

Of the two assertions contained in the above short passage, the
inaccuracy and disingenuousness of the first, as far as the Bengal
Tenancy Bill is concerned, has already been shown in this paper at
pages 9 and 10; and regarding the latter assertion it will perhaps
suffice to observe that, although very voluminous papers were
published with the Bill, not a single petition from ryots was among
them, while the district officers distinctly stated in their reports on
the Bill that they were not aware of any demand having been made
or any desire manifested by the ryots for legislation touching rents.
Then as regards the charge of illegal ejectment, it is supported by no
evidence whatever, while evidence of its groundlessness is supplied
by the Viceroy's despatch to the Secretary of State on the subject
of the Bill, in which a statement of Mr. Reynolds' is quoted at
paragraph 103, to the effect that *the right of eviction is never exercised in the eastern districts, and that exemption from eviction
would be a worthless boon in Behar where ryots are hardly ever
evicted.*

It may be unnecessary to go further into the subject of the many
inaccuracies contained in the Lieutenant-Governor's despatch, as
they have been serially discussed and exposed in a Memorial which
the Central Committee of the Bengal and Behar landowners presented to the Viceroy in November last soon after that despatch was
published.

The foregoing remarks on the Bengal Tenancy Bill will, it is
earnestly hoped, induce the reader to peruse the Bill itself and the
documents relating to it, which have been published in the Government Gazette of India of the 20th October 1883. It is impossible to
rise from a perusal of those papers and of the Chief Justice's Minute
of 6th September 1882 without feeling a clear conviction—

1st. That the avowed objects of the Bill cannot be attained under
its provisions.

2nd. That its inevitable effect will be to create a new class of
middlemen from among the money-lenders and other outsiders, who

are not likely to have any sympathy or community of feeling with the cultivating tenants.

3rd. That the tenants of the new middlemen would, under the Bill, be debarred from ever acquiring any occupancy right, such as are possessed at present by a large number of ryots; and would be liable to eviction at the will of their new landlords.

4th. That the power of rack-renting the land, which the Bill places in the hands of the new middlemen, would deprive the cultivating tenants of the protection which the existing law provides against the undue enhancement of rents.

5th. That the proposed interference with the freedom of contract, the attempt to settle rents by tables of rates, and the supersession of the Civil Courts by executive officers, would be productive of great injustice and inconvenience, and offer the strongest encouragement to devices for eluding the law, a condition of things which cannot fail to demoralise the people.

6th. That the proposed infringement of proprietary rights which have been solemnly guaranteed by the Government of India with the concurrence of the Crown and Parliament of Great Britain, would constitute a breach of public faith which would seriously reflect on the character of the British Government in India, and destroy the confidence of the people of that country in the honesty and good intentions of their rulers.

POSTSCRIPT.

London, February 18, 1884.

Since the foregoing pages were written, a report has been received of the public meeting which was held at the Town Hall of Calcutta, on the 29th of December last, for the purpose of protesting once more against the proposed legislation on the tenure of land in Bengal.

The meeting was very largely attended by zemindars from all parts of the country. Extracts from the speeches delivered on the occasion will be found at the end of the Appendix.

A just idea of the effect which the Bill, if enacted, would have on the position of all who, relying on the good faith of the Government, have invested their capital in land, or advanced it for agricultural purposes in Bengal, is afforded in the following words with which Mr. Gregor Grant, proprietor of extensive estates in the hill tracts inhabited by the aboriginal race called the Sonthals, concluded his thoughtful and instructive address on the occasion :—

"I have been a resident in the Bhaugulpore district for over forty-two years . . . My whole life's earnings have been invested in the security of landed property. If the present Bill becomes law, the zemindar to whom I have lent all my earnings on the mortgage of his estates will not be able to repay me the money I have given him, as his property will become greatly depreciated in value, and I will be unjustly deprived of my life's earnings, on which I had relied as a provision for my old age."

J. DACOSTA.

APPENDIX

CONTAINING

Extracts from the Reports of the Twenty-one Commissioners, District Judges, and District Officers consulted by the Government, through the High Court and the Board of Revenue, on the Provisions of THE BENGAL TENANCY BILL of 1883.

From J. P. GRANT, Esq., District Judge of Hooghly.

13th July 1883.

I shall content myself with criticising the provisions of the Bill from the point of view of what I understand to be its two-fold object, viz. to give security to the tenant in the occupation and enjoyment of his land, and to give facilities to the landlord for the settlement and recovery of his rent.

Section 3, *Clause* 5.—The definitions of "tenure-holder" and "ryot" are not satisfactory. If these definitions are maintained, the conventional meaning of the word "ryot," the nearest equivalent of which is "yeoman," will disappear, as will indeed the class itself; for the inevitable tendency of the proposed law is to make *right-of-occupancy ryots*, in fact as well as in name, middlemen. I would take occupancy ryots out of the category of tenure-holders. There is nothing in common in their position and the position of those who are really middlemen, such as *putneedars* and farmers. The law should recognise the existing two classes of ryots, viz. those having and those not having rights of occupancy ; and in defining them, should employ the word ryot for both. The definition of tenure-holder should be altered to signify exclusively a middleman between a proprietor and a ryot.

CHAPTER II. purports to limit for the future *khamar*, or private estate land, to what was such land at the passing of the Bill. I doubt both the policy which would enact this and the possibility of enforcing it, if enacted, in the face of the provisions of Section 141.

CHAPTER III. A., *Sections* 14 *and* 15, convert an occupancy-ryot into a tenure-holder. I have already pointed out the confusion of ideas here indicated, which is certain to breed confusion in practice. You cannot alter the conventional meaning of words by Act of Parliament. Section 16 converts the *bhag-jotedar* into a ryot who may possibly acquire a right of occupancy. This is totally opposed to all the existing notions of a *bhag-jotedar's* status and position. He is, in fact, only a labourer under another name. His share of the crop is the wages for which he has engaged to cultivate it.

2 *

CHAPTER IV.—I do not see why the Putnee Regulation should be incorporated with the Bill. The character of a complete code is repudiated by the Bill; and I see no more reason for incorporating this Regulation than for incorporating the Regulation containing the permanent settlement, which is still left as a separate law, and is, in its nature, as much connected with the Bill as the Putnee Regulation.

CHAPTER VI. provides for the drawing-up of a local table of rates of rents and produce. I believe that it will be practically impossible to draw up such tables. Indeed, I understand that an attempt has been already made on a considerable scale and has signally failed. This was only to be expected. . . . I do not know how the market-rate at harvest-time is to be authoritatively settled.

CHAPTER VIII. deals with what are mistakenly called "ordinary" ryots. The ordinary ryot of the country is the ryot having rights of occupancy; it is all other classes of ryots that are exceptional. I do not see why the every-day terms of "ryots having a right of occupancy" and "ryots not having a right of occupancy," should not be maintained. But the mistake goes deeper than the mere names. The difference between the two classes of ryots is that one has fixity of tenure and the other has not. The provisions of this chapter would seem to imply that the former class possesses some privilege of setting at a lower rate of rent also; for the "ordinary" ryot may by the Bill be rack-rented up to a certain maximum. All classes of ryots have now, and ought always to have, equal protection at the hands of the law, in respect of the rate of rent payable by them; the only difference is that, while one class holds from year to year or for a term of years on lease, the other holds in perpetuity, if he only pays his rent.

CHAPTER XI. introduces a state of things which the preamble of Regulation II. of 1793 states was then found unsatisfactory. The principle therein enunciated is that disputes between landlord and tenant shall be adjudicated by Civil Courts and not by the Revenue authorities who, otherwise, would, in many cases, be deciding upon their own acts.

From JOHN BEAMES, Esq., Commissioner of the Burdwan Division.

22nd June 1883.

2. I have already submitted two lengthy reports on this subject, the first of which commented on the Bill drafted by the Rent Commission in 1880, and the second on the amended Bill put forward by the Government in 1881. I am still very much in doubt whether any enactment of the kind is really required, except in Behar.

3. It is not to be expected that the Bill will escape opposition, nor do I think such opposition altogether unreasonable. It is all very well to say that the framers of the permanent settlement reserved to themselves and their successors the right to interfere between zemindars and ryots, whenever such a step might seem necessary for the protection of the latter; and that, though no such interference practically did take place during the sixty-six years that intervened between 1793 and 1859, yet that it was never too late to mend, and that consequently we are going to interfere now. The answer to that argument is that during all those years we have allowed men to buy zemindaries and tenures on the belief, fully justified by our action, that no interference would take place, and that it is not fair to these persons suddenly to uproot the conditions on the faith of which they have invested their money. I so far agree with this argument as to think that, in any changes which may now be made, it is not sufficient to go back to first principles, and base our enactment solely on what we understand to be the relation between.

landlord and tenant, as established by Lord Cornwallis's Regulations; we must go further than this, and take into consideration the present status and vested interests of the proprietary body whom we have called into existence and whom we have, during nearly a century, allowed to acquire rights and privileges which are none the less deserving of respect now, because their growth and development were not contemplated by the statesmen of the last century.

4. The question I ask myself, as I examine one section of the Bill after another, is "does this provision deprive either the landlord or tenant of any right or any status which he legally holds *at present*, whether in virtue of the terms of the permanent settlement or in virtue of any custom which the Government has tacitly allowed to grow up since that time?" We have nothing to do with the historical zemindar of 1793. If he existed at all, that is, if there was any class of men so situated as we are apt to figure them to ourselves, he exists no longer. We have to deal with the zemindar in the position which he holds in the present day.

5. This is the view which most of the officers and private gentlemen with whom I have from time to time consulted take of the matter, and I think that it is the only practical and reasonable view to take. . . . The Bengal of to-day offers a startling contrast to the Bengal of 1793. The wealth and prosperity of the country have marvellously increased —increased beyond all precedent—under the permanent settlement. There is much force in the remark that a great portion of this increase is due to the zemindari body as a whole, and that they have been very active and powerful factors in the development of this prosperity.

7. Section 3, Sub-Sections 3 and 5.—The definition of ryot has purposely been left obscure. We are told that certain persons are not ryots, but we are not told who are ryots. The definition of the Rent Commission was not satisfactory, because no other test was applied than that of the extent of the holdings. The Bill, in Sections 14 and 15, also fixes an arbitrary line between a tenure-holder and a ryot by making what are at present known as ryots with occupancy at fixed rates of rent into tenure-holders. If this definition be maintained, we get an exceedingly simple definition of ryots by merely saying that all persons who hold land under a zemindar, except those mentioned in Sections 14 and 15, are ryots.

8. This, however, introduces considerable confusion in another way; for it has never, as far as I am aware, been the custom to regard as tenure-holders persons who have a right of occupancy at fixed rates. Such persons are always regarded by themselves and by others as ryots; and the adoption of the classification of the present Bill will very much modify our conception on this point, and introduce changes which will not be readily understood or acquiesced in by the classes connected with the land.

10. When a zemindar lets land to a tenure-holder, he considers that he is granting, and the tenure-holder considers that he is obtaining, the right to collect rents from a number of cultivators already actually in occupation of the land so granted. When, however, a zemindar lets land to a ryot, he grants and the ryot takes the permission to cultivate the land himself, it not being, at the time of granting the lease, actually occupied by cultivators. The ryot, who thus takes land, may subsequently, without ceasing to be considered by the zemindar or himself a ryot, sublet portions or even the whole of such land; but at the time of taking the *pottah* (lease) the land is not in occupation of others.

11. This, I think, is the broad line of demarcation between "talookdar" and "ryot"; and if we use tenure-holder strictly for talookdar, this

demarcation will practically hold good everywhere, with very few and unimportant modifications. It is the intent with which the land is granted and taken that shows where to draw the line; and the intent is clearly understood in all cases by the parties at the time the transaction occurs.

12. The definition might be formulated thus:

A tenure-holder is a person who takes land from a proprietor with the intent of collecting the rents from the ryots, and against whom the proprietor has the remedy mentioned in Section 15 of this Act (sale).

A ryot is a person who takes land from a proprietor with the intent of cultivating it himself or by hired labour, or of sub-letting it, and against whom the proprietor, &c., has the remedy specified in Chapter XIII. of this Act (distraint).

13. If the difficulty is great in distinguishing between a ryot and a tenure-holder, it is equally great in distinguishing between a ryot and an under-ryot; and we cannot rest contented with the definition of an under-ryot given in sub-section (6), that an under-ryot means "a tenant holding below a ryot," unless we know what a ryot is. What we must know for purposes of settlement, and what the zemindar also must know for the same purpose, is who is the person in whose name the *jummabundi* is to be made. Section 164 of the present Bill, indeed, contemplates that, in compiling a record of rights, which is practically what we know as a *jummabundi*, tenure-holders, occupancy-ryots, *bastu*-ryots, ryots, under-ryots, shall all be jumbled up together. But this will never do. Something more definite will be necessary, unless the whole of our system of settlement-procedure is to be reversed, in which case a good deal of Regulation VII. of 1822 will have to be repealed. Bengal Act VIII. of 1869 is, I see, to be repealed; but Chapter XI. of this Bill, as I shall notice further on, makes the same requirements as the Act does on Settlement officers, in respect of defining the status of various kinds of tenants, so that I am afraid we shall not be able to get on without some definition of "ryot."

18. I have already noticed that Sections 14 and 15 turn an occupancy-ryot into a tenure-holder. I see that this is said to have been done for the convenience of the draftsman. It is unfortunate that we hear so much of this person now-a-days. It seems to me that it is a matter of no moment at all whether he finds an Act easy or difficult to draft. That is his affair, and should not for an instant occupy the mind of the legislator, whose attention should be directed solely to the justice and the utility of the law. The mechanical operation of putting an idea into plain English is beneath consideration. I venture to think that by turning the occupancy-ryot at fixed rates into a tenure-holder, we are creating a state of things foreign to the ideas and customs of the people, and likely to give rise to much confusion.

31. I think Section 45 goes a great deal too far. It allows a man who has held land anywhere in an *estate*, no matter how often it may have been changed, to become a settled ryot; and a settled ryot acquires a right of occupancy in any land he may happen to hold on the 2nd of March last, so that in case of a large zemindari, say the Burdwan estate for instance, a man may come to a village from another village sixty miles off in that estate, take lands there, and have rights of occupancy from a few days' possession.

33. There may be some justice in the rule that a ryot who has lived twelve years in a village shall be considered a settled ryot. The village, even in Bengal, still preserves some sort of solidarity; the estate has none, and it would certainly be unfair to allow a ryot to acquire a right of occupancy in a plot of land which he has held only for one year, in a

village in which he is, to all intents and purposes, an outsider and a stranger, simply on the ground that he has held land for twelve years in other disconnected parts of the same estate. Such a concession as this is not looked for by the cultivating class, is opposed to their own views and to the custom of the country, and would operate very hardly on the zemindars.

37. The illustration to Section 4 of the Bill recognises the custom that under-ryots may acquire a right of occupancy, but leaves the conditions under which such a right may be acquired undefined, and the under-ryots consequently unprotected.

38. There are in Midnapore many thousands of these ryots whose forefathers have tilled the land they now occupy for many generations, and I agree with Mr. Wilson in thinking that there is no reason why they should be left unprotected.

41. Section 56 has given rise to much discussion.

42. Here there is some confusion in the laws. Section 47 provides that no occupancy rights shall accrue on land held by any person as owner. One would suppose that when a landlord exercised the right of pre-emption, and bought a ryot's holding, he would thenceforth hold it as owner.

43. Yet the sections on pre-emption and Section 56 speak of the ryot selling his "occupancy right" and the landlord purchasing the same. What is this but selling and purchasing the land itself? I do not see why, if the landlord thus purchased the land, it should not be open to him to extinguish the occupancy right. In fact, under Section 47, that right should be extinguished by the mere fact that he, the owner, purchases it. But, to prevent this consequence, the fine distinction is introduced that he, the owner, holds it not as owner, but as an occupancy ryot under himself.

45. Moreover, as pointed out by Mr. Reynolds in his speech in Council, the landlord will, by this provision, be led to keep the land in his own hands, thus virtually turning it into *khamar*. The whole section seems to me to involve an erroneous idea. It is not the land that acquires rights, but the man who holds it. If he holds it for a certain term of years, equity and custom demand that he should acquire occupancy rights in it. But one fails to see why the land itself should carry those rights with it when it passes into the hands of a man who has done nothing to earn or merit those rights.

79. Section 151.—The procedure of Chapter XI. virtually amounts to making a regular settlement of part or the whole of a permanently-settled estate. It involves not merely the settlement of rents, but the preparation of a *jummabundi*; in fact all the proceedings of an ordinary settlement, excepting only the fixing of the revenue. And in some respects this procedure gives more power to revenue officers than do the existing Settlement Laws. This is stated to be intentional, and the procedure has been invented with a view to removing from the Civil Courts the power they now exercise in reversing the decision of revenue officers on many points in a settlement; accordingly, Bengal Act VIII. of 1869 is repealed.

80. The revenue officers will, under such a provision, pursue their course in settling an estate in peace without having the fear of interference by the civil court constantly before their eyes.

81. All this is very pleasant and gratifying for us revenue officers. I do not, however, quite see how it is to be reconciled with the remarks in the preamble to Regulation II. of 1793, which, after stating that " all questions between Government and the landholders respecting the assessment and collection of the land revenue, &c. &c., have hitherto been cognizable in the courts of *mal adalut* or revenue courts," goes

on to say that, "the proprietors can never consider the privileges which have been conferred upon them as secure while the revenue officers are vested with these judicial powers." This is not forgotten by the zemindars in the present day, and it is to be feared that the provision ot this chapter is, by many nomindars, looked upon as an infringement of the principle laid down in the above Regulation, which has, for nearly a century, been one of the fundamental principles of British rule.

85. It is no light thing to enter on to a permanently settled estate and turn it upside down, with the result, perhaps, of crippling the land-lord's resources for one lifetime or more.

From E. E. Lowis, Esq., Commissioner of the Chittagong Division.

30th June 1883.

3. The introduction of this measure is viewed by all whom I have consulted on the subject with the gravest apprehensions, as tending to embitter the relations between landlord and tenant, and likely to lead to a great amount of litigation with its accompanying fraud and chicanery, which must in the end injure, and not benefit the ryot. These views are based on the conviction that the provisions of the Bill do not deal with facts as they really exist, but seek to evolve and insist on theoretical privileges as appertaining to the ryots, which that class never enjoyed, and which they are for the future to enjoy at the expense of the landlord.

4. These apprehensions are not allayed by the remark contained in the *Statement of Objects and Reasons*, that the present Bill is a mere prelude to what may be expected to follow when the whole law on the subject comes to be codified; and it is urged that, if this measure is not to be considered in itself as complete, it is hardly worth while introducing it, seeing that the effect will most inevitably be a crop of litigation and general disturbance of the agricultural community.

5. I most certainly concur in the opinion that its provisions are quite inapplicable to the condition of things and the system of land tenure existing in this division.

6. I feel sure that any change in the existing law is not urgently called for.

8. The essence of the Bill is the protection of the ryot; and though no definition of a ryot has been given, it is plain that, in the proposed law, the term is almost synonymous with cultivator.

(*The intervening paragraphs endeavour to show the inapplicability of the provisions of the Bill to the condition of things existing in the Chittagong division in particular.*)

31. As to the voidance of contracts, the proposed law appears to introduce a dangerous precedent. In certain cases the provisions of the law are to be held to over-ride contracts entered into with deliberation; and this without any inquiry whether the contract was voluntary or not. So far as my experience goes, the ryots are very well able to look after their own interests, and hardly require to be thus hedged round with protective enactments, as appears to be thought necessary; they are only too ready to evade their contracts, if it is to their interests to do so, and are quite prepared to support such evasion by every artifice that the law renders possible, as well as by means not strictly lawful; it seems hardly expedient, therefore, to teach such men that the law does not recognise the keeping of contract, and that self-interest can be held, to be a valid excuse for contravening the terms of an agreement. Cases may arise where it is

evident that an unjust and one-sided contract has been entered into, as the result of deception or force; but surely such cases may be left to be dealt with by the application of the law of equity.

Clause 2, *Section* 73, says that a contract, in a certain case, made in favour of a ryot must be enforced, while Section 50 protects him from contracts which are against him. *Clause* 2, *Section* 74, enforces a contract which is against a zemindar, while Sections 87 and 90 repudiate contracts which are in his favour. These instances will teach the ryots that there is no moral obligation in promises, and that he must always consider his own convenience in dealing with others. This is a dangerous doctrine to teach. If ninety per cent. of the tenantry have been able to acquire tenant rights under a system when contracts have been held valid, there is no need to make them now invalid.

34. When the whole set of tradition and custom in a tract of country is against the fundamental principle of the proposed law, it seems to me inadvisable to extend such law to that tract.

From R. Towers, Esq., District Judge of Tipperah.

12th May 1883.

2. The tenant acquires (under this Bill) advantages at the landlord's expense, which, in many cases, exceed the tenant's demands, which are entirely novel in their character, and appear to be derived rather from a consideration of what has been found expedient in foreign countries than Indian law or custom.

3. Among those I would class :—

(1.) The easy terms on which occupancy rights are conferred.

(2.) The confiscation of the landlord's right to deal as he chooses with land that has once been ryoti, when it reverts to his private possession.

(3.) The almost entire abolition of the right of private contract between parties.

(4.) Compensation for disturbance.

(5.) The power given to ryots to make improvements against the landlord's wish.

I admit the difficulty of conceding to the zemindar his demand for greater facility in the realisation of his dues, but I am not prepared to say that it could not be satisfied to a certain extent. There is, however, hardly any attempt made to do so in the Bill.

4. The next general observation which occurs to me is that litigation will be enormously fostered by the Bill. The parties are driven into Court or before the Revenue authorities at every step.

5. Then, not a few of the provisions of the Bill seem unsuited to practical working. Among these I would instance the procedure regulating the transfer of occupancy rights, the preparation of tables of rates, the apportionment of expenses, the rules for enhancement which seem very intricate.

CHAPTER II.—The survey and register under Section 7 will, I believe, be a work of enormous difficulty: Every plot will be disputed, and there will be in effect a civil suit contested in every stage, before the Survey officer, the Commissioner, the Board, and the Government. It seems to me to be more expedient to allow each case to be settled by the Courts on its own merits in case of dispute, than to cause a widespread discord by sending a roving Commission about the country to agitate questions on which the parties concerned are themselves quiescent. I believe there is no injustice felt in this part of the country.

Chapter V.—The two chief points open to criticism in this chapter seem to be (1) the definition of occupancy ryots, and (2) the provision that any ryot taking land from a landlord, of which the latter has himself acquired the occupancy right, shall have a right of occupancy in it.

With regard to the first of these, extreme care has been taken that, uuder the Bill, a ryot that held two cottahs of land in a village A for twelve years, may acquire rights of occupancy in 200 beegahs in villages B, C and D, though he may have had possession of the same land for only three or four months. The necessity of the provision has been maintained on the ground that otherwise the landlord, by shifting the ryot from one plot to another, might prevent the acquirement of the right in any one plot. There may be parts of the country where this is done, but I do not believe in the existence of the practice in Bengal.

I have received some strong representations as to the delay which will be caused to the landlord by his not being allowed to eject any occupancy ryot for arrears of rent, his remedy under the Bill being the sale of the holding. This is one of the points when the zemindar asking for bread (i.e. greater facility for realising his rents) has been given a stone.

Then with regard to Section 56, except in the very rare cases of ejectment and lapse, the only way in which the landlord can acquire the right is by purchase. But if he is compelled to treat any person to whom he subsequently lets the land as an occupancy ryot, what consideration has he had for his purchase money? In my opinion there is an economic mistake, as well as a serious injustice in the provisions of this section.

Chapter VI. Section 58, 61.—Here, I think, there is too much interference with private contract, and that Section 61 is not defensible. Why should a settled ryot, who wishes to take on more land than that in respect of which he has acquired his status, be allowed to hold any further land he may take from the zemindar on privileged terms?

The preparation of rates will be practically impossible in most places.

From J. Monro, Esq., Commissioner of the Presidency Division.

2nd July 1883.

3. I have had many conversations on the subject with officials, zemindars, and others, and have omitted no opportunity of ascertaining the feeling of the people generally in connection with this important measure.

4. The landholding class is most strenuously opposed to the Bill, and there is no doubt that a most uncompromising resistance to its provisions will be manifested. There is a general feeling amongst the members of the landholding class that zemindars will practically be effaced and reduced to the position of annuitants, and that the Bill constitutes a distinct infringement of the rights which they conceive were guaranteed under the terms of the permanent settlement, and which they have certainly exercised for nearly a century.

6. The ryots are ignorantly apathetic on the subject. They have heard rumours of some impending changes, and, in some instances, agitators have made them believe that the millennium of the ryots is at hand, when they will pay only nominal rents for, and reap all the benefits from the land; but, as a rule, they have no intelligent idea on the subject, and it is difficult to define any feeling they may have in the matter.

7. Upon the question of the rights of the zemindars under the permanent settlement, I have already expressed an opinion, and after the authoritative declaration of the Government of India of their views upon that point, it is not for me to reopen the discussion . . . The Bill is framed for the purpose of carrying out a pledge given by the Government with regard to the rights of ryots at the time of the permanent settlement. And in pursuance of the effort to fulfil this pledge, it is now proposed to give the ryots fixity of tenure, fair rent, and freedom of sale of their holdings.

8. How far these privileges or rights were guaranteed under the terms of the settlement has been disputed; how far the ryot requires fixity of tenure which he has in Lower Bengal practically got, is also a question upon which there have been differences of opinion; whether freedom of sale will, in reality, confer on the ryots the boon which it is intended to give them, is also an open question; but there is and can be no difference of opinion as to the ryot being required to pay a fair rent for any holding which he possesses.

16. Holding the views which I have on another occasion expressed, I cannot consider many of the provisions of the Bill as fair to the zemindar with reference to the rights which they have enjoyed for a century; and yet I am precluded from calling into question the principles upon which the Bill is founded.

27. With reference to the provisions of the Bill regarding occupancy ryots, I object to the extension of the provisions of Act X. of 1859, specially with reference to—

1. The definition of a settled ryot in Section 45.
2. What seems to me the unjust provision of Section 47.
3. Transferability of the tenure.
4. Sub-letting.
5. The abolition of freedom of contract.
6. The Provisions of Sections 59 and 61.

28. I have nothing new to add to the arguments of those who object to the extension of occupancy rights proposed by the Bill. It seems to me as to them unjust that the element of residence should not be an essential feature of the status of a settled ryot. I see no reason why a settled ryot, having a right of occupancy in certain lands, should, as a matter of right, have the same status in lands which may be miles away from his village, although within the same estate; and the accrual of the rights of occupancy to a settled ryot in any lands subsequently acquired by virtue of his tenancy of lands at the time of his becoming a settled ryot, seems to me an unjust extension of occupancy right.

29. There is no doubt that the unfettered power of transfer will encourage disputes and faction quarrels, which have already been a prominent feature in native families; and if, in addition to this power of transfer, is given the privilege of sub-letting without the consent of the landlord, the latter will very soon find his estate full of occupancy ryots or their dependents, in the shape of his bitterest enemies.

31. If the tenure is allowed to be transferable, I would on no account permit sub-letting, which will simply encourage ryots to let out their tenures and prey upon the sub-tenants. Such a system will, in the end, lead to sub-tenants or ordinary ryots (i.e. the cultivators) under occupancy holders being much more rack-rented than they are now.

32. As to the abolition of freedom of contract, I altogether fail to see the justice of the provision. I do not find anything of the kind in any of the Settlement Regulations, and I fail to see how the ryot is ever to learn how to stand alone if he is to be rigidly protected against himself. The ryot is to be allowed freedom in every respect, except

when he enters into an agreement with his landlord. If this is not setting class against class, and teaching the ryot to look upon his landlord as his natural enemy, words have no meaning. I would certainly leave parties to contract as they please, and the Courts should not, in my opinion, refuse to recognise such contracts. Denial of the ryot of contract has a distinct tendency to make the landlord resort to illegal cesses, and the ryots acquiesce in such improper exactions. . . . I must confess that, according to my experience, the ryot of Lower Bengal is not such a down-trodden or helpless creature, with reference to his own interests, as he is represented to be. . . . I can point to the majority of ryots having occupancy rights in Dacca, Tipperah, Chittagong, Jessore, Noakhaly, and other districts, as being men who are eminently calculated to look after their interests. It seems hardly consistent to inculcate upon the people by one enactment their fitness to govern themselves, and in another to provide them with a means of protection against their own acts : to give them power to vote with reference to matters about which they express little concern, and to deny them a right to contract with regard to their rent, about which they are supremely interested.

34. I am not of opinion that it will be practicable to frame tables of rates such as are proposed, without an amount of harassment and expense to both landlords and tenants which would be ruinous to them ; and, even when prepared, I question very much whether it would be fair to either party to keep them in force even for ten years.

36. With regard to the ordinary ryots, the provisions of the Bill militate against all previous practice, at which a tenant-at-will was allowed to hold in accordance with agreement entered into between him and his landlord. I think it unwise that such a practice should be disturbed, and am not prepared to support those provisions which fix a maximum of rent to be demanded, and which introduce the entirely new system of compensation for disturbance of the tenancy of a man who has no right to such tenancy, except under an agreement with his landlord.

37. Throughout Lower Bengal there is no necessity for recognising any other principle than that of mutual interest between landlords and tenants in determining the relations which should exist on the part of the landlords to tenants-at-will. No landholder in his senses will now aim at extravagant enhancements, for such a policy will very soon relieve him of his ryots. Most landlords are now anxious to get ryots to settle ; and evictions, even of tenants-at-will, is a procedure, I imagine, more sparingly resorted to in Lower Bengal than in any country that I know of. The relations, therefore, between landlords and tenants-at-will may safely be left to determine themselves according to the economic laws of supply and demand.

41. The chapter upon compensation for improvement seems based upon an entirely mistaken theory.

42. There have been for centuries, and are now, millions of ryots who have had fixity of tenure. Have these ryots shown any inclination to invest capital in improving their land ; have they evinced any desire to increase the productive powers of the land, even by the elementary process of manuring it ? Have they done anything under the influence of fixity of tenure in the way of constructing for the benefit of their lands any of the numerous works specified in Section 26 as agricultural improvements ?

43. In Lower Bengal the ryots with rights of occupancy have done nothing to improve their lands. Any such improvements as have been made have, so far as my experience goes, been carried out by landlords, and not by ryots ; and I see no reason to believe that the ryots, when

they have more capital, will change their nature or their habits as regards expenditure which they think ought to be incurred by the zemindar.

45. The ryot, so far as my experience goes, does not want to improve his land (which has for ages yielded crops without expenditure on his part on agricultural improvements), nor does he want to be improved himself; he wants to be let alone, and this Chapter on agricultural improvements introduces a system which is perfectly new in the bucolic history of Bengal: it is certainly not needed with reference to the acts or wants of ryots at present, and will infallibly lead to litigation and false claims of every description. Such a system will also most certainly lead to landlords declining to undertake, or give any assistance to villagers in undertaking, village improvements; and when villagers with opposing interests are left to themselves, to carry such improvements, the result may easily be imagined.

46. I do not object to seeing the whole chapter excised from the Bill.

50. I am quite prepared to admit that if the provisions of Chapters XI. and XII. can be successfully carried out, and if we can have a record of rights made out and rents ascertained, great progress will have been made in reaching a solution of many vexed questions at issue between landlords and tenants. The expense of such proceedings as are contemplated under these two chapters will be enormous, and, I suspect, ruinous to both parties. Before making these provisions of universal application Government should, in my opinion, try the experiment thoroughly in Crown estates. We have not yet, in the similar operations which have been carried on in settlements, sufficient data to work upon, and I much fear that the amount of litigation which would be at once excited by the application of these provisions generally, would be very injurious to both ryots and landlords.

51. As to the provisions for the recovery of rents, which was the beginning of the legislation which has found its outcome in the present Bill, I am afraid that the landlords will hardly be satisfied with the relief which has been given them.

53. *On the principle on which this Bill is drawn* the zemindars could not expect further relief. I suspect, however, that they expected, and I am not prepared to say that they had not a good right to expect, very much more substantial relief, as the outcome of their application for a summary method of realising rents preferred during the last twelve years.

55. Under such circumstances I cannot convince myself that the Bill, if passed into law, will render practicable a satisfactory solution of the difficulties attending the disposal of the questions at issue; on the contrary, I feel constrained to believe that the application of the various provisions of the Bill must result in endless litigation, active hostility between landlords and tenants, and injury to the property of both.

From J. F. STEVENS, Esq., District Judge of Sáran.

14th May 1883.

CHAPTER I.—I think that an attempt should be made to define the terms "tenure" and "under-tenure." In Chapter III. we find important provisions on the subject of tenures; but when we turn to the definition in order to ascertain what a tenure is, we only find that it includes an under-tenure (which term is left altogether undefined) and the interest of every tenant of the class referred to in Section 14.

CHAPTER II.—I do not see why a landlord should be prevented from acquiring, as *khamar*, uncultivated land which he brings under cultivation by hired labourers.

CHAPTER V.—The term "estimated value" in Sections 51 and 54 is not perfectly clear. By whom is the value to be estimated, and how are the parties to be bound by the estimate?

Section 56 appears to me exceedingly hard upon the landlord. . . . If he is allowed to buy the occupancy right, he is fairly entitled to obtain by his purchase the full advantages that would be obtained by any other purchaser.

CHAPTER VI.—There should be some attempt to define the term "staple crops," as a good deal may turn on its precise meaning. The table of rates would be of great utility; it will be for the Revenue authorities to ascertain how far its preparation is possible.

CHAPTER VII., *Section* 86.—1 doubt the justice of giving compensation in the case of the ejectment of a ryot through his own fault.

CHAPTER VIII.—I should like to see it stated what are the rights of an ordinary ryot as to the use of the land. An occupancy ryot may, under Section 50, use it in any manner which does not render it unfit for the purposes of the tenancy. Is it intended to be implied, from the absence of such an express provision in the case of the ordinary ryot, that his right to use the land is more restricted?

Section 90.—It appears to me that the ordinary ryot under the Bill acquires something very like a right of occupancy. Is a landlord never to let to an ordinary ryot for a fixed time? and if he is to have that power, is not the ryot to be liable to ejectment, on the ground that the lease has expired? There is no provision, apparently, for such a case in Section 90. Again, it seems to me only equitable that the landlord should have the power of ejecting an ordinary ryot, after due notice, on paying compensation for improvements.

CHAPTER IX., *Section* 125 (2).—The difficulty is, how the landlord is to know when the tenant's right, title, and interest is brought to sale. Ought not a notice to be served upon him? There is the same difficulty as to Section 52.

From F. M. HALLIDAY, Esq., Commissioner of the Patna Division, in Conference with Six Collectors.

7th to 13th July 1883.

Sections 43, 45, *and* 47.—We were unanimously and decidedly of opinion that the extension of the right of occupancy to all lands held in the same village or estate should be conditional on residence; and I would submit that the distinction which exists according to the custom of the country between a resident and a non-resident ryot, and which has constantly been affirmed and re-affirmed by subsequent Regulations and Acts, has been entirely lost sight of in the Bill. The definition of estate in Section 3 should be adhered to, and hence Section 43 (*b*) should be expunged. In Behar the retention of this clause would lead to endless confusion and complication.

Section 48 has already been noticed by Mr. Reynolds in his speech in Council, where he speaks of it as practically an admission of the vicious principle that the occupancy right may be made a matter of bargain. This section appears altogether unnecessary. A proprietor, before his estate was sold for arrears of revenue, might go about granting occupancy rights all round, and thereby diminish the value of the estate, occupancy rights not being voidable under the sale law. As Mr. Reynolds remarked, the occupancy right is not the landlord's to grant; it is essentially inherent to the status of the resident cultivator. We would, therefore, record our protest against this section.

Section 50.—The Collector of Durbhunga states: " I think the sub-letting power given to occupancy ryots the most doubtful and only dangerous part of the Bill." A long string of rentpayers and receivers must be bad. As far as an occupancy ryot is a rent-receiver, he is one of the objectional class of land-jobbers. His under-ryot is the important man. It is as a cultivator we wish to protect the ryot ; not as a land-jobber.

The Collector of Mozufferpore has recorded that he cannot admit the necessity or advisability of framing the Bill in such a manner as to lead to consequences such as Clause 41 of the *Statement of Objects and Reasons* admits to be possible. It seems difficult to understand how such a result can be contemplated with equanimity, or how an intention can be deliberately expressed of encouraging the growth of another class of idle annuitants upon the land in addition to those who already cumber it. The Bill will undoubtedly enhance the value of occupancy rights, which will naturally be bought up right and left by the money-lending class. The net result of the Bill will, therefore, be the extinction of the present class of occupancy ryots and the transfer of their rights to money-lenders.

Section 62.—We were unanimous in thinking that the preparation of a table of rates was impracticable. These sections, on the preparation of a table of rates and produce, and of suits to enhance money-rents where such table is in force, contain a Procrustian scheme of enforcing uniformity in matters in which, from the nature of things, no uniformity exists. The rates in a village are about as numerous as the fields of the ryots, and cannot be classified without an arbitrary disregard of actual facts.

Section 90.—I express the unanimous opinion of the Conference in saying that the freedom of contract should not be withheld from a zemindar, giving land to a new, and possibly an unknown, ryot.

From J. F. Bradbury, Esq., District Judge of Backergunge.

2nd June 1883.

The interpretation clauses are defective in that they do not include the definition of a tenure. The term " under-tenure" is misleading.

Section 6.—Why is land which is admittedly not *khamar*, but is com prehended in a permanent, heritable, and transferable tenure within an estate, and cultivated by the holder of such tenure, to be deemed *ryoti* land of such estate? The framers of the section seem to have ignored estates not consisting exclusively of *khamar* and *ryoti* land.

Section 20.—Who is an authority empowered by the Government to make settlements definitively? The Commissioners and the Board of Revenue confirm settlements, but make none. The collector and his subordinate makes them, but not definitively, for their orders are not final till confirmed.

Section 21.—What is a " beneficial rent "? The term is novel in Indian law and requires explanation.

This report contains a large number of exceptions taken to the Bill chiefly on technical grounds, and terminates thus :

The Court will observe that I have abstained from discussing the policy of the Bill. . . . I trust that some of my comments have revealed defects, the correction of which may hereafter prevent litigation.

From N. S. Alexander, Esq., Commissioner of the Dacca Division.

23rd to 29th June 1883.

The right of occupancy is for the protection of the cultivator of the land, and the land was originally let to the cultivator for cultivation ;

it seems to be inequitable, therefore, to allow a non-cultivator to be thrust upon a zemindar as an occupancy ryot.

The Dacca zemindars say :—"If a ryot is evicted from a holding in default of payment of rent, there is nothing in this Section 129 that will prevent his demanding compensation from the landlord. This is very unfair; it is encouraging a defaulter, while it is the duty of the Government (considering the stringent sun-set law under which it claims the revenue from the zemindar) to afford every facility to the landlord in the realisation of rent."

From G. N. BARLOW, Esq., Commissioner of the Bhaugulpore Division and Sonthal Pergunahs, in Conference with Four Collectors.

20th June 1883.

Section 56.—It was observed at the meeting that although at different times and by different objectors it had been urged that if an occupancy right were made transferable by law, zemindars, or planters, or mahajuns would buy up occupancy rights on a great scale ; yet, on zemindars alone had been imposed the condition contained in this section. It appeared to the meeting that there was not sufficient reason for making such a distinction. Section 56 was unanimously condemned by the meeting.

CHAPTER VI., *Part B.*—It was agreed (Mr. Porch alone dissenting) that this part ought to be entirely omitted, owing to—

(1.) The difficulty or impossibility of ascertaining the rates in the way proposed.

(2.) The necessity that would still exist, even if a table of rates were prepared and sanctioned for any area, of holding a local inquiry in each case for enhancement of rent in order to identify the class under which each field in the holding would fall.

(3.) The want of proper establishments and experienced or scientific officers to classify the lands.

(4.) The cost of making a local inquiry in each case,

CHAPTER XIV.—It was unanimously agreed that in suits for arrears of rent, which involve no questions of right or title, the procedure of the civil court in regard to the recording of evidence ought to be made as summary as is the procedure of magistrates in summary criminal trials.

The following passages occur in the Memorandum appended to the Commissioner's report by W. Hastings D'Oyly, Collector of Bhangulpore.

Sections 76, 77, 78.—Some exception should be made in respect of recently reclaimed lands. A ryot has held such land, say, for five years, at first rent-free, latterly at a nominal rent of two annas per beegah, as a concession granted for the cost of clearance. Under Section 76 the enhanced rent cannot be more than four annas, and under Section 78 it cannot be raised for ten years. Supposing the land in 1884 to be equal to lands for which three rupees per beegah is paid as rent, the landlord will have to wait fifty years before he can legally recover a fair rent ! ! ! These remarks also apply to the provisions of Section 59 (2).

Section 82.—I should be glad if occupancy rights could be restricted to the actual cultivators.

CHAPTER XIII.—It has been asserted that one of the objects of the present legislation is to afford facilities to the landlord for the settlement and recovery of his rent, whereas there can be but little doubt that the recovery of rent has been made more difficult than it previously was.

Memorandum of R. Porch, Esq., Collector of Maldah.

Section 50, when enacted, will lead to a very general loss of right of occupancy holdings by the present generation of ryots, whose holdings will be at once bought up by the money-lending classes, the ryots becoming rack-rented pauper cottiers or landless labourers.

From A. C. BRETT, Esq., District Judge of Tirhoot.

14th May 1883.

Occupancy ryot.—The fundamental idea conveyed by the word *Khudkast* was permanence. The test in old days of permanence was residence.

Ordinary ryot.—To tell a zemindar that he cannot evict without paying ten times the increment of rent demanded, is to tell him he cannot evict at all. We are supposed to be interpreting the permanent settlement, not altering it.

Transferability of occupancy rights.—I think a zemindar has a right to be protected from the incoming of an objectionable tenant. The proposed right of pre-emption is saddled with the provision that the next tenant, whether a settled ryot or not, shall have a right of occupancy immediately. Therefore, unless the zemindar cultivates the land by his own ploughs, the only way he can secure himself from an objectionable tenant is to throw away his money; and the operation may be repeated *ad infinitum*

Enhancement of rent.—The task of framing records of rights and tables of rates is, no doubt, a formidable one; but in the resolute facing of this difficulty lies the only chance of success for a rent law in this country, however equitable may be its spirit and however scientific its drafting.

From C. B. GARRET, Esq., Officiating District Judge, 24 Pergannahs.

18th May 1883.

Section 21, *Sub-section* 4, appears to press unfairly on the landlord. Surely in no conceivable case could it be fair that the whole net profits of a tenure, of which even the whole was unreclaimed when the tenure was created, should be perpetually enjoyed by the tenant. Surely the landlord who owned the land before it was reclaimed, is entitled to something for the use of what I may call the raw material on which the tenant has operated his reclamation.

Section 49, I think, is open to very serious objection. I have known in these districts many small proprietors whose sole wealth was their *khamar*. I have always understood *khamar* to be land which was admitted to be the peculium of the zemindar, and which he had every right to dispose of to the very best advantage that the state of the market allowed him to do. I do not think that we need be apprehensive that he will now-a-days be able to do more than this.

Section 50.—Does this mean simply that he may sublet a portion of his land, remaining liable to the landlord for the rent assessed on the whole, or he may, at his option, apportion his liability to his landlord? If the latter, I think it is a provision obviously unfair to the landlord.

Section 85.—A ryot should not be allowed to sell his arable land, and entirely abandon the occupation of husbandry, and still retain a permanent heritable and transferable right in his *bastu* in an agricultural village.

CHAPTER XIII.—I confess I should have been glad to see the power of distraint entirely abolished. I am convinced, however, that it would be unjust to the landlords to do so at present. My experience is that it is a power very greatly abused. At the same time I admit that, when Collector and Manager of Wards' Estates, under Act XL. of 1858, having had experience of villages from which I could never realise my rents except by distraint.

From BABOO RAJENDRA COOMAR SEAL, District Judge of Bankoora.

16th May 1883.

Section 3 (3).—Ryots of the class described in *Section* 14 ought not to be brought under the category of tenure-holders. Paragraph 13 of the *Statement of Objects and Reasons* explains that it is necessary to call them tenure-holders, simply because it is convenient to do so from the draftsman's point of view; but in course of time the ground on which they have been called tenure-holders would be lost sight of, and they themselves would lose the privileges of a ryot.

Section 15.—Throughout the Bill it is provided that a man should first go to the Revenue Court and then to the Civil Court. This procedure will not only be expensive but inconvenient. The best course would be at once to go to the Civil Court, where he will get the final relief.

Section 130.—The Bill itself ought to make provision for the appointment of assessors on the line of the Land Acquisition Act, and it ought not to be left to the local Government to do so.

From W. F. MERES, Esq., Judge, Midnapore.

26th May 1883.

Section 3.—It is to be regretted that the border-line between a ryot and a tenure-holder has not been drawn in the Bill. There is along the coast a large tract of land formerly occupied by Government for the manufacture of salt. On the abolition of the manufacture the land was surrendered to the zemindars in whose estates it lay, and who have let it to speculators. The lessee clears a portion, protects it by an embankment, and induces cultivators to take up small blocks and bring them under cultivation. These cultivators are fairly entitled to acquire occupancy rights against the speculators, but cannot do so (under the Bill) if he is classed as a ryot. The same thing occurs in the jungle mehals of this district.

The definition of a ryot should be so drawn as to include the case of a man who takes up land for cultivation by himself, or by his family or servants, and it should exclude the case of a man who takes land merely to sub-let as a speculation. A maximum limit of a ryot's holding is, therefore, necessary, and I may say that after eighteen years' service in the lower provinces, I have never met with an instance of a genuine cultivating tenant who held fifty beegahs of arable land.

CHAPTER VI. B.—The consequence of an error by the officer who prepares the table of rates, in over-estimating the normal produce of its average money value, or in fixing too high a minimum, will be nothing short of the ruin of the tenantry of the tract dealt with. The difficulty of collecting really accurate data for the table of rates will be found to be very great.

From C. A. SAMUELLS, Esq., Collector of Bankoora.

21st June 1883.

Section 16 seems to go too far. A *bhag-jotedar* is only a labourer under another name. This means of cultivating land (giving a share of its

-crop) is simply employed in lieu of wages, being preferable to wages in giving a man an interest in his work; and no one will be more surprised at the sudden change in his condition than the *bhag-jotedar* himself.

CHAPTER V.—The principle involved in Section 47 seems almost a ludicrous way of making out an occupancy right. There is to be a perfect transformation scene on a day yet to be fixed. In this draft it is the 3rd March 1883. On that day villagers, who may be mere tenants-at-will, and may never have held one piece of land for more than three days at a time, will suddenly become ryots with rights of occupancy in the plot last held, all contracts to the contrary notwithstanding. This is directly opposed to the law of 1869 (Act VIII. Section 7), and renders all contracts under that Act mere waste-paper. They would probably convert this right into cash at the first opportunity; but I cannot think the circumstances of the case will justify such flagrant infringement of the rights of the zemindars.

Section 49 appears to be the result of a confusion of ideas—a confounding a *khamar* land as it is and as it ought to be (*i.e. as it is desired to make it*). It is a contradiction of terms to speak of anyone holding *khamar* land as a ryot, unless a *bhag-jotedar* is considered such; and I have pointed out that he is not looked on as a ryot, but as another form of labourer.

Section 50 bestows a number of valuable privileges on the ryot: would it be too much to ask that one provision be added on behalf of the man at whose expense we are generous? viz. that the occupancy right be liable to be revoked for non-payment of the "fair and equitable rent" on the due date? We have taken great trouble to insure the ryot against exaction. We have gone so far as to interfere with the liberty of contract between him and his master, and it will surely be only just to the zemindar that we insist on punctual payment from the ryot, as we insist on his punctually paying the revenue. If the zemindar is liable to lose his estate for non-payment of revenue on a fixed date, there can be no injustice in holding this right and interest conferred on ryots liable to sale for the same reasons.

Section 61 is subversive of the laws of political economy and justice. If the land is capable of bearing a higher rent, why should the zemindar be compelled to let it at a lower rate (*to a middleman who may exact much more from the cultivating tenant*)?

B.—Admitting that rents are no longer to be fixed by consent, the next best thing is a table of rates. It is another question how such a table is to be prepared, and it pre-supposes a certain dead level in the out-turn of lands, as if improvement and industry were of no account.

Section 76.—I can see no reason for an arbitrary limit. The only recognised limit should be what is fair and equitable.

Section 89.—The ordinary ryot, who most requires protection, appears to get very little, and yet to be competent to make an agreement which his landlord will respect. Section 129 would be harmless as far as any class of improvements is concerned; but it will afford a spur to law-suits founded on imaginary improvements, and supported with all the wit and ingenuity shown on such occasions by a people prone to litigation.

CHAPTER XIII.—I think it must be allowed that the position of the zemindar under the Bill will be scarcely better than that of a mere rent-charger. Neither he nor his tenant could effect a compromise in future; they must be ranged in hostile camps, and the rules of the contest are rigidly fixed. A member of the Council has stated that 90 per cent. of the ryots in Bengal have occupancy rights. In another place I find it stated that "it is on all hands admitted to be the fact that, with or without right, the great peasant population of Bengal has long held the land at very low rates, far below the market rack-rent": these are Sir G. Campbell's very words. If the above statements be correct, then the mere fact of a few disturbances in Pubna, due, perhaps, to an over-zealous officer, are not a sufficient plea for legislation.

I regard an Act which abolishes freedom of contract between landlord and tenant as a backward step in legislation.

I cannot help observing in conclusion that the zemindars suffer from a daily increasing difficulty in the collection of their rents and the Government cesses; and I think that it behoves us to strengthen their hands to the utmost.

Consider the large arrear in Government estates, where the manager is armed with an exceptional procedure and the whole power of the Government; what must be the difficulties of a private individual whose only remedy is a civil suit, which is worthless as a resource, if his ryots combine against him?

From HERBERT MOSLEY, Esq., Collector of Moorshedabad.

18th May 1883.

In my opinion, the new Rent Bill goes much too far, and will result in difficulties to zemindars, which may have a prejudicial effect on the Government revenue.

2. Generally, the effect left on my mind after reading the Bill is that it has been drawn up for the purpose of supporting an ignorant and easily-deluded peasantry against zemindars who are always trying to get the better of them. In some parts of the country it may be that the ryot is unable to look after himself, but it is certainly not the case everywhere. In this district, as in many others, the zemindars have by no means the best of it; and little more is wanted than a much cheaper and a very much more expeditious mode of deciding suits than exists at present.

4. CHAPTER I., *Section* 3 (5).—I would strike out the latter part of this clause. I do not see why, in a law for the protection of the cultivator, the same protection should be extended to him after he ceases to be one. He should, I think, cease to be a ryot when he ceases to cultivate, using the land for other purposes. In the same section, I would strike out everything relating to sub-letting, for reasons given further on.

17. There is, in Sections 45, 47 and 50, the same disabling of a certain class to make contracts which I think so objectionable throughout the Bill; this is likely often to inflict hardship. For instance, it is often highly advantageous to the ryot to hold certain lands for a year or two, and this may suit the zemindar too, except for this new law, which would void any contract to give it back after the term, and so the ryot will not get it.

18. *Section* 47 will cause injustice by handing over, as occupancy land, land which has expressly been let for a term only.

19. In *Section* 50 I would alter Clause A to one expressing that he may only use the land for cultivation, and Clause E I would eliminate. If, as I think is the case, this Bill is intended to protect ryots, I fail to see why it should allow sub-letting. A ryot ceases to be a ryot when he ceases to cultivate; and when he sub-lets he becomes the most oppressive of all landlords, a petty middleman. To protect the actual cultivator is well; to put a man between him and the zemindar can only injure one or the other. If the sub-tenant only pays a fair and equitable rent to the middleman, it is very evident that the latter pays

a less than fair and equitable rent to the zemindar, which would be contrary to Clause C; and if the ryot turned middleman does pay a fair and equitable rent to the zemindar, then it is evident that the sub-tenant, the actual cultivator, pays an unfair and inequitable rent; and how does this improve the condition of the cultivating class?

22. As regards the sections providing for tables of rates, I can only say that I do not believe that such tables could possibly be prepared accurately. My experience in settlements shows that no two villages are alike, or can fairly have one table of rates assigned to them; and the Special Officer who was sent up here to inquire about this matter told me that his inquiries led to exactly the same result.

23. I also doubt very much whether such a list (of the market prices at harvest time) as that contemplated in Section 83 can ever possibly be prepared with any accuracy; and without accuracy the provision would be very mischievous.

24. Turning now to ordinary ryots, I see, by Section 90, that a zemindar cannot let land for a term at all, and Section 95 will effec-tually stop a zemindar from spending money on improvements whenever rents have been enhanced a short time previously.

25. And letting for a short term at a nominal rent to improve the land will be put a stop to, for the ryot, when he is called on for an enhanced rent, will refuse, and then, by Section 93, the landlord may have to pay compensation for improvements, and must have to pay compensation for disturbance, though all this was allowed for in the shape of nominal rent.

29. I think Section 171 (on the right to reap during distraint) should specifically declare how the cost of cutting, &c. (Clause 2) is to be met, and, as I remarked at the commencement of this letter, I should prefer to see a simpler and quicker procedure for suits. And I cannot but again say that I am afraid the Bill, if passed, will result in ruin to many zemindars, and I may add that the agitation among the ryots that, you may remember, occurred to the south of this district some time ago, when a Bill was being prepared, shadows forth pretty dis-tinctly what may be expected if this Bill passes.

From E. J. BARTON, Esq., Collector of Jessore.

31st May 1883.

3. I have doubts if it would be expedient to pass the Bill in its present shape. I think that a more speedy and cheaper means of realising rent is desirable, and that the Bill which secures this would do all that is necessary.

4. The parts of the Bill which are open to objection are those which introduce changes in the respective rights of landlord and tenant, and raise the tenant into the position of a co-partner at the expense of the landlord, without giving the latter any compensation for the property of which he is deprived.

5. Constant changes in legislation are greatly to be deprecated in this country, and should only be made when a clear and undoubted necessity arises. In the present case I do not think that any such necessity has arisen. I here speak of Lower Bengal. . . . The Bill, in important matters, deprives a landlord of liberty to contract with his ryots. I consider that some of its provisions, instead of conferring a benefit upon the cultivating ryots, as they seem intended to do, will injure them. I consider that the Legislature should interfere with the liberty of contract only in cases of most pressing necessity, and that no case of this kind has been established, so far as the landlords and tenants of Lower Bengal are concerned. In my opinion, the Bill will not improve

matters as regards the condition of the ryots, and there is grave reason to fear that it will aggravate the evils which it professes to remedy.

From F. Wyer, Esq., Collector of Hooghly.

26th June 1883.

8. It seems to me that the right of occupancy should be acquired only by the actual cultivator, and that it should not be transferable; otherwise the right will, in all probability, pass in a few years into the hands of the money-lenders.

11. It is the general opinion that the table of rates cannot be prepared, and in that opinion I agree.

16. Sections 93 and 94, Clauses A and B, and Sub-section 2 should, I think, be struck out. If (under them) the ryot does not choose to pay a fair and equitable rent, the landlord has to suffer. He has to pay compensation for disturbance. Does he disturb when the ryot refuses to pay his just rent?

19. Section 166.—If the power of distraining crops for current arrears is continued the procedure should be very much less complex than that proposed in the Bill. The costs (under the Bill) would be very heavy, and would ultimately fall on the ryot.

22. The Bill excites great apprehensions in the minds of the zemindars, and will, I think, not effect any permanent settlement of the rent question.

From E. V. Westmacott, Esq., Collector of Dacca.

23rd July 1883.

5. The action of the proposed law will only be to make the occupancy ryot the rack-renter instead of the present landlord, and the actual cultivator will not be the better for it.

9. I do not believe that the proposed law will have any effect whatever in raising the condition of the masses.

11. To speak of the wretchedness of Bengal ryots as notorious argues absolute ignorance of the facts of the case, and can only excite ridicule in those who know anything of the ryots of Dinagepore, Backergunge, Noakhaly, to say nothing of other Bengal districts.

27. Section 50 (a) appears to open the door to endless litigation.

35. Section 79 (c).—Why should a ryot be allowed to apply for a reduction year after year when a landlord cannot apply for enhancement, even on proved increase of area, oftener than once in ten years?

38. Section 91.—Any law fixing the rent of a ryot without a right of occupancy, will always be a dead letter.

40. Section 93 (b).—I think this compensation to a ryot, who has no right of occupancy, is iniquitous. If the ryot does not agree to pay the enhanced rent, and does not give up his holding, he is considered liable to pay the enhanced rent for the next year. I do not see why the law should change this.

45. Section 119.—I think it objectionable to pass a law which will, in practice, be evaded, as will certainly be the case with the limitation of the rent to $\frac{5}{16}$ of the gross produce. In Noakhaly there is a quantity of land which remains uncultivated for years, and is only taken up when the price of rice is exceptionally high. I think it impossible to interfere with the free contracts which they make. I have never had any trouble in the settlement of any question arising from such free contract. I think that any attempt at legislative interference with free contract in these cases will hinder cultivation, if not practically evaded.

48. If the zemindar has power enough to compel the ryot to pay illegal cesses against his will, I do not object to the interference of the State; but where both landlord and tenant are content with the indefinite relations between them, understood and freely accepted by both parties, but indefinite when brought before the tribunal of the moonsif, I think that very serious economic evils are likely to ensue from any attempt at legal definition or limitation, however attractive to a theoretic and sentimental statesman. The result of such an attempt will be to set class against class where relations are now friendly, as following the cherished customs of the country and the natural economic laws.

55. I think the proposed Act will do generally more harm than good in the Bengal districts, with which I am well acquainted.

From W. V. G. TAYLOR, Esq., Collector of Nuddea.

7th June 1883.

Among all whom I have consulted, the consensus of opinion is against the Bill as being one-sided and tending to lower the status of the zemindar.

2. I consider that portions of it are unsuited to this district, that they would unnecessarily deprive zemindars of privileges which they have long enjoyed and to which they are entitled, without conferring on the old ryots any corresponding advantage, and only benefiting new comers who have no claims on the estate. On the other hand, some of the benefits conferred on the ryots appear to me of a very doubtful nature, notably the transfer of occupancy rights by sale.

3. *Sections* 5 *and* 6 appear to me to be inapplicable to this district, in which the *utbandi* system prevails to a very great extent. Lands let out on this system have hitherto been considered to belong to the land-lords as their private property. Under the Bill such lands will become ryoti; and it seems questionable whether privileges so long enjoyed, and from which no injury to the ryots accrued, should be taken away.

Section 45.—The *utbandi* system will make almost every ryot a settled ryot, with a right of occupancy in the lands he may be holding since March. It cannot be the intention of the Bill to take advantage of a special system such as this.

Section 93.—I presume the Court has to decide whether the claim for enhancement is just and fair and in accordance to the law, before ejecting the ryot. In that case it seems hard that the landlord should have to grant compensation for disturbance which would never have occurred but for the obstinate rejection of such just claim by the ryot.

From Lord H. ULICK BROWN, Commissioner of the Rajshahve and Cooch Behar Division.

22nd September 1883.

9. The Bill proposes to effect a violent revolution in the ownership of landed property, and to change the landed system over a large and important tract of country, affecting one way or the other the interests of above fifty-five millions of people. The magnitude and importance of the measure can hardly be over-rated.

10. I think that such important changes, affecting detrimentally the rights and interests of a large and important class, should only be made on very strong grounds; such as, for instance, the grounds advanced by Mr. Gladstone when introducing a somewhat similar measure for Ireland in 1870. . . . The result of such a measure as this in that case might well make thinking men pause before introducing it into another

country, even if the circumstances under which the Irish measure was applied existed here. . . . The result of a similar measure in Ireland was almost disastrous, but it was tried to meet circumstances which seemed to the Government to require special treatment.

11. What are the circumstances under which it is proposed to introduce the present measure ? They are about as different to those found in Ireland as it is possible to conceive. No special and strong grounds, political or other, exist in the present case, nor have any been asserted in support of this Bill. . . . It is well known that in Eastern Bengal the ryots are very much the stronger, and that if protection or assistance is required there, it is required by the zemindar.

In 1877, so far from any measure to assist the ryots being thought necessary or advisable, the Lieut.-Governor thought special legislation necessary to enable the zemindars all over Bengal to recover their rents in cases where there was no dispute, combinations among some ryots and a general disinclination to meet their undisputed liabilities having called for such legislation in aid of the weaker party—the zemindars. . . . Matters have in no way changed since then. There has been no general feeling of discontent among the ryots of the country as a body. I am sure that all Government officers will agree in this, and in thinking that the ryots of Bengal are, as a body, in a contented prosperous condition, nor will it be denied that there has been no general request on the part of the ryots for such legislation as is now proposed.

12. It is clear, then, that the present measure is proposed, not because it is necessary, but because, in the opinion of the Government, the land system of the Bill is preferable to the existing one. It seems to me that the passing of such a Bill would not be justified by the circumstances under which it is proposed, and that, even if there were no other objections, it would not be right to pass it.

13. But there are other, and, in my opinion, serious objections to the Bill. There is, first, the one, argued so universally and strongly by the zemindars, that it is an infringement of the rights guaranteed to them by the permanent settlement.

The representations of the zemindars on this point seem to me to be most reasonable, and entitled to the fullest consideration. I have always thought that the quotations from the writings of Mr. Francis, Sir John Shore, Lord Cornwallis, and others, as to whether the zemindars had proprietary rights or not before the permanent settlement, which quotations have been so often brought forward by both sides when discussing the question of the infringement of the permanent settlement by the passing of Act X. of 1859, and such Bills as this one, are not really much to the point, as the case of the zemindars rests on a much stronger ground, viz. the declaration of the Permanent Settlement Regulation that they are proprietors of their estates.

The zemindars do not stand alone in thinking that Act X. of 1859, and such bills as this are breaches of the conditions of the permanent settlement. The English barrister-judges of the High Court, and especially the chief justice of the year when Act X. of 1859 was passed, and the present chief justice, are entirely in accord on that question.

I do not deny that on grave grounds of public necessity, such as apprehensions of general disturbances, it may be necessary to depart from even such engagements as the permanent settlement; but no one says that they exist in the present case. Nor do I forget that the permanent settlement allows Government to interfere for the welfare and protection of the ryot. But if it had been intended that such interference could amount to the destruction of the proprietary rights then conferred, such rights would never have been conferred; and then I request reference to paragraph 11 of this letter, as it can scarcely be alleged that interference is necessary in the very slightest degree for the protection of the ryots who are in Bengal proper stronger than the zemindars.

14. Next, we have for ninety years treated the zemindars as real proprietors, making them discharge the duties of proprietors as regards matters connected with police, crime, furnishing, supplies to troops on the march, and, above all, the collection of public demands. Is it fair or just to deprive them now of several of the most important rights of a proprietor?

15. In what I have said as to the ryots being stronger than the zemindars, as to the former not requiring assistance against the latter, and as to the latter (as admitted by the Governments of Bengal and India in 1877) requiring assistance against the former, I have had principally in view the ryots of Bengal Proper. I know that in Behar the zemindars are, generally speaking, the stronger; but if any measures nearly approaching those in the Bill had been necessary in that province, some measure or other would assuredly have been proposed by Sir Richard Temple or Sir Ashley Eden in 1876 and 1877 to assist the ryots of Behar, who have not asked for this Bill any more than have the ryots of Bengal.

16. Another objection is, that it is a serious thing to create among the nobility and gentry of a population of fifty-five millions, a feeling that the Government have injured such an important class, and that without nearly sufficient cause, and without any demand for it on the part of the classes for whose sake the injury is done.

17. Another objection is the possibly disturbing effect the Bill might have on the ryots throughout the country. Though, happily, they are of a very different mould to the Irish, still when the ryots of Bengal and Behar see that, without any general representation on their part—without, so far as they know, any reason at all for the action of the Government—the zemindars are deprived of rights, while others are at the same time conferred on the ryots, I think it very possible that the idea may occur to the latter, that, as they have got so much without asking for it, Government must be actuated by a great desire to please them and to injure the zemindars who are sacrificed for their sake, and that by agitation further concessions may be obtained. Such agitation might before long grow and gain strength till it became a source of much trouble to the Government.

18. For these reasons I am opposed to the most important provisions of the Bill, and think that none of them should be applied to Bengal proper. But provisions for facilitating the recovery of rent should be enacted.

23. In conclusion, I hope that, after all that was said and done in 1877, and the unchanged circumstances since then, a provision will be made for the recovery of undisputed rents. It seems to me very unjust to omit such a provision in favour of the zemindar from a Bill which proposes to deprive him of so much. In 1877 the zemindar asked for bread; his claim to it was admitted by the Governments of Bengal and India; in 1883 he is refused a crumb and given a very large stone.

THE LATEST MEETING OF THE ZEMINDARS.

ONE of the largest meetings yet held in India, to express dissatisfaction with the Bengal Tenancy Bill, was held in the Town Hall of Calcutta on the 29th December 1883.

The chair was taken by the MAHARAJAH OF DURBHUNGA, and the MAHARAJAH OF DOOMROAN moved the first Resolution, to the effect that *the Government has entirely failed to show that any grounds exist for introducing into the Bengal Tenancy Bill revolutionary provisions which are a novel departure from the ancient custom and the existing law relating to landlord and tenant, and which will most injuriously affect all classes of the community who are in any way interested in land.*

The Maharajah, addressing the meeting in *Urdu*, made the following remarks: " You are aware of the revolutionary provisions embodied in the Bill. Nothing has been so clearly made out in recent discussions than that these revolutionary provisions are a departure from the ancient custom of the land. Under the worst of the Moguls your proprietary rights were always respected : he was extortionate, but never confiscated your proprietary rights. It has been said that the zemindars were then mere collectors of Government revenue. The histories of many of the families, whose representatives I see around me, give a flat contradiction to that statement. The zemindaries which have descended to me from a long line of ancestors, existed, as I learn from my family records, from a long time anterior to the Mahomedan conquest of the country, and my ancestors possessed greater rights and privileges than I have come to enjoy under the permanent settlement. The rights recognized by that settlement have never, before this, been questioned by the Government or the Courts of Law.

" Gentlemen, it has been said that the tenants under you had greater rights before the introduction of the permanent settlement than they enjoy at present ; and that it is the duty of the Legislature to rehabilitate them in their old rights. The assertion as to such rights having existed, is refuted by the two highest judicial authorities in the land.

" The advocates of the Bill admit that its provisions will sweep away your vested rights guaranteed under the permanent settlement ; but they add that the Government reserved the power to enact laws for the protection and welfare of your ryots, and that the Legislature is simply exercising that power. It cannot be denied that, in certain contingencies, under certain political necessities, the Government of a country would be justified in trenching on vested rights. But no such grave political necessity exists in the present instance. If the reservation is held to justify the Government in taking away your proprietary rights guaranteed by the permanent settlement, then that settlement would have no meaning.

" It has been said, Gentlemen, that you, zemindars in Bengal Proper, are weak and your ryots are strong ; and that we in Behar are strong and our ryots are low and depressed. Why is then the same nostrum prescribed for two evils which are so entirely opposed to each other in their nature ? The provision intended to make the Behar ryots strong would necessarily, if also applied to ryots of Bengal, aggravate the evil, by making the strength of the latter excessive. But what is the actual condition of things in our much-maligned province of Behar ? I need only quote in answer what the Lieut.-Governor said on the subject."

The Maharajah, after citing passages in Sir Ashley Eden's speeches in 1881 and 1882 testifying to the growing prosperity of the cultivators, said : " This opinion must have been available to the Government when it indited its despatch to the Secretary of State on the Rent Bill in March 1882, and to the members of the Legislative Council when they made their furious denunciations of our zemindari system in March 1883. But it did not suit their purpose to give place, in their speeches, to Sir Ashley Eden's publicly-expressed opinions on the question.

" You have heard it said that a drowning man catches at a straw, and you may, therefore, understand why our mighty legislators caught at a straw like the opinion of a Government pleader at Gya, in defence of the position they had taken up in the Council. They could find nothing better. Why was not an inquiry instituted before we were so ruthlessly denounced in Council? The Government despatch relies on certain figures taken from the Road Cess returns. Those figures go on the assumption that all lands in a district are equally cultivated. This is an error ; besides, the figures do not show that higher rents prevail in Behar than in Bengal. The despatch quotes the opinions of Messrs. Metcalfe, Geddes and McDonnel; but it forgets that these opinions, which, as far as I know, never before were deemed worthy of facing the light, were followed by the Behar Rent Commission ; and that that body, composed of experienced officials and non-officials, never recommended the violent and radical changes which have been embodied in the Bengal Tenancy Bill. Then, two officers, Messrs. Tobin and Finucane, were appointed to determine what was called equitable rents, the former being deputed to Shahabad and the latter to a selected tract in the North Gangetic districts. What was the result of the inquiry ? Mr. Tobin found that the rents had not been changed for the last forty years and were exceptionally low. When this result was made known to the authorities, the inquiry in the Southern districts was immediately stopped, because the result militated against opinions pronounced in certain quarters. Mr. Finucane's report, on the other hand, was extensively quoted in Council. The rent-rates found by Mr. Finucane in the Mozufferpore district, are not, however, higher than those found to prevail in Bengal Proper, as will appear when the larger size and the greater productiveness of the tract selected for Mr. Finucane's examination is considered. These, Gentlemen, are the sum and substance of the evidence on which a whole class of zemindars has been condemned. A great portion of Behar consists of lands occupied by indigo-planters, of Crown estates and of escheated estates. If you compare the position and condition of our ryots with those of the ryots in the Crown and escheated estates, you will find, as you well know, that our ryots are far better off. The reason is obvious. The ryots belong to the same castes as the zemindars ; they are Brahmins, Rajputs, Palhuns, Kaysts, Gowalas and Kurmis ; and Mahomedans likewise are represented in both classes. Indeed, zemindars have often many of their own kith and kin among their ryots. Woe, therefore, to the zemindars who would disregard the voice of the community among whom they live, and try to play the part of the rapacious or tyrannical landlord. All these are facts which a little inquiry would have brought out; but no inquiry was instituted, we were condemned unheard, and it is now proposed to confiscate our rights by this revolutionary measure. I ask you, Gentlemen, to record your emphatic opinion that the measure has no justification in the actual condition of things. A common danger has brought us together from distant parts of the country. We have come, respectfully and loyally, to submit this our last appeal to the Government, in the metropolis of India. We have come to ask the Government to have regard for its plighted faith, and to protect the vested rights of an important section of its subjects ; to show to the Government that the revolutionary changes, which it proposes to effect by the Bengal Tenancy Bill, have neither been asked for by the ryots nor are calculated to do them good. The alarm and consternation that have come on the zemindars throughout the country can hardly be described. Our mighty Government may afford to disregard that alarm and consternation; but it should not forget that the foundation of the British rule in India is justice—justice to all alike ; and that all cases of injustice, of broken faith, tend directly or indirectly to sap that foundation. It is the duty of all loyal subjects to speak out on an occasion like this ; and I would deem myself unworthy of that character of loyalty which has always distinguished the family to which I have the honour to belong, if I had not spoken out as I have done."

Mr. J. J. J. KESWICK, in seconding the Resolution, said : " Maharajahs, Rajahs, and Gentlemen,—It is unnecessary for me to trouble you with a speech, as I spoke on the subject on a former occasion, and my views against the Bill are well known. I would much rather listen to those gentlemen who have not spoken before, and I am glad to see this great meeting of influential zemindars, as it shows the earnestness of your protest against this uncalled-for and unnecessary measure."

Baboo DWARKANATH CHUCKERBUTTY supported the Resolution, and observed, in the course of his speech, that the Government of the late Viceroy had been taunted for his aggressive policy. " We have been told," he said, " of the wickedness and folly of the wars it carried on, and of the perpetual unrest in which it kept the Empire ; but the Government of the present Viceroy seems actuated by the same spirit, only the scene is changed : we had war with foreign nations, and now we have a war of races at home. Lord Lytton fought with gunpowder and cannon. Lord Ripon delights in legislative explosives ; and, if this Bill becomes law, it will cause a fearful upheaval of society."

The MAHARAJAH OF DINAGEPORE moved the second Resolution to the effect that *the Bill, if passed into law, will be detrimental to the peace and tranquillity of the country, by fostering disputes and litigation between all classes of the agricultural population, and thereby interfere with the general welfare of the community.*

Mr. BELL, in seconding the Resolution, made the following observations in a clear and forcible speech, which could not be condensed without detriment, and should, therefore, be read in a full report of the meeting : " I was struck with what my friend said when he contrasted the aggressive policy of Lord Ripon with the aggressive policy of Lord Lytton ; but he omitted to say that Lord Lytton's arms were directed against the enemies of his country, while Lord Ripon is attacking those who have always been the support of the British Government. . . . It is proposed in the Bill that no agreement between the landlord and his tenant shall be valid, unless it receives the sanction of a revenue officer. It seems to me that a landlord and his tenant can agree about the rates of rent, considering that they know the land and the produce that it grows, far better than any revenue officer can do. It is simply preposterous to press a proposition that no engagement shall be made between landlord and tenant except with the sanction of a Government officer." Then, referring to the approval which the Bengal Tenancy Bill received from the Lieutenant-Governor, Mr. Bell said : " Although I am opposed to the Lieutenant-Governor on this Bill, he is a gentleman for whom I entertain profound respect, and whose opinion I would not oppose were I not supported by the almost unanimous opinion of the officials and non-officials throughout the country. . . . What I complain of and deeply deplore, is the injudicious indifference with which this unanimous consensus of opinion has been received. At the same time, though the odds are against us, I do not despair, for I feel we are fighting a righteous cause. I feel that it is impossible for Lord Ripon, if he regards his reputation as a statesman, to turn a deaf ear to the almost unanimous voice—both official and non-official—of India. I myself have confidence that the settlement to which my friend, the Maharajah, alludes—of Lord Cornwallis—will not be permitted to be torn to shreds, and I am sure that you will agree with me that the name of Cornwallis ought never to be mentioned without exciting in your breasts the profoundest feelings of gratitude. I read the other day the epitaph on his monument, and I think that the words upon it correctly describe our feelings, that *after the monument is crumbled into dust, millions will still attest the wisdom of his conduct and the virtue of his life.*"

RAJAH HURBULLUB NARAINSING moved the third Resolution to *the effect that if the deprivation of the landlords of their just rights, inherited from generation to generation, confirmed by the permanent settlement and consecrated by a century of British rule, be deemed essential to the welfare of the tenantry, the Government be solicited to consider the justice of allowing the zemindars to surrender their estates on receiving such compensation in money as will, when invested in Government securities, produce a permanent return equal to their present income.*

Mr. GREGOR GRANT, from whose speech a passage has already been quoted, made also the following statement: "About nine years ago, Sir George Campbell, *for the sake of peace and good government of the Sonthal Pergunnahs,* deprived the zemindars of the power to settle their own lands with the ryots, and appointed Government officials to grant leases to them instead. The effect has been that, whereas suits for the recovery of rent were formerly almost unknown when the zemindar made his own settlement, they have, under the Government settlements, multiplied a hundredfold."

The HONOURABLE HARBANS SAHAI, in supporting the Resolution, said: "There can be no two opinions as to the justice of our demand. There is no revolution in the land; and if unfortunately there were one, a settled Government would confiscate the rights only of the guilty; and if it became necessary to trench on the vested rights of the innocent, it would, in honour and justice, deem itself bound to offer compensation. The state of things in Ireland does not exist in India; your ryots have not complained of you, have not sought relief against you, nor have they asked for additional rights. You have heard from preceding speakers the overwhelming testimony there is, that the condition of our tenantry is improving from year to year under the existing conditions. Were the Bill to become law, your zemindari office would have to be transferred to the Revenue officer's *cutcherry* or to the Civil Court, with, at every step, a law-suit or some legal proceeding, fines, harassment from surveys, records of rights, settlements, and the like. You know what law-suits mean—simply ruin to those engaged in them. The visit of a Common Court peon to a village is justly dreaded by those on whom it is inflicted: under the Tenancy Bill you will have no end of such visits."

RAJAH SHYAMA SUNKER RAI CHOWDHREE, in moving the fourth Resolution, went into the origin and history of the rights of the zemindars, and added the following remarks: "Among the fifty thousand or more proprietors of land in Bengal and Behar, about a thousand are descendants of persons who were proprietors at the time of the permanent settlement; the rest derive their title from purchase at Government revenue sales, or at other public or private sales. The one thousand original proprietors and their descendants have spent a large amount of capital on their estates since 1793: therefore, the whole of the fifty thousand proprietors have invested capital in land, in good faith and perfect reliance on the guarantee of rights afforded by the permanent settlement Regulations. Surely they are entitled to compensation for any of those rights which may be taken from them." The resolution was to the effect that, *as thousand of estates have been made of waste and other lands upon the faith of the zemindars being entitled to their present rights, suitable clauses may be introduced into the Bill for providing compensation to the zemindars for the loss of their rights.*

Mr. J. G. APCAR, in seconding the Resolution, made the following observations in the course of his speech: "When an injustice is perpetrated to any class, it is an injury to the whole State; and the Tenancy Bill is a measure that certainly calls for the active sympathy with the zemindars of all who are interested in the welfare of India. The zemindars are a class on whom the stability of the Empire greatly rests; and when we find legislation proposed that has offended the officials, angered the European community, and is beginning to alienate the zemindars, I think it is time for us to take alarm. In what manner has this Bill come before us? It has been brought forward, not merely on insufficient evidence, but on no evidence at all. It has been framed upon assumption: it is pressed forward by men selected for the purpose. I would ask, why is it and how is it that those who have ripe experience, and could form a correct judgment on the subject, have been studiously kept from dealing with it? Why has the assistance of Mr. Dampier, of Mr. Monro, and of our learned Advocate-General not been called in? In our opposition to this measure there is no question of party politics. Liberals oppose it. I would instance my friend, Mr. Keswick, who is a strong Liberal, or at least was so, until the definition of that term came to be a person who is generous at other persons' expense. But this is not all; there have been reasonable representations made, and they have been treated with contempt; there have been opinions given—official opinions—and I would ask the Government how it is that that most able minute of our honoured Chief Justice has not had place given to it in the opinions published by the Government?

"Is it for the sake of the ryot that this measure has been brought out? We shall find that, if passed into law, it will reduce him to a worse state than that which he now occupies. For whose good, then, is the measure proposed? Government takes no heed that the value of property is being reduced thirty per cent.; it ignores the fact that people have been dealing with the property in the belief that it had been permanently settled, and on the faith of the British Government. Is it not paying too heavy a price for a policy by which the Government forfeits the confidence of all who have anything to lose. and imperils the peace and prosperity of the country? I ask you, Gentlemen, is not that too heavy a cost?"

Baboo SOORJ NARAIN SING, of Bhangulpore, in a long speech supporting the Resolution, observed: "Government has, for a long series of years, from the Permanent Settlement to the present day, sold estates on the understanding that the purchasers would have in them the rights which the existing law gives to landed proprietors. I have seen documents in which the authorised officers of the Government stated that certain zemindaris purchased from the State were free from *mourosi* and other tenant rights. Is it just that those who have invested their capital in such estates should be deprived of the rights they bought, without receiving any compensation for the same?"

Nawab VELAYET ALI KHAN, who spoke in Urdu, proposed the fifth Resolution, to the effect that *in view of the provisions of the Bengal Tenancy Bill, which will deprive the landlords of their legitimate prestige and influence, and reduce them to a state of helplessness, the Government should be requested to relieve the zemindars of the duty of collecting the road and public works cesses, and of such other services and obligations as are now cast upon them by law or custom.*

Baboo SALIGRAM SING, in seconding the Resolution, referred to the many important duties which now devolve upon zemindars, such as aiding in the demarcation of land, assisting the police in the apprehension of offenders, supplying provisions to the troops that pass through their lands, collecting the Government cesses, and furnishing information on various matters. He also recalled the eminent services which the zemindars had rendered to the Government in critical times ; and argued that their altered position under the Bill, and the loss of prestige which would ensue, would deprive them of the power of dulv fulfilling such duties.

The MAHARAJAH OF GHIDORE moved the sixth Resolution, which was that *the Viceroy in Council be moved to publish for general information, in English and in the vernaculars, the Bengal Tenancy Bill as it may be amended by the Select Committee, and to grant sufficient time to the public for the consideration of the amended Bill.*

Baboo PROSONNO CHUNDER ROY, Zemindar of Nuddea, in seconding the Resolution, explained that, according to the custom prevailing in his district, lands were not let out on lease, but that the cultivators were each year allowed to plough and sow such lands as they pleased, the zemindar's agent being afterwards sent to see what land each had cultivated, and to compute the rent according to customary rules mutually accepted. The Bill would convert these casual cultivators, and even trespassers, into middlemen of the class it proposes to create, giving them the right to sub-let their zemindar's land, and to sell their new rights to outsiders.

Baboo TROYLUCKO NATH MITTER, in supporting the Resolution, observed that the changes which the Bill had undergone were so numerous, and some of them so important and so novel in their character, that, unless the Bill was before the public for a reasonable period, it would be impossible for those whose interests are affected by it, to consider its provisions and express their opinion on them. He added : "To justify hasty legislation, necessity for the same must be made out. It must be shown that the circumstances of the country had attained a critical position ; that the relations of the different classes were strained ; that their attitude was menacing, and that conflict and calamity would ensue without immediate legislative interference. But can this be said of the present relations between the rent-paying and the rent-receiving classes? Is it not a fact that, two months before the Bill was introduced, their relations were perfectly amicable ? I may add, without fear of contradiction, that even its introduction has not yet excited any general bitterness of feeling between the two classes. Why, then, force this legislative measure with undue speed ? "

Baboo SHEO PROTAB NARAIN, Delegate for the MAHARAJAH OF HUTWA, who had been prevented from attending the meeting by a heavy domestic affliction, said, in supporting the sixth Resolution : "The history of the Bill shows what great changes it has undergone, not always at the hands of the Select Committee, but also at those of certain gentlemen who have been charged ever and anon with the making of the Bill ; how, with its many revolutionary changes, we find in it but little of Sir Ashley Eden's original Bill for the speedy realisation of rents. The dwarf has grown into the monster which threatens to swallow up all our rights. In the Select Committee, Gentlemen, the public has no access, and its few members are left to re-arrange things according to their idiosyncrasies, without any light from outside. It is nothing but just, therefore, that the fullest opportunity of discussing its recommendations should be given to the public. But while those acquainted with the English language will thus be in a position to know and discuss the changes recommended, there is an infinitely more numerous class who, on account of their ignorance of that language, will not be able to form any idea of those changes, and the ryots come in this category. We ask, therefore, the Government not to proceed with this Bill until accurate translations of it in the vernaculars, embodying the recommendations of the Select Committee, have been for some time before the public.

Baboo CHUCKEN LALL SING, Zemindar of Chuckdiggee, proposed, and Baboo HUROCHUNDER ROY CHOWDHREE, Zemindar of Mymemsing, seconded the seventh Resolution, that *a memorial be presented to the Viceroy in Council embodying the Resolutions passed at the meeting, and that it be forwarded with the signature of the Chairman.*

A vote of thanks to His Highness the Chairman was proposed by Maharajah JOTENDRO MOHUN TAGORE, and seconded by Baboo JOY KISSEN MOOKERJEE, and unanimously carried, as were the seven preceding Resolutions.

The meeting then separated.

London: Printed by W. H. Allen & Co., 13 Waterloo Place, Pall Mall. S.W.

REMARKS

AND

EXTRACTS FROM OFFICIAL REPORTS

ON THE

BENGAL TENANCY BILL.

BY

J. DACOSTA.

LONDON:

W. H. ALLEN & CO., 13 WATERLOO PLACE. S.W.

————

1884.

PRICE ONE SHILLING.

THE

BENGAL TENANCY BILL.

London, February 1884.

Great excitement and alarm have been occasioned in Bengal by the introduction, in the Legislative Council of India, of a measure bearing the above title, which deals with the rights of property, proposes to abolish the freedom of contract, and would deprive a large class of the people of the protection they now receive from the law courts.

The avowed objects of the Bill are—

" (1) to give reasonable security to the tenant in the occupation " and enjoyment of his land ; and

" (2) to give reasonable facilities to the landlord for the settlement " and recovery of his rent " ;

but an examination of its provisions renders it clear that these objects are unattainable under their operation, and that the Bill is calculated to produce effects exactly opposed to them. Such is the view taken by the Bengal officials (Commissioners, District Judges, and Collectors) whom the Government consulted on the subject last summer, and extracts from whose reports will be found in the Appendix to this paper.

The weight due to the opinions of these officials, who are members of the Covenanted Civil Service of India, may be gathered from the fact that they form the principal and most trusted channel by which the Government receives its information on the state of the country, the condition and feelings of the people, and the details of the administration ; they have, indeed, not inaptly been called " the eyes and ears of the Government." It is, moreover, by them that the new Bill would have to be administered ; and their strong condemnation of it is the more significant, that their feelings and training would incline them, one would think, rather to support than to oppose the Government whom they serve, and on whose

1 *

good-will in no small degree depend their advancement and' welfare.

For such a body of men to condemn the main provisions of the Bill as unjust, iniquitous, unnecessary, calculated to set class against class, to incite to strife and litigation, and to result in grievous injury to both the landowners and the cultivators, would argue a very strong conviction against the proposed legislation ; and when their administrative experience and their daily intercourse with the people are taken into consideration, can any doubt exist as to their opinion, expressed under official responsibility, being entitled to greater confidence than the views of the author or originator of the Bengal Tenancy Bill, whose very name is unknown to the public, and who is, therefore, but an irresponsible adviser of the Government?

The promoters of the measure have said that legislation was undertaken on this occasion at the instance of the zemindars, and that the necessity of introducing the clauses which relate to the position of the tenants arose from the pledge which the Government gave to the ryots in 1793. How far these pleas can be accepted as a justification of the Bill will appear from the following statement.

To begin with the pledge alluded to, it is inferred from the following passage in Regulation I. of 1793 :—

" It being the duty of the ruling power to protect all classes of " people, and more particularly those who, from their situation, are " most helpless, the Governor-General in Council will, whenever he " may deem it proper, enact such regulations as he may think neces- " sary for the protection and welfare of the dependent talookdars, " ryots, and other cultivators of the soil."

The pledge, it will be seen—if there be one in the above passage —is to protect the talookdars and cultivators, while the Bill would despoil those very talookdars and the zemindars in order to create a new class of middlemen; and would take away from the cultivators, whom it professes to protect, the protection they now enjoy against the undue enhancement of their rents. In other words, the measure has been put forward under a delusive plea which has gained for it the sympathy and support of many in this country ; while few have studied its clauses and ascertained its real tendency and scope.

The ryots or cultivating tenants in Bengal may be classed under two distinct heads, viz. those who have and those who have not occu. pancy rights. The former are entitled, from prolonged residence, to hold their land so long as they pay their rents punctually, and they are protected by existing laws from the undue enhancement of their rents : the bulk of the ryots belong to this class, and their number has been increasing steadily. The other class con.

·sists of yearly tenants, or tenants who hold their land under a lease.

Now, the Bill proposes to cancel every lease, and confer on the lessee, and generally on every ryot, a permanent right of occupancy, provided he has held his land for twelve years, or tenanted any plot, however small, in the same estate for that period, or even held various plots in it for shorter periods amounting to twelve years : it proposes, moreover, to do away with the payment of rent as a necessary condition for the preservation of an occupancy right, and to render occupancy rights transferable by sale without the consent of the landlord ; also to confer such rights, permanently and at once, in respect of all lands of which the new occupancy ryot may become the tenant in the same estate, although he may have held them only for a few days. At the same time elaborate provisions are made for preventing that the landlord should demand a full rent from the new occupancy ryot, the maximum being fixed at less than half the rate sanctioned by custom and general usage, and, indeed, of the rate which the Government itself continues to claim in the Crown estates of Bengal and in the other provinces where the Government is the landlord. Protected by these conditions, the new occupancy ryot is to be allowed to sublet all the land over which he may acquire the newly-invented occupancy right, free from the restrictions as to rent which are to be imposed on the landlord.

The inevitable result of these provisions must be to enrich the new middleman (misnamed occupancy ryot, since neither residence nor cultivation is required for his qualification) at the expense of the zemindars and talookdars on the one hand, and of the ryots or cultivating tenants on the other, regardless of the faith we have pledged to the former, and of our bounden duty, irrespective of all pledges, to protect the latter.

The effect of the Bill would, in short, be to despoil the zemindar of proprietary rights solemnly guaranteed to him in 1793; to take from the cultivator (for whose benefit the measure has professedly been framed) the protection he now has against excessive rents, and to call in a new class of middlemen, under the fictitious name of occupancy ryots, to share in the profit from land, vesting them with the power of absorbing the lion's share, although they would have to contribute neither labour nor capital for its production.

The marvellous equanimity and complacency with which a result so deplorable and so contrary to the avowed objects of the Bill, is viewed by its promoters at Section 41 of the *Statement of Objects and Reasons,* would betray the fact that such is actually the end for which the measure has been prepared, and that it represents its real object. The passage in the *Statement* runs thus :—

" That the powers of transferring and subletting which the Bill

" recognises, may in time lead to a state of things in which the bulk
" of the cultivators would not be occupancy ryots, but under-ryots
" with but little protection from the law, is, indeed, within the range
" of possibility; but if such a state of things should arise, we may
" rest assured that the Government of the day will know how to deal
" with it."

Unjustifiable and disastrous as a similar result might be, it would
not be difficult to point to the motives which may have rendered it
desirable in the estimation of the author of the measure.

Bengal, under the permanent settlement of 1793, has attained a
degree of prosperity unknown in the other provinces of our Indian
Empire, and the official reports on the condition of the country have,
for years, represented its peasantry in a thriving and progressive
state. Before 1793 one-third of the land was jungle, the bulk of the
ryots lived on the verge of starvation, and the land-tax, which formed
the only source of State revenue, could never be recovered in its
entirety. At the same time there was no prospect of improvement in
the existing state of things, as capitalists stood aloof from agricultural
enterprise, owing to the prevailing system of periodically re-assessing
the land-tax; a system under which the fruit of the capital invested
in the clearance, improvement, and cultivation of land was exposed
to be absorbed in the Government demand at the next assessment of
the tax.

At present not only is the land revenue collected in Bengal with
an ease and regularity never attained in the other provinces of India,
but new and growing sources of revenue have been opened out,
which already yield almost three times as much as the land-tax. In
short—

" *The Bengal of to-day offers a startling contrast to the Bengal*
" *of* 1793; *the wealth and prosperity of the country have marvellously*
" *increased—increased beyond all precedent under the permanent*
" *settlement . . . A great portion of this increase is due to the zemin-*
" *dari body as a whole, and they have been very active and powerful*
" *factors in the development of this prosperity.*"—Report of the
Commissioner of Burdwan, *Gazette of India*, 20th October 1883.

This growing prosperity has, for many years, excited the cupidity
of a certain class of financiers. The salt duty was raised in Bengal
to fifteen hundred per cent. of the value of the salt when shipped at
Liverpool. Direct taxation, Excise, Stamp, and Customs duties were
greatly increased, and cesses were imposed on the landholding and
agricultural classes under the colour of local taxation.

All this, however, did not satisfy financiers whose mind seemed
bent upon intercepting the profit from land before it could reach the
hands of those who had produced it. These financiers were not contented to wait until such profit should accumulate in the form of

national wealth; as then a portion of it only could be obtained through taxation. They resolved, therefore, on increasing the land-tax under some disguised form that would conceal its violation of the public faith pledged in 1793; and their first attempt took the shape of local and provincial cesses. The disguise, however, deceived neither the people nor the official class, a majority of whom strongly protested against the step; and a member of the Secretary of State's Council recorded his opinion on its character in the following remarkable but apposite terms :—" *We have no standing ground in* " *India except brute force, if we forfeit our character for truth.*"

A different scheme had, therefore, to be devised for attaining the object in view, and the Bengal Tenancy Bill would appear to be the form under which the new scheme is to be inaugurated.

At present the wealth produced by the labour of the cultivator, from the land supplied by the zemindar, and with the aid of the funds advanced by the capitalist, after satisfying the legitimate claim of the State, is distributed among those three agents or factors; and a residue, left in the hands of each, goes yearly to increase the national wealth in one form or another, whence the people and the Government both derive substantial benefit.

Under the Bill the landowner would scarcely receive enough to discharge the revenue, and the cultivator would be ground down by the [new middleman; while the latter, who is to be vested with unrestricted power to rack-rent the land, would absorb all the surplus profit yielded by it. This surplus could then be diverted into the coffers of the State, simply by the necessary taxation being imposed on the middleman; a process against which he could claim no protection under the permanent settlement, seeing that he was not a party to that compact.

There seems little room to doubt that such is the actual scheme in furtherance of which the Bengal Tenancy Bill has been introduced. The avowed objects of that Bill, at all events, are unattainable under its provisions, and common-sense will not permit us to believe that the ultimate object can be limited to enriching the money-lenders and other outsiders who are invited to acquire the extraordinary rights which it proposes to create.

Corroborative evidence of the intentions of the Government being at variance with the avowed objects of the Bill, is also supplied by the fact that, while so much stress is laid on the importance of restoring to the ryots the rights they are alleged to have possessed at the time of the permanent settlement, the Bill specially provides that no such rights shall be recognised in the Crown estates; and the Commissioner of the Presidency Division remarks in his report of the 31st December 1880 :—

" So far as the practice of the Government is concerned, I fail to

" find in their dealings with the ryots upon Crown lands any indica-
" tions of the recognition of a living tenant-right among any class of
" ryots save those known as *khudkash* and *kudeemi*."

While the policy inaugurated by this Bill appears to be regulated
by no fixed principle, it is, at the same time, a very short-sighted
policy, seeing that, for the sake of a temporary accretion of revenue,
to be obtained through breach of faith and spoliation, it would
arrest the whole course of prosperity which has flowed from the
permanent settlement, and reduce the agricultural population of
Bengal to the destitute and precarious condition of the Madras
and Bombay ryots, among whom millions drag a miserable existence on insufficient food, and a deficient harvest brings famine
with its many sufferings and horrors. Capital, in obedience to the
same laws which controlled its application before the introduction of
the permanent settlement, would once more stand aloof from agricultural enterprise in Bengal, and auction sales of estates for arrears of
revenue, fields abandoned by the cultivators and increasing difficulty
in the collection of the land-tax would mark in the official reports of
Bengal, as similar results have marked in those of Madras and
Bombay, the decline in the prosperity of the province.

That this is not the first time that the plea of protecting the ryot
would be used for supporting schemes of spoliation, may be seen
from the following passage in a Minute written by Sir Phillip Francis
in 1776 :—

" It is proposed to secure to the ryots the perpetual and undis-
" turbed possession of their lands. This language, I know, is popular,
" and has often been used to give countenance and colour to acts of
" violence and injustice against the zemindars and others of superior
" rank of the natives. Before we give perpetual possession we ought
" to determine the property. The State does not consist of nothing
" but the ruler and the ryot, nor is it true that the ryot is the pro-
" prietor of the land . . . . but it does not follow that because the
" ryot has no direct permanent property in the land, he should there-
" fore have no right, or that no care should be taken to protect him.
" Without his assistance, the land is useless to the zemindar. If
" they are left to themselves, they will soon come to an agreement in
" which each party will find his advantage. . . . . To dictate the
" specific terms of any lease is an invasion of the rights of property
" . . . . the intervention of the Government between the zemindar
" and the ryot should have no object but to enforce the execution of
" their respective engagements."

Having now seen how delusive is the professed object of securing
the ryot or cultivating tenant in the occupation and enjoyment of
his land, let us see what the Bill proposes for attaining its other

avowed object, *i.e.* to give acilities to the landlord for the recovery ot nis rent.

The promoters of the measure tell us that legislation on this occasion was undertaken at the instance of the zemindars. The facts to which this interpretation has been given, are as follows :—

In 1871, when the Government imposed an additional burden on land in Bengal, in the shape of a Road Cess payable partly by the zemindars, partly by their tenants, and requested the former to collect the tenant's portion free of charge and at their risk (a risk which involved the attachment and sale of their estates in case the full amount of the Cess was not paid into the treasury on the due date), the zemindars observed that they already experienced much trouble, delay, and expense in the collection of their rents, owing to the defective state of the law on the subject; that in order to save their estates from attachment, they had often to make good from other sources the deficiency which occurred in their rent collections, and that their difficulties would increase if they undertook the collection of the Government Cess on the conditions proposed. Finally, however, they accepted the duty and the risk, upon a promise which the Government then made to simplify the law for the recovery of rent.

The zemindars have, ever since, punctually fulfilled that duty which, in following years, was rendered more onerous, in consequence of new Cesses having been imposed in addition to the Cess of 1871 ; but the promise of the Government has not been redeemed to this day, while the opportunity it afforded for legislation has been turned to account for making the present attempt to despoil those very zemindars from whom a valuable consideration had been accepted and to whom assistance had been promised in return.

The course pursued in this instance is so extraordinary, so derogatory to the dignity of the ruling power, so repugnant to all sense of fairness, that it seems advisable, in stating it, to cite authentic testimony in support of the statement.

The District Judge of Tipperah in his report on the Bill, dated 12th May 1883, says :—

" I admit the difficulty of conceding to the zemindar his demand " for greater facility in the realisation of his dues ; but I am not " prepared to say that it could not be satisfied to a certain extent. " There is not, however, any attempt made to do so in the Bill. " This is one of the points where the zemindar, asking for bread, " has been given a stone."

The Commissioner of the Presidency Division, in his report of the 2nd July 1883, observes :—

" As to the recovery of rents, which was the beginning of the " legislation which has found its outcome in the present Bill, the

" landlords will hardly be satisfied with the relief given them. *On*
" *the principles on which the Bill is drawn* * the zemindars could not
" expect further relief. I suspect, however, that they expected, and
" I am not prepared to say that they have not a good right to expect,
" very much more substantial relief, as the outcome of their applica-
" tion for a summary method of realising rents, preferred during the
" last twelve years."

Reverting now to the promise which the Government made in
1871, we find that no step whatever was taken for redeeming it until
1873, when a Bill was sketched for the purpose, but was not pro--
ceeded with for reasons which have remained unknown to the public.
The next apparent step was taken in 1877, when Sir Ashley Eden,
on assuming the Government of Bengal, said :—

" The landlords have not such facility as they should have for the
" ready and prompt realisation of their rent and the Government
" cesses. My predecessor recorded a Minute expressing the intention
" of at once applying for the sanction of the Government of India to
" pass a short Bill to provide a system for the realisation of rent by
" a somewhat more summary and prompt process than that which
" now exists. I hope it will not be long before I shall be in a posi-
" tion to ask the Council to pass a Bill of the sort."

In 1878 a Bill was at last introduced by the Government of
Bengal ; and the following remarks made on the occasion by the
officer in charge of the Bill, will show how great was the necessity
for a measure of the kind :—

" Notwithstanding the fact that, in about seventy-five per cent. of
" the suits for arrears of rent, the claim is really not contested, the
" zemindars and other rent-receivers have often found themselves
" unable to recover their just dues without submitting to a process
" which entails costs that may possibly never be recovered, and
" delays that are frequently embarrassing and ruinous ; and even
" when the zemindar has got his decree, it by no means follows that
" he has got his rent. The Road Cess and Public Works Cess Acts
" have thrown upon the zemindars the responsibility of collecting,
" with their rents, and paying into the treasuries, all that portion of
" the fresh local and provincial taxation which falls upon tenants
" of every degree. If they cannot recover this easily and effectually
" from their tenants, they must, under penalty, pay the amount
" themselves—a position which the State is obviously bound to
" render as little burdensome as possible."

Notwithstanding the above encouraging statement, this Bill also
was dropped after a time, upon the vague and inconclusive plea that,
as the law on rent seemed to require revision, it was advisable to

* These words were underlined obviously for the purpose of drawing attention to the
unprincipled character of the Bill.

deal with both subjects in one measure. A Rent Commission was thereupon appointed, consisting almost exclusively of Government servants, which held numerous meetings, but took no evidence and abstained even from examining the parties concerned; and it ultimately submitted in 1880 a draft Bill of a most complicated and revolutionary character. The following extracts from the official reports made on the Rent Commission's Bill will give a clearer idea of its nature.

The Commissioner of the Presidency Division said, on the 31st of December 1880 :—

"The proposed Bill seems to me to contemplate grave infringe-" ments on the rights of zemindars as hitherto recognised; to destroy "such rights, and to give the holders no compensation for such "damage done to their interests. It seems to me, moreover, "peculiarly unjust to contemplate such restrictive legislation with "reference to the rights of zemindars, when the whole tendency of "recent legislation on the part of the Government has been to "throw more responsibility on the landholders in the way of "providing funds for improvements connected with the land."

The Commissioner of the Cooch Behar and Rajshahya Division, observed in his report, dated the 1st of February 1881 :—

"Such important changes deeply affecting the rights and pecu-" niary interests of a large and important class should only be made "on very strong grounds, such as, for instance, the grounds advanced "by Mr. Gladstone when introducing a somewhat similar measure "for Ireland in 1870. He then urged that, as good general laws had "failed to dispel the serious ill-feeling of the mass of the population, "it was necessary to take an extreme step in a direction specially "acceptable to that population, in the hope that it would put an end "to what was always a serious political danger. No strong and "special grounds, political or other, exist in the present case, nor are "they asserted by the Rent Commission, who, indeed, seem to be "unanimous in holding what is a nearly unanimous opinion, viz. "that the ryots of Bengal are stronger than the zemindars."

The Commissioner of the Burdwan Division wrote on the 26th of April 1881 :—

"From the experience I have had of the very great difficulty "which officers of the Government feel in managing wards and "attached estates in the Chittagong and Dacca Divisions, I am con-" vinced that the position of the zemindar (landlord) in those parts "is a precarious one. As far as I am able to judge, it will be "rendered more so if the present Bill becomes law. . . . I am not "aware that any section of the community in Bengal has suggested "or manifested any desire for new legislation on the rent question."

The Bill of 1880 was the first indication that the Government had really no intention of keeping its promise of 1871, but only sougnt an opportunity for passing a confiscatory measure, in violation of the engagement entered into in 1793. The Bill, however, not having gone sufficiently far in the direction desired by the Government, another Bill was drawn on its lines with new and still more objectionable provisions. The new Bill was published under the title of the Bengal Rent Bill, and discussion on it was ostentatiously invited ; but it was afterwards twice materially altered before being submitted to the Secretary of State, without the public being allowed to know what were the changes made in it. This tortuous course evoked the following remarks from the Chief Justice of Bengal, when the Bill, in its original form, showing none of the alterations which had already been introduced into it, was submitted for the opinion of the High Court of Calcutta :—

" The Bill as it was first drafted by the Rent Commission differed " in many respects from that which has since been prepared by Mr. " Reynolds ; and we are now in still greater uncertainty as to what " is really proposed, because we learn that Mr. Reynolds' draft was " again materially altered before it was sent to the Government of " India, and that it has now been submitted with still further altera- " tions for the consideration of the Secretary of State.

" This method of dealing with important legislative measures is " inconvenient, and seems hardly fair to those classes of the com- " munity whose interests may be most seriously threatened.

" The Bill, for aught we know, may be submitted to the Secretary " of State in a form which the Bengal public has never seen, and " upon which they had no opportunity of making a single comment. " In this form it will be discussed, and probably approved, at the " India Office ; and if it is then to be sent back to this country to be " dealt with in accordance with the views of the Secretary of State, it " is clear that those classes whose interests it is calculated to injure " may be placed at very great disadvantage."

The course apprehended by the Chief Justice was precisely the one followed in this instance ; and its unfairness and danger will become apparent when it is considered that the constitution of the Legislative Council is such as to enable the Government, at all times, to secure in it an official majority ; its ordinary members being made to understand that it is their duty to give their vote to the Government, irrespective of their personal opinion. The deliberations of the Legislative Council are thus reduced to a sham, and its functions are made to consist simply in the enactment of measures which have received the sanction of the Secretary of State ; a sanction neces- sarily granted upon a one-sided representation of the case, without the aid of the light which public and free discussion alone can throw upon all sides of a question. This dangerous course is now being followed, as far as the Government of India is concerned, in a matter affecting the rights and interests of fifty millions of our Indian fellow-subjects.

The Bengal Tenancy Bill consists of no less than 230 sections; but as the greater number refer to details which it would be useless to examine while the provisions they are intended to carry out are condemned, it might suffice here to point to the unsound principle on which many of the details have been framed, namely, on the principle of superseding the jurisdiction of the Law Courts by the intervention of Executive officers. Considering how large a portion of the produce of the land is claimed by the State as revenue, and how often the fiscal regulations have led to the acquirement of private estates by the Government at a nominal price, the Government is by no means a disinterested party in the differences which arise between its officers and the landowners, and between the latter and their tenants. By appointing, therefore, its own servants to adjudicate on such differences, the Government assumes the right of being the judge in its own case, and often of its own acts, seeing that the differences in question frequently arise from the action of the Revenue officers themselves.

This proposed supercession of the Law Courts by Executive officers has accordingly been condemned by officials, and strongly protested against by the landed classes, not only as conflicting with the Regulations of 1793, and likely, therefore, to lead to confusion and litigation, but as calculated to prevent a complete and impartial inquiry into the circumstances connected with the matter in dispute. The District Judge of Hoogly remarks :—

" It re-introduces a state of things which the preamble of Regu-"lation II. of 1793 states was then found unsatisfactory."

The Commissioner of Burdwan says :—

" This (the preamble) is not forgotten by the zemindars in the "present day, and Chapter XI. is looked upon as an infringement of "the principle laid down in the above Regulation, which has, nearly "for a century, been one of the fundamental principles of British "rule."

The injustice which would be perpetrated if the provisions in Chapter XI. became law will appear more clearly on a perusal of the preamble in question, in which the following passage occurs :—

" All questions between the Government and the landholders "respecting the assessment and collection of the public revenue, and "disputed claims between the latter and their ryots (tenants), have "hitherto been cognisable in the Courts of Maal Adawlut, or "Revenue Courts. The collectors of revenue preside in these Courts "as judges, and an appeal lies from their decision to the Board of

" Revenue, and from the decrees of that Board to the Governor-
" General in Council in the department of revenue. The proprietors
" can never consider the privileges which have been conferred upon
" them as secure whilst the revenue officers are vested with these
" judicial powers. Exclusive of the objections arising to these
" Courts from their irregular, summary, and often *ex parte* pro-
" ceedings, and from the collectors being obliged to suspend the
" exercise of their judicial functions whenever they interfere with
" their financial duties, it is obvious that, if the regulations for
" assessing and collecting the public revenue are infringed, the
" revenue officers themselves must be the aggressors, and that indi-
" viduals who have been wronged by them in one capacity can
" never hope to obtain redress from them in another. Their financial
" occupations equally disqualify them for administering the laws
" between the proprietors of land and their tenants. Other security
" must be given to landed property, and to the rights attached to it,
" before the desired improvements in agriculture can be expected
" to be effected. Government must divest itself of the power of
" infringing, in its executive capacity, the rights and privileges which,
" as exercising the legislative authority, it has conferred on the land-
" holders. The revenue officers must be deprived of their judicial
" powers. All financial claims of the public, when disputed under
" the Regulations, must be subjected to the cognisance of courts of
" judicature, superintended by judges who, from their official situa-
" tions and the nature of their trusts, shall not only be wholly unin-
" terested in the result of their decisions, but bound to decide
" impartially between the public and the proprietors of land, and
" also between the latter and their tenants. The collectors of the
" revenue must not only be divested of the power of deciding upon
" their own acts, but rendered amenable for them to the Courts of
" Judicature, and collect the public dues, subject to a personal pro-
" secution for every exaction exceeding the amount which they are
" authorised to demand on behalf of the public, and for every
" deviation from the regulations prescribed for the collection of it.
" No power will then exist in the country by which the rights vested
" in the landholders by the Regulations can be infringed, or the
" value of landed property affected. Land must, in consequence,
" become the most desirable of all property, and the industry of
" the people will be directed to those improvements in agriculture
" which are as essential to their own welfare as to the prosperity of
" the State."

From the above passage it will be seen how justice was administered in Bengal before the introduction of the permanent settlement,
and the principle which has regulated its administration subsequently.
Under the former *régime* the condition and prospects of the country

were described in the following terms in a letter of the Governor-General to the Court of Directors, dated the 18th September 1783 ·—

"I may safely assert that one-third of the Company's territory in " Hindoostan is now a jungle inhabited only by wild beasts. Will " a ten years' lease induce any proprietor to clear away that jungle, " and encourage the ryots to come and cultivate his lands, when at " the end of that lease he must either submit to be taxed *ad libitum* " for the newly-cultivated lands, or lose all hopes of deriving any " benefit from his labours, for which, perhaps, by that time he will " hardly be repaid ? "

The effect produced by the permanent settlement and improved administration of justice, inaugurated in 1793, will be seen from the following extract, already quoted at page 6 :—" *The Bengal of to-day* " *offers a startling contrast to the Bengal of* 1793; *the wealth and* " *prosperity of the country have marvellously increased—increased* " *beyond all precedent—under the permanent settlement. A great* " *portion of this increase is due to the zemindari body ·as a whole."*

It is now proposed, under the Bengal Tenancy Bill, to set aside the permanent settlement as interpreted and carried out during the last ninety years, and to revert, in the administration of justice in ' Bengal, to the unsound principle and previously condemned system of vesting revenue officers with judicial powers. This proposal is the more startling that no urgent necessity has been pleaded for the change, nor any substantial advantage been shown as likely to accrue from it and from the Bill generally, to either of the two parties for whose benefit the measure has professedly been introduced. On the contrary, it is admitted that the Bill is calculated to deprive the landowners of valuable proprietary rights which they have hitherto possessed, and to leave the bulk of the cultivating tenants with but little protection from the law.

The principle and the main provisions of the proposed legislation, as will be seen from the extracts in the Appendix, have been condemned by every high official in Bengal, excepting the Lieutenant-Governor, who expressed his dissent from their opinions in a lengthy despatch covering twenty-five pages of the Government *Gazette* of 20th October 1883. It must be remembered, however, that the Lieutenant-Governor, having been a Member of the Viceroy's Council when the Bill was adopted, was committed to its support long before the district officials sent in the reports which condemn it. A perusal of his despatch, moreover, will show that his dissent is supported partly by declamatory arguments, and partly by groundless allegations. For instance, in order to prove the necessity of the proposed legislation, he says :—

" If there really be any persons who, in the face of the over-

" whelming accumulation of evidence afforded by the discussions of " the past ten years, still question the necessity of legislation on the " broad lines of the Bill, then it is quite hopeless that anything the " Lieutenant-Governor could say would convince him."

Hollow declamation of this sort, affording no ground whatever for the formation of any opinion on the question at issue, seems out of place in the discussion of a matter of literally vital importance. Then, as regards alleged facts, the Lieutenant-Governor says :—

" In Bengal the demand for legislation came, in the first instance, " from the landlords; while in Behar the cry was from the ryots for " protection from illegal enhancement and ejectment."

Of the two assertions contained in the above short passage, the inaccuracy and disingenuousness of the first, as far as the Bengal Tenancy Bill is concerned, has already been shown in this paper at pages 9 and 10; and regarding the latter assertion it will perhaps suffice to observe that, although very voluminous papers were published with the Bill, not a single petition from ryots was among them, while the district officers distinctly stated in their reports on the Bill that they were not aware of any demand having been made or any desire manifested by the ryots for legislation touching rents. Then as regards the charge of illegal ejectment, it is supported by no evidence whatever, while evidence of its groundlessness is supplied by the Viceroy's despatch to the Secretary of State on the subject of the Bill, in which a statement of Mr. Reynolds' is quoted at paragraph 103, to the effect that *the right of eviction is never exercised in the eastern districts, and that exemption from eviction would be a worthless boon in Behar where ryots are hardly ever evicted.*

It may be unnecessary to go further into the subject of the many inaccuracies contained in the Lieutenant-Governor's despatch, as they have been serially discussed and exposed in a Memorial which the Central Committee of the Bengal and Behar landowners presented to the Viceroy in November last soon after that despatch was published.

The foregoing remarks on the Bengal Tenancy Bill will, it is earnestly hoped, induce the reader to peruse the Bill itself and the documents relating to it, which have been published in the Government Gazette of India of the 20th October 1883. It is impossible to rise from a perusal of those papers and of the Chief Justice's Minute of 6th September 1882 without feeling a clear conviction—

1st. That the avowed objects of the Bill cannot be attained under its provisions.

2nd. That its inevitable effect will be to create a new class of middlemen from among the money-lenders and other outsiders, who are not likely to have any sympathy or community of feeling with the cultivating tenants.

3rd. That the tenants of the new middlemen would, under the Bill, be debarred from ever acquiring any occupancy right, such as are possessed at present by a large number of ryots; and would be liable to eviction at the will of their new landlords.

4th. That the power of rack-renting the land, which the Bill places in the hands of the new middlemen, would deprive the cultivating tenants of the protection which the existing law provides against the undue enhancement of rents.

5th. That the proposed interference with the freedom of contract, the attempt to settle rents by tables of rates, and the supersession of the Civil Courts by executive officers, would be productive of great injustice and inconvenience, and offer the strongest encouragement to devices for eluding the law, a condition of things which cannot fail to demoralise the people.

6th. That the proposed infringement of proprietary rights which have been solemnly guaranteed by the Government of India with the concurrence of the Crown and Parliament of Great Britain, would constitute a breach of public faith which would seriously reflect on the character of the British Government in India, and destroy the confidence of the people of that country in the honesty and good intentions of their rulers.

POSTSCRIPT.

London, February 18, 1884.

SINCE the foregoing pages were written, a report has been received of the public meeting which was held at the Town Hall of Calcutta, on the 29th of December last, for the purpose of protesting once more against the proposed legislation on the tenure of land in Bengal.

The meeting was very largely attended by zemindars from all parts of the country. Extracts from the speeches delivered on the occasion will be found at the end of the Appendix.

A just idea of the effect which the Bill, if enacted, would have on the position of all who, relying on the good faith of the Government, have invested their capital in land, or advanced it for agricultural purposes in Bengal, is afforded in the following words with which Mr. Gregor Grant, proprietor of extensive estates in the hill tracts inhabited by the aboriginal race called the Sonthals, concluded his thoughtful and instructive address on the occasion :—

"I have been a resident in the Bhaugulpore district for over forty-two years . . . My whole life's earnings have been invested in the security of landed property. If the present Bill becomes law, the zemindar to whom I have lent all my earnings on the mortgage of his estates will not be able to repay me the money I have given him, as his property will become greatly depreciated in value, and I will be unjustly deprived of my life's earnings, on which I had relied as a provision for my old age."

J. DACOSTA.

APPENDIX

·CONTAINING

Extracts from the Reports of the Twenty-one Commissioners, District Judges, and District Officers consulted by the Government, through the High Court and the Board of Revenue, on the Provisions of THE BENGAL TENANCY BILL of 1883.

From J. P. GRANT, Esq., District Judge of Hooghly.

13th July 1883.

I shall content myself with criticising the provisions of the Bill from the point of view of what I understand to be its two-fold object, viz. to give security to the tenant in the occupation and enjoyment of his land, and to give facilities to the landlord for the settlement and recovery of his rent.

Section 3, *Clause* 5.—The definitions of "tenure-holder" and "ryot" are not satisfactory. If these definitions are maintained, the conventional meaning of the word "ryot," the nearest equivalent of which is "yeoman," will disappear, as will indeed the class itself; for the inevitable tendency of the proposed law is to make *right-of-occupancy ryots*, in fact as well as in name, middlemen. I would take occupancy ryots out of the category of tenure-holders. There is nothing in common in their position and the position of those who are really middlemen, such as *putneedars* and farmers. The law should recognise the existing two classes of ryots, viz. those having and those not having rights of occupancy ; and in defining them, should employ the word ryot for both. The definition of tenure-holder should be altered to signify exclusively a middleman between a proprietor and a ryot.

CHAPTER II. purports to limit for the future *khamar,* or private estate land, to what was such land at the passing of the Bill. I doubt both the policy which would enact this and the possibility of enforcing it, if enacted, in the face of the provisions of Section 141.

CHAPTER III. A., *Sections* 14 *and* 15, convert an occupancy-ryot into a tenure-holder. ·I have already pointed out the confusion of ideas here indicated, which is certain to breed confusion in practice. You cannot alter the conventional meaning of words by Act of Parliament. Section 16 converts the *bhag-jotedar* into a ryot who may possibly acquire a right of occupancy. This is totally opposed to all the existing notions of a *bhag-jotedar's* status and position. He is, in fact, only a labourer under another name. His share of the crop is the wages for which he has engaged to cultivate it.

2 *

CHAPTER IV.—I do not see why the Putnee Regulation should be incorporated with the Bill. The character of a complete code is re-pudiated by the Bill; and I see no more reason for incorporating this Regulation than for incorporating the Regulation containing the permanent settlement, which is still left as a separate law, and is, in its nature, as much connected with the Bill as the Putnee Regulation.

CHAPTER VI. provides for the drawing-up of a local table of rates of rents and produce. I believe that it will be practically impossible to draw up such tables. Indeed, I understand that an attempt has been already made on a considerable scale and has signally failed. This was only to be expected. . . . I do not know how the market-rate at harvest-time is to be authoritatively settled.

CHAPTER VIII. deals with what are, mistakenly called "ordinary" ryots. The ordinary ryot of the country is the ryot having rights of occupancy; it is all other classes of ryots that are exceptional. I do not see why the every-day terms of "ryots having a right of occupancy" and "ryots not having a right of occupancy," should not be maintained. But the mistake goes deeper than the mere names. The difference between the two classes of ryots is that one has fixity of tenure and the other has not. The provisions of this chapter would seem to imply that the former class possesses some privilege of setting at a lower rate of rent also; for the "ordinary" ryot may by the Bill be rack-rented up to a certain maximum. All classes of ryots have now, and ought always to have, equal protection at the hands of the law, in respect of the rate of rent payable by them; the only difference is that, while one class holds from year to year or for a term of years on lease, the other holds in perpetuity, if he only pays his rent.

CHAPTER XI. introduces a state of things which the preamble of Regulation II. of 1793 states was then found unsatisfactory. The principle therein enunciated is that disputes between landlord and tenant shall be adjudicated by Civil Courts and not by the Revenue authorities who, otherwise, would, in many cases, be deciding upon their own acts.

From JOHN BEAMES, Esq., Commissioner of the Burdwan Division.

22nd June 1883.

2. I have already submitted two lengthy reports on this subject, the first of which commented on the Bill drafted by the Rent Commission in 1880, and the second on the amended Bill put forward by the Government in 1881. I am still very much in doubt whether any enactment of the kind is really required, except in Behar.

3. It is not to be expected that the Bill will escape opposition, nor do I think such opposition altogether unreasonable. It is all very well to say that the framers of the permanent settlement reserved to themselves and their successors the right to interfere between zemindars and ryots, whenever such a step might seem necessary for the protection of the latter; and that, though no such interference practically did take place during the sixty-six years that intervened between 1793 and 1859, yet that it was never too late to mend, and that consequently we are going to interfere now. The answer to that argument is that during all those years we have allowed men to buy zemindaries and tenures on the belief, fully justified by our action, that no interference would take place, and that it is not fair to these persons suddenly to uproot the conditions on the faith of which they have invested their money. I so far agree with this argument as to think that, in any changes which may now be made, it is not sufficient to go back to first principles, and base our enactment solely on what we understand to be the relation between

landlord and tenant, as established by Lord Cornwallis's Regulations; we must go further than this, and take into consideration the present status and vested interests of the proprietary body whom we have called into existence and whom we have, during nearly a century, allowed to acquire rights and privileges which are none the less deserving of respect now, because their growth and development were not contemplated by the statesmen of the last century.

4. The question I ask myself, as I examine one section of the Bill after another, is "does this provision deprive either the landlord or tenant of any right or any status which he legally holds *at present*, whether in virtue of the terms of the permanent settlement or in virtue of any custom which the Government has tacitly allowed to grow up since that time?" We have nothing to do with the historical zemindar of 1793. If he existed at all, that is, if there was any class of men so situated as we are apt to figure them to ourselves, he exists no longer. We have to deal with the zemindar in the position which he holds in the present day.

5. This is the view which most of the officers and private gentlemen with whom I have from time to time consulted take of the matter, and I think that it is the only practical and reasonable view to take. . . . The Bengal of to-day offers a startling contrast to the Bengal of 1793. The wealth and prosperity of the country have marvellously increased —increased beyond all precedent—under the permanent settlement. There is much force in the remark that a great portion of this increase is due to the zemindari body as a whole, and that they have been very active and powerful factors in the development of this prosperity.

7. Section 3, Sub-Sections 3 and 5.—The definition of ryot has purposely been left obscure. We are told that certain persons are not ryots, but we are not told who are ryots. The definition of the Rent Commission was not satisfactory, because no other test was applied than that of the extent of the holdings. The Bill, in Sections 14 and 15, also fixes an arbitrary line between a tenure-holder and a ryot by making what are at present known as ryots with occupancy at fixed rates of rent into tenure-holders. If this definition be maintained, we get an exceedingly simple definition of ryots by merely saying that all persons who hold land under a zemindar, except those mentioned in Sections 14 and 15, are ryots.

8. This, however, introduces considerable confusion in another way; for it has never, as far as I am aware, been the custom to regard as tenure-holders persons who have a right of occupancy at fixed rates. Such persons are always regarded by themselves and by others as ryots; and the adoption of the classification of the present Bill will very much modify our conception on this point, and introduce changes which will not be readily understood or acquiesced in by the classes connected with the land.

10. When a zemindar lets land to a tenure-holder, he considers that he is granting, and the tenure-holder considers that he is obtaining, the right to collect rents from a number of cultivators already actually in occupation of the land so granted. When, however, a zemindar lets land to a ryot, he grants and the ryot takes the permission to cultivate the land himself, it not being, at the time of granting the lease, actually occupied by cultivators. The ryot, who thus takes land, may subsequently, without ceasing to be considered by the zemindar or himself a ryot, sublet portions or even the whole of such land; but at the time of taking the *pottah* (lease) the land is not in occupation of others.

11. This, I think, is the broad line of demarcation between "talookdar" and "ryot"; and if we use tenure-holder strictly for talookdar, this

demarcation will practically hold good everywhere, with very few and unimportant modifications. It is the intent with which the land is granted and taken that shows where to draw the line ; and the intent is clearly understood in all cases by the parties at the time the trans- action occurs.

12. The definition might be formulated thus :

A tenure-holder is a person who takes land from a proprietor with the intent of collecting the rents from the ryots, and against whom the proprietor has the remedy mentioned in Section 15 of this Act (sale).

A ryot is a person who takes land from a proprietor with the intent of cultivating it himself or by hired labour, or of sub-letting it, and against whom the proprietor, &c., has the remedy specified in Chapter XIII. of this Act (distraint).

13. If the difficulty is great in distinguishing between a ryot and a tenure-holder, it is equally great in distinguishing between a ryot and an under-ryot ; and we cannot rest contented with the definition of an under-ryot given in sub-section (6), that an under-ryot means "a tenant holding below a ryot," unless we know what a ryot is. What we must know for purposes of settlement, and what the zemindar also must know for the same purpose, is who is the person in whose name the *jummabundi* is to be made. Section 164 of the present Bill, indeed, contemplates that, in compiling a record of rights, which is practically what we know as a *jummabundi*, tenure-holders, occupancy-ryots, *bastu*-ryots, ryots, under-ryots, shall all be jumbled up together. But this will never do. Something more definite will be necessary, unless the whole of our system of settlement-procedure is to be reversed, in which case a good deal of Regulation VII. of 1822 will have to be repealed. Bengal Act VIII. of 1869 is, I see, to be repealed ; but Chapter XI. of this Bill, as I shall notice further on, makes the same requirements as the Act does on Settlement officers, in respect of defining the status of various kinds of tenants, so that I am afraid we shall not be able to get on without some definition of "ryot."

18. I have already noticed that Sections 14 and 15 turn an occupancy-ryot into a tenure-holder. I see that this is said to have been done for the convenience of the draftsman. It is unfortunate that we hear so much of this person now-a-days. It seems to me that it is a matter of no moment at all whether he finds an Act easy or difficult to draft. That is his affair, and should not for an instant occupy the mind of the legislator, whose attention should be directed solely to the justice and the utility of the law. The mechanical operation of putting an idea into plain English is beneath consideration. I venture to think that by turning the occupancy-ryot at fixed rates into a tenure-holder, we are creating a state of things foreign to the ideas and customs of the people, and likely to give rise to much confusion.

31. I think Section 45 goes a great deal too far. It allows a man who has held land anywhere in an *estate*, no matter how often it may have been changed, to become a settled ryot; and a settled ryot acquires a right of occupancy in any land he may happen to hold on the 2nd of March last, so that in case of a large zemindari, say the Burdwan estate for instance, a man may come to a village from another village sixty miles off in that estate, take lands there, and have rights of occupancy from a few days' possession.

33. There may be some justice in the rule that a ryot who has lived twelve years in a village shall be considered a settled ryot. The village, even in Bengal, still preserves some sort of solidarity ; the estate has none, and it would certainly be unfair to allow a ryot to acquire a right of occupancy in a plot of land which he has held only for one year, in a

village in which he is, to all intents and purposes, an outsider and a stranger, simply on the ground that he has held land for twelve years in other disconnected parts of the same estate. Such a concession as this is not looked for by the cultivating class, is opposed to their own views and to the custom of the country, and would operate very hardly on the zemindars.

37. The illustration to Section 4 of the Bill recognises the custom that under-ryots may acquire a right of occupancy, but leaves the conditions under which such a right may be acquired undefined, and the under-ryots consequently unprotected.

38. There are in Midnapore many thousands of these ryots whose forefathers have tilled the land they now occupy for many generations, and I agree with Mr. Wilson in thinking that there is no reason why they should be left unprotected.

41. Section 56 has given rise to much discussion.

42. Here there is some confusion in the laws. Section 47 provides that no occupancy rights shall accrue on land held by any person as owner. One would suppose that when a landlord exercised the right of pre-emption, and bought a ryot's holding, he would thenceforth hold it as owner.

43. Yet the sections on pre-emption and Section 56 speak of the ryot selling his "occupancy right" and the landlord purchasing the same. What is this but selling and purchasing the land itself? I do not see why, if the landlord thus purchased the land, it should not be open to him to extinguish the occupancy right. In fact, under Section 47, that right should be extinguished by the mere fact that he, the owner, purchases it. But, to prevent this consequence, the fine distinction is introduced that he, the owner, holds it not as owner, but as an occupancy ryot under himself.

45. Moreover, as pointed out by Mr. Reynolds in his speech in Council, the landlord will, by this provision, be led to keep the land in his own hands, thus virtually turning it into *khamar*. The whole section seems to me to involve an erroneous idea. It is not the land that acquires rights, but the man who holds it. If he holds it for a certain term of years, equity and custom demand that he should acquire occupancy rights in it. But one fails to see why the land itself should carry those rights with it when it passes into the hands of a man who has done nothing to earn or merit those rights.

79. Section 151.—The procedure of Chapter XI. virtually amounts to making a regular settlement of part or the whole of a permanently-settled estate. It involves not merely the settlement of rents, but the preparation of a *jummabundi* ; in fact all the proceedings of an ordinary settlement, excepting only the fixing of the revenue. And in some respects this procedure gives more power to revenue officers than do the existing Settlement Laws. This is stated to be intentional, and the procedure has been invented with a view to removing from the Civil Courts the power they now exercise in reversing the decision of revenue officers on many points in a settlement ; accordingly, Bengal Act VIII. of 1869 is repealed.

80. The revenue officers will, under such a provision, pursue their course in settling an estate in peace without having the fear of inter-ference by the civil court constantly before their eyes.

81. All this is very pleasant and gratifying for us revenue officers. I do not, however, quite see how it is to be reconciled with the remarks in the preamble to Regulation II. of 1793, which, after stating that " all questions between Government and the landholders respecting the assessment and collection of the land revenue, &c. &c., have hitherto been cognizable in the courts of *mal adalut* or revenue courts," goes

on to say that, "the proprietors can never consider the privileges which have been conferred upon them as secure while the revenue officers are vested with these judicial powers." This is not forgotten by the zemindars in the present day, and it is to be feared that the provision of this chapter is, by many zemindars, looked upon as an infringement of the principle laid down in the above Regulation, which has, for nearly a century, been one of the fundamental principles of British rule.

85. It is no light thing to enter on to a permanently settled estate and turn it upside down, with the result, perhaps, of crippling the land-lord's resources for one lifetime or more.

From E. E. Lowis, Esq., Commissioner of the Chittagong Division.

30th June 1883.

3. The introduction of this measure is viewed by all whom I have consulted on the subject with the gravest apprehensions, as tending to embitter the relations between landlord and tenant, and likely to lead to a great amount of litigation with its accompanying fraud and chicanery, which must in the end injure, and not benefit the ryot. These views are based on the conviction that the provisions of the Bill do not deal with facts as they really exist, but seek to evolve and insist on theoretical privileges as appertaining to the ryots, which that class never enjoyed, and which they are for the future to enjoy at the expense of the landlord.

4. These apprehensions are not allayed by the remark contained in the *Statement of Objects and Reasons*, that the present Bill is a mere prelude to what may be expected to follow when the whole law on the subject comes to be codified; and it is urged that, if this measure is not to be considered in itself as complete, it is hardly worth while introducing it, seeing that the effect will most inevitably be a crop of litigation and general disturbance of the agricultural community.

5. I most certainly concur in the opinion that its provisions are quite inapplicable to the condition of things and the system of land tenure existing in this division.

6. I feel sure that any change in the existing law is not urgently called for.

8. The essence of the Bill is the protection of the ryot; and though no definition of a ryot has been given, it is plain that, in the proposed law, the term is almost synonymous with cultivator.

(*The intervening paragraphs endeavour to show the inapplicability of the provisions of the Bill to the condition of things existing in the Chittagong division in particular.*)

31. As to the voidance of contracts, the proposed law appears to introduce a dangerous precedent. In certain cases the provisions of the law are to be held to over-ride contracts entered into with deliberation; and this without any inquiry whether the contract was voluntary or not. So far as my experience goes, the ryots are very well able to look after their own interests, and hardly require to be thus hedged round with protective enactments, as appears to be thought necessary; they are only too ready to evade their contracts, if it is to their interests to do so, and are quite prepared to support such evasion by every artifice that the law renders possible, as well as by means not strictly lawful; it seems hardly expedient, therefore, to teach such men that the law does not recognise the keeping of contract, and that self-interest can be held to be a valid excuse for contravening the terms of an agreement. Cases may arise where it is

evident that an unjust and one-sided contract has been entered into, as the result of deception or force; bnt surely such cases may be left to be dealt with by the application of the law of equity.

Clause 2, *Section* 73, says that a contract, in a certain case, made in favour of a ryot must be enforced, while Section 50 protects him from contracts which are against him. *Clause* 2, *Section* 74, enforces a contract which is against a zemindar, while Sections 87 and 90 repudiate contracts which are in his favour. These instances will teach the ryots that there is no moral obligation in promises, and that he must always consider his own convenience in dealing with others. This is a dangerous doctrine to teach. If ninety per cent. of the tenantry have been able to acquire tenant rights under a system when contracts have been held valid, there is no need to make them now invalid.

34. When the whole set of tradition and custom in a tract of country is against the fundamental principle of the proposed law, it seems to me inadvisable to extend such law to that tract.

From R. Towers, Esq., District Judge of Tipperah.

12th May 1883.

2. The tenant acquires (under this Bill) advantages at the landlord's expense, which, in many cases, exceed the tenant's demands, which are entirely novel in their character, and appear to be derived rather from a consideration of what has been found expedient in foreign countries than Indian law or custom.

3. Among those I would class :—

(1.) The easy terms on which occupancy rights are conferred.

(2.) The confiscatiou of the landlord's right to deal as he chooses with land that has once been ryoti, when it reverts to his private possession.

(3.) The almost entire abolition of the right of private contract between parties.

(4.) Compensation for disturbancor

(5.) The power given to ryots to make improvements against the landlord's wish.

I admit the difficulty of conceding to the zemindar his demand for greater facility in the realisation of his dues, but I am not prepared to say that it could not be satisfied to a certain extent. There is, however, hardly any attempt made to do so in the Bill.

4. The next general observation which occurs to me is that litigation will be enormously fostered by the Bill. The parties are driven into Court or before the Revenue authorities at every step.

5. Then, not a few of the provisions of the Bill seem unsuited to practical working. Among these I would instance the procedure regulating the transfer of occupancy rights, the preparation of tables of rates, the apportionment of expenses, the rules for enhancement which seem very intricate.

CHAPTER II.—The survey and register under Section 7 will, I believe, be a work of enormous difficulty. Every plot will be disputed, and there will be in effect a civil suit contested in every stage, before the Survey officer, the Commissioner, the Board, and the Government. It seems to me to be more expedient to allow each case to be settled by the Courts on its own merits in case of dispute, than to cause a widespread discord by sending a roving Commission about the country to agitate questions on which the parties concerned are themselves quiescent. I believe there is no injustice felt in this part of the country.

CHAPTER V.—The two chief points open to criticism in this chapter seem to be (1) the definition of occupancy ryots, and (2) the provision that any ryot taking land from a landlord, of which the latter has himself acquired the occupancy right, shall have a right of occupancy in it.

With regard to the first of these, extreme care has been taken that, uuder the Bill, a ryot that held two cottahs of land in a village A for twelve years, may acquire rights of occupancy in 200 beegahs in villages B, C and D, though he may have had possession of the same land for only three or four months. The necessity of the provision has been maintained on the ground that otherwise the landlord, by shifting the ryot from one plot to another, might prevent the acquirement of the right in any one plot. There may be parts of the country where this is done, but I do not believe in the existence of the practice in Bengal.

I have received some strong representations as to the delay which will be caused to the landlord by his not being allowed to eject any occupancy ryot for arrears of rent, his remedy under the Bill being the sale of the holding. This is one of the points when the zemindar asking for bread (*i.e.* greater facility for realising his rents) has been given a stone.

Then with regard to Section 56, except in the very rare cases of ejectment and lapse, the only way in which the landlord can acquire the right is by purchase. But if he is compelled to treat any person to whom he subsequently lets the land as an occupancy ryot, what consideration has he had for his purchase money? In my opinion there is an economic mistake, as well as a serious injustice in the provisions of this section.

CHAPTER VI. *Section* 58, 61.—Here, I think, there is too much interference with private contract, and that Section 61 is not defensible. Why should a settled ryot, who wishes to take on more land than that in respect of which he has acquired his status, be allowed to hold any further land he may take from the zemindar on privileged terms?

The preparation of rates will be practically impossible in most places.

From J. MONRO, Esq., Commissioner of the Presidency Division.

2nd July 1883.

3. I have had many conversations on the subject with officials, zemindars, and others, and have omitted no opportunity of ascertaining the feeling of the people generally in connection with this important measure.

4. The landholding class is most strenuously opposed to the Bill, and there is no doubt that a most uncompromising resistance to its provisions will be manifested. There is a general feeling amongst the members of the landholding class that zemindars will practically be effaced and reduced to the position of annuitants, and that the Bill constitutes a distinct infringement of the rights which they conceive were guaranteed under the terms of the permanent settlement, and which they have certainly exercised for nearly a century.

6. The ryots are ignorantly apathetic on the subject. They have heard rumours of some impending changes, and, in some instances, agitators have made them believe that the millennium of the ryots is at hand, when they will pay only nominal rents for, and reap all the benefits from the land; but, as a rule, they have no intelligent idea on the subject, and it is difficult to define any feeling they may have in the matter.

7. Upon the question of the rights of the zemindars under the permanent settlement, I have already expressed an opinion, and after the authoritative declaration of the Government of India of their views upon that point, it is not for me to reopen the discussion . . . The Bill is framed for the purpose of carrying out a pledge given by the Government with regard to the rights of ryots at the time of the permanent settlement. And in pursuance of the effort to fulfil this pledge, it is now proposed to give the ryots fixity of tenure, fair rent, and freedom of sale of their holdings.

8. How far these privileges or rights were guaranteed under the terms of the settlement has been disputed; how far the ryot requires fixity of tenure which he has in Lower Bengal practically got, is also a question upon which there have been differences of opinion; whether freedom of sale will, in reality, confer on the ryots the boon which it is intended to give them, is also an open question; but there is and can be no difference of opinion as to the ryot being required to pay a fair rent for any holding which he possesses.

16. Holding the views which I have on another occasion expressed, I cannot consider many of the provisions of the Bill as fair to the zemindar with reference to the rights which they have enjoyed for a century; and yet I am precluded from calling into question the principles upon which the Bill is founded.

27. With reference to the provisions of the Bill regarding occupancy ryots, I object to the extension of the provisions of Act X. of 1859, specially with reference to—

    1. The definition of a settled ryot in Section 45.
    2. What seems to me the unjust provision of Section 47.
    3. Transferability of the tenure.
    4. Sub-letting.
    5. The abolition of freedom of contract.
    6. The Provisions of Sections 59 and 61.

28. I have nothing new to add to the arguments of those who object to the extension of occupancy rights proposed by the Bill. It seems to me as to them unjust that the element of residence should not be an essential feature of the status of a settled ryot. I see no reason why a settled ryot, having a right of occupancy in certain lands, should, as a matter of right, have the same status in lands which may be miles away from his village, although within the same estate; and the accrual of the rights of occupancy to a settled ryot in any lands subsequently acquired by virtue of his tenancy of lands at the time of his becoming a settled ryot, seems to me an unjust extension of occupancy right.

29. There is no doubt that the unfettered power of transfer will encourage disputes and faction quarrels, which have already been a prominent feature in native families; and if, in addition to this power of transfer, is given the privilege of sub-letting without the consent of the landlord, the latter will very soon find his estate full of occupancy ryots or their dependents, in the shape of his bitterest enemies.

31. If the tenure is allowed to be transferable, I would on no account permit sub-letting, which will simply encourage ryots to let out their tenures and prey upon the sub-tenants. Such a system will, in the end, lead to sub-tenants or ordinary ryots (i.e. the cultivators) under occupancy holders being much more rack-rented than they are now.

32. As to the abolition of freedom of contract, I altogether fail to see the justice of the provision. I do not find anything of the kind in any of the Settlement Regulations, and I fail to see how the ryot is ever to learn how to stand alone if he is to be rigidly protected against himself. The ryot is to be allowed freedom in every respect, except

when he enters into an agreement with his landlord. If this is not setting class against class, and teaching the ryot to look upon his landlord as his natural enemy, words have no meaning. I would certainly leave parties to contract as they please, and the Courts should not, in my opinion, refuse to recognise such contracts. Denial of the ryot of contract has a distinct tendency to make the landlord resort to illegal cesses, and the ryots acquiesce in such improper exactions. . . . I must confess that, according to my experience, the ryot of Lower Bengal is not such a down-trodden or helpless creature, with reference to his own interests, as he is represented to be. . . . I can point to the majority of ryots having occupancy rights in Dacca, Tipperah, Chittagong, Jessore, Noakhaly, and other districts, as being men who are eminently calculated to look after their interests. It seems hardly consistent to inculcate upon the people by one enactment their fitness to govern themselves, and in another to provide them with a means of protection against their own acts : to give them power to vote with reference to matters about which they express little concern, and to deny them a right to contract with regard to their rent, about which they are supremely interested.

34. I am not of opinion that it will be practicable to frame tables of rates such as are proposed, without an amount of harassment and expense to both landlords and tenants which would be ruinous to them ; and, even when prepared, I question very much whether it would be fair to either party to keep them in force even for ten years.

36. With regard to the ordinary ryots, the provisions of the Bill militate against all previous practice, at which a tenant-at-will was allowed to hold in accordance with agreement entered into between him and his landlord. I think it unwise that such a practice should be disturbed, and am not prepared to support those provisions which fix a maximum of rent to be demanded, and which introduce the entirely new system of compensation for disturbance of the tenancy of a man who has no right to such tenancy, except under an agreement with his landlord.

37. Throughout Lower Bengal there is no necessity for recognising any other principle than that of mutual interest between landlords and tenants in determining the relations which should exist on the part of the landlords to tenants-at-will. No landholder in his senses will now aim at extravagant enhancements, for such a policy will very soon relieve him of his ryots. Most landlords are now anxious to get ryots to settle ; and evictions, even of tenants-at-will, is a procedure, I imagine, more sparingly resorted to in Lower Bengal than in any country that I know of. The relations, therefore, between landlords and tenants-at-will may safely be left to determine themselves according to the economic laws of supply and demand.

41. The chapter upon compensation for improvement seems based upon an entirely mistaken theory.

42. There have been for centuries, and are now, millions of ryots who have had fixity of tenure. Have these ryots shown any inclination to invest capital in improving their land ; have they evinced any desire to increase the productive powers of the land, even by the elementary process of manuring it ? Have they done anything under the influence of fixity of tenure in the way of constructing for the benefit of their lands any of the numerous works specified in Section 26 as agricultural improvements ?

43. In Lower Bengal the ryots with rights of occupancy have done nothing to improve their lands. Any such improvements as have been made have, so far as my experience goes, been carried out by landlords, and not by ryots ; and I see no reason to believe that the ryots, when

they have more capital, will change their nature or their habits as regards expenditure which they think ought to be incurred by the zemindar.

45. The ryot, so far as my experience goes, does not want to improve his land (which has for ages yielded crops without expenditure on his part on agricultural improvements), nor does he want to be improved himself; he wants to be let alone, and this Chapter on agricultural improvements introduces a system which is perfectly new in the bucolic history of Bengal: it is certainly not needed with reference to the acts or wants of ryots at present, and will infallibly lead to litigation and false claims of every description. Such a system will also most certainly lead to landlords declining to undertake, or give any assistance to villagers in undertaking, village improvements; and when villagers with opposing interests are left to themselves, to carry such improvements, the result may easily be imagined.

46. I do not object to seeing the whole chapter excised from the Bill.

50. I am quite prepared to admit that if the provisions of Chapters XI. and XII. can be successfully carried out, and if we can have a record of rights made out and rents ascertained, great progress will have been made in reaching a solution of many vexed questions at issue between landlords and tenants. The expense of such proceedings as are contemplated under these two chapters will be enormous, and, I suspect, ruinous to both parties. Before making these provisions of universal application Government should, in my opinion, try the experiment thoroughly in Crown estates. We have not yet, in the similar operations which have been carried on in settlements, sufficient data to work upon, and I much fear that the amount of litigation which would be at once excited by the application of these provisions generally, would be very injurious to both ryots and landlords.

51. As to the provisions for the recovery of rents, which was the beginning of the legislation which has found its outcome in the present Bill, I am afraid that the landlords will hardly be satisfied with the relief which has been given them.

53. *On the principle on which this Bill is drawn* the zemindars could not expect further relief. I suspect, however, that they expected, and I am not prepared to say that they had not a good right to expect, very much more substantial relief, as the outcome of their application for a summary method of realising rents preferred during the last twelve years.

55. Under such circumstances I cannot convince myself that the Bill, if passed into law, will render practicable a satisfactory solution of the difficulties attending the disposal of the questions at issue; on the contrary, I feel constrained to believe that the application of the various provisions of the Bill must result in endless litigation, active hostility between landlords and tenants, and injury to the property of both.

From J. F. STEVENS, Esq., District Judge of Sáran.

14th May 1883.

CHAPTER I.—I think that an attempt should be made to define the terms " tenure " and "under-tenure." In Chapter III. we find important provisions on the subject of tenures; but when we turn to the definition in order to ascertain what a tenure is, we only find that it includes an under-tenure (which term is left altogether undefined) and the interest of every tenant of the class referred to in Section 14.

CHAPTER II.—I do not see why a landlord should be prevented from acquiring, as *khamar*, uncultivated land which he brings under cultivation by hired labourers.

CHAPTER V.—The term "estimated value" in Sections 51 and 54 is not perfectly clear. By whom is the value to be estimated, and how are the parties to be bound by the estimate?

Section 56 appears to me exceedingly hard upon the landlord. . . . If he is allowed to buy the occupancy right, he is fairly entitled to obtain by his purchase the full advantages that would be obtained by any other purchaser.

CHAPTER VI.—There should be some attempt to' define the term "staple crops," as a good deal may turn on its precise meaning. The table of rates would be of great utility; it will be for the Revenue authorities to ascertain how far its preparation is possible.

CHAPTER VII., *Section* 86.—1 doubt the justice of giving compensation in the case of the ejectment of a ryot through his own fault.

CHAPTER VIII.—I should like to see it stated what are the rights of an ordinary ryot as to the use of the land. An occupancy ryot may, under Section 50, use it in any manner which does not render it unfit for the purposes of the tenancy. Is it intended to be implied, from the absence of such an express provision in the case of the ordinary ryot, that his right to use the land is more restricted?

Section 90.—It appears to me that the ordinary ryot under the Bill acquires something very like a right of occupancy. Is a landlord never to let to an ordinary ryot for a fixed time? and if he is to have that power, is not the ryot to be liable to ejectment, on the ground that the lease has expired? There is no provision, apparently, for such a case in Section 90. Again, it seems to me only equitable that the landlord should have the power of ejecting an ordinary ryot, after due notice, on paying compensation for improvements.

CHAPTER IX., *Section* 125 (2).—The difficulty is, how the landlord is to know when the tenant's right, title, and interest is brought to sale. Ought not a notice to be served upon him? There is the same difficulty as to Section 52.

From F. M. HALLIDAY, Esq., Commissioner of the Patna Division, in Conference with Six Collectors.

7th to 13th July 1883.

Sections 43, 45, *and* 47.—We were unanimously and decidedly of opinion that the extension of the right of occupancy to all lands held in the same village or estate should be conditional on residence; and I would submit that the distinction which exists according to the custom of the country between a resident and a non-resident ryot, and which has constantly been affirmed and re-affirmed by subsequent Regulations and Acts, has been entirely lost sight of in the Bill. The definition of estate in Section 3 should be adhered to, and hence Section 43 (*b*) should be expunged. In Behar the retention of this clause would lead to endless confusion and complication.

Section 48 has already been noticed by Mr. Reynolds in his speech in Council, where he speaks of it as practically an admission of the vicious principle that the occupancy right may be made a matter of bargain. This section appears altogether unnecessary. A proprietor, before his estate was sold for arrears of revenue, might go about granting occupancy rights all round, and thereby diminish the value of the estate, occupancy rights not being voidable under the sale law. As Mr. Reynolds remarked, the occupancy right is not the landlord's to grant; it is essentially inherent to the status of the resident cultivator. We would, therefore, record our protest against this section.

Section 50.—The Collector of Durbhunga states: " I think the sub-letting power given to occupancy ryots the most doubtful and only dangerous part of the Bill." A long string of rentpayers and receivers must be bad. As far as an occupancy ryot is a rent-receiver, he is one of the objectional class of land-jobbers. His under-ryot is the important man. It is as a cultivator we wish to protect the ryot; not as a land-jobber.

The Collector of Mozufferpore has recorded that he cannot admit the necessity or advisability of framing the Bill in such a manner as to lead to consequences such as Clause 41 of the *Statement of Objects and Reasons* admits to be possible. It seems difficult to understand how such a result can be contemplated with equanimity, or how an intention can be deliberately expressed of encouraging the growth of another class of idle annuitants upon the land in addition to those who already cumber it. The Bill will undoubtedly enhance the value of occupancy rights, which will naturally be bought up right and left by the money-lending class. The net result of the Bill will, therefore, be the extinction of the present class of occupancy ryots and the transfer of their rights to money-lenders.

Section 62.—We were unanimous in thinking that the preparation of a table of rates was impracticable. These sections, on the preparation of a table of rates and produce, and of suits to enhance money-rents where such table is in force, contain a Procrustian scheme of enforcing uniformity in matters in which, from the nature of things, no uniformity exists. The rates in a village are about as numerous as the fields of the ryots, and cannot be classified without an arbitrary disregard of actual facts.

Section 90.—I express the unanimous opinion of the Conference in saying that the freedom of contract should not be withheld from a zemindar, giving land to a new, and possibly an unknown, ryot.

From J. F. BRADBURY, Esq., District Judge of Backergunge.

2nd June 1883.

The interpretation clauses are defective in that they do not include the definition of a tenure. The term "under-tenure" is misleading.

Section 6.—Why is land which is admittedly not *khamar*, but is comprehended in a permanent, heritable, and transferable tenure within an estate, and cultivated by the holder of such tenure, to be deemed *ryoti* land of such estate? The framers of the section seem to have ignored estates not consisting exclusively of *khamar* and *ryoti* land.

Section 20.—Who is an authority empowered by the Government to make settlements definitively? The Commissioners and the Board of Revenue confirm settlements, but make none. The collector and his subordinate makes them, but not definitively, for their orders are not final till confirmed.

Section 21.—What is a "beneficial rent"? The term is novel in Indian law and requires explanation.

This report contains a large number of exceptions taken to the Bill chiefly on technical grounds, and terminates thus :

The Court will observe that I have abstained from discussing the policy of the Bill. . . . I trust that some of my comments have revealed defects, the correction of which may hereafter prevent litigation.

From N. S. ALEXANDER, Esq., Commissioner of the Dacca Division.

23rd to 29th June 1883.

The right of occupancy is for the protection of the cultivator of the land, and the land was originally let to the cultivator for cultivation ;

it seems to be inequitable, therefore, to allow a non-cultivator to be thrust upon a zemindar as an occupancy ryot.

The Dacca zemindars say :—" If a ryot is evicted from a holding in default of payment of rent, there is nothing in this Section 129 that will prevent his demanding compensation from the landlord. This is very unfair; it is encouraging a defaulter, while it is the duty of the Government (considering the stringent sun-set law under which it claims the revenue from the zemindar) to afford every facility to the landlord in the realisation of rent."

From G. N. BARLOW, Esq., Commissioner of the Bhaugulpore Division and Sonthal Pergunahs, in Conference with Four Collectors.

20th June 1883.

Section 56.—It was observed at the meeting that although at different times and by different objectors it had been urged that if an occupancy right were made transferable by law, zemindars, or planters, or mahajuns would buy up occupancy rights on a great scale ; yet, on zemindars alone had been imposed the condition contained in this section. It appeared to the meeting that there was not sufficient reason for making such a distinction. Section 56 was unanimously condemned by the meeting.

CHAPTER VI., *Part B.*—It was agreed (Mr. Porch alone dissenting) that this part ought to be entirely omitted, owing to—

(1.) The difficulty or impossibility of ascertaining the rates in the way proposed.

(2.) The necessity that would still exist, even if a table of rates were prepared and sanctioned for any area, of holding a local inquiry in each case for enhancement of rent in order to identify the class under which each field in the holding would fall.

(3.) The want of proper establishments and experienced or scientific officers to classify the lands.

(4.) The cost of making a local inquiry in each case,

CHAPTER XIV.—It was unanimously agreed that in suits for arrears of rent, which involve no questions of right or title, the procedure of the civil court in regard to the recording of evidence ought to be made as summary as is the procedure of magistrates in summary criminal trials.

The following passages occur in the Memorandum appended to the Commissioner's report by W. Hastings D'Oyly, Collector of Bhangulpore.

Sections 76, 77, 78.—Some exception should be made in respect of recently reclaimed lands. A ryot has held such land, say, for five years, at first rent-free, latterly at a nominal rent of two annas per beegah, as a concession granted for the cost of clearance. Under Section 76 the enhanced rent cannot be more than four annas, and under Section 78 it cannot be raised for ten years. Supposing the land in 1884 to be equal to lands for which three rupees per beegah is paid as rent, the landlord will have to wait fifty years before he can legally recover a fair rent !!! These remarks also apply to the provisions of Section 59 (2).

Section 82.—I should be glad if occupancy rights could be restricted to the actual cultivators.

CHAPTER XIII.—It has been asserted that one of the objects of the present legislation is to afford facilities to the landlord for the settlement and recovery of his rent, whereas there can be but little doubt that the recovery of rent has been made more difficult than it previously was.

Memorandum of R. Porch, Esq., Collector of Maldah.

Section 50, when enacted, will lead to a very general loss of right of occupancy holdings by the present generation of ryots, whose holdings will be at once bought up by the money-lending classes, the ryots becoming rack-rented pauper cottiers or landless labourers.

From A. C. BRETT, Esq., District Judge of Tirhoot.

14th May 1883.

Occupancy ryot.—The fundamental idea conveyed by the word *Khudkast* was permanence. The test in old days of permanence was residence.

Ordinary ryot.—To tell a zemindar that he cannot evict without paying ten times the increment of rent demanded, is to tell him he cannot evict at all. We are supposed to be interpreting the permanent settlement, not altering it.

Transferability of occupancy rights.—I think a zemindar has a right to be protected from the incoming of an objectionable tenant. The proposed right of pre-emption is saddled with the provision that the next tenant, whether a settled ryot or not, shall have a right of occupancy immediately. Therefore, unless the zemindar cultivates the land by his own ploughs, the only way he can secure himself from an objectionable tenant is to throw away his money; and the operation may be repeated *ad infinitum*

Enhancement of rent.—The task of framing records of rights and tables of rates is, no doubt, a formidable one; but in the resolute facing of this difficulty lies the only chance of success for a rent law in this country, however equitable may be its spirit and however scientific its drafting.

From C. B. GARRET, Esq., Officiating District Judge, 24 Pergannahs.

18th May 1883.

Section 21, *Sub-section* 4, appears to press unfairly on the landlord. Surely in no conceivable case could it be fair that the whole net profits of a tenure, of which even the whole was unreclaimed when the tenure was created, should be perpetually enjoyed by the tenant. Surely the landlord who owned the land before it was reclaimed, is entitled to something for the use of what I may call the raw material on which the tenant has operated his reclamation.

Section 49, I think, is open to very serious objection. I have known in these districts many small proprietors whose sole wealth was their *khamar*. I have always understood *khamar* to be land which was admitted to be the peculium of the zemindar, and which he had every right to dispose of to the very best advantage that the state of the market allowed him to do. I do not think that we need be apprehensive that he will now-a-days be able to do more than this.

Section 50.—Does this mean simply that he may sublet a portion of his land, remaining liable to the landlord for the rent assessed on the whole, or he may, at his option, apportion his liability to his landlord? If the latter, I think it is a provision obviously unfair to the landlord.

Section 85.—A ryot should not be allowed to sell his arable land, and entirely abandon the occupation of husbandry, and still retain a permanent heritable and transferable right in his *bastu* in an agricultural village.

CHAPTER XIII.—I confess I should have been glad to see the power of distraint entirely abolished. I am convinced, however, that it would be unjust to the landlords to do so at present. My experience is that it is a power very greatly abused. At the same time I admit that, when Collector and Manager of Wards' Estates, under Act XL. of 1858, having had experience of villages from which I could never realise my rents except by distraint.

From BABOO RAJENDRA COOMAR SEAL, District Judge of Bankoora.

16th May 1883.

Section 3 (3).—Ryots of the class described in Section 14 ought not to be brought under the category of tenure-holders. Paragraph 13 of the *Statement of Objects and Reasons* explains that it is necessary to call them tenure-holders, simply because it is convenient to do so from the draftsman's point of view; but in course of time the ground on which they have been called tenure-holders would be lost sight of, and they themselves would lose the privileges of a ryot.

Section 15.—Throughout the Bill it is provided that a man should first go to the Revenue Court and then to the Civil Court. This procedure will not only be expensive but inconvenient. The best course would be at once to go to the Civil Court, where he will get the final relief.

Section 130.—The Bill itself ought to make provision for the appointment of assessors on the line of the Land Acquisition Act, and it ought not to be left to the local Government to do so.

From W. F. MERES, Esq., Judge, Midnapore.

26th May 1883.

Section 3.—It is to be regretted that the border-line between a ryot and a tenure-holder has not been drawn in the Bill. There is along the coast a large tract of land formerly occupied by Government for the manufacture of salt. On the abolition of the manufacture the land was surrendered to the zemindars in whose estates it lay, and who have let it to speculators. The lessee clears a portion, protects it by an embankment, and induces cultivators to take up small blocks and bring them under cultivation. These cultivators are fairly entitled to acquire occupancy rights against the speculators, but cannot do so (under the Bill) if he is classed as a ryot. The same thing occurs in the jungle mehals of this district.

The definition of a ryot should be so drawn as to include the case of a man who takes up land for cultivation by himself, or by his family or servants, and it should exclude the case of a man who takes land merely to sub-let as a speculation. A maximum limit of a ryot's holding is, therefore, necessary, and I may say that after eighteen years' service in the lower provinces, I have never met with an instance of a genuine cultivating tenant who held fifty beegahs of arable land.

CHAPTER VI. B.—The consequence of an error by the officer who prepares the table of rates, in over-estimating the normal produce of its average money value, or in fixing too high a minimum, will be nothing short of the ruin of the tenantry of the tract dealt with. The difficulty of collecting really accurate data for the table of rates will be found to be very great.

From C. A. SAMUELLS, Esq., Collector of Bankoora.

21st June 1883.

Section 16 seems to go too far. A *bhag-jotedar* is only a labourer under another name. This means of cultivating land (giving a share of its crop) is simply employed in lieu of wages, being preferable to wages in giving a man an interest in his work; and no one will be more surprised at the sudden change in his condition than the *bhag-jotedar* himself.

CHAPTER V.—The principle involved in Section 47 seems almost a ludicrous way of making out an occupancy right. There is to be a perfect transformation scene on a day yet to be fixed. In this draft it is the 3rd March 1883. On that day villagers, who may be mere tenants-at-will, and may never have held one piece of land for more than three days at a time, will suddenly become ryots with rights of occupancy in the plot last held, all contracts to the contrary notwithstanding. This is directly opposed to the law of 1869 (Act VIII. Section 7), and renders all contracts under that Act mere waste-paper. They would probably convert this right into cash at the first opportunity; but I cannot think the circumstances of the case will justify such flagrant infringement of the rights of the zemindars.

Section 49 appears to be the result of a confusion of ideas—a confounding a *khamar* land as it is and as it ought to be (*i.e. as it is desired to make it*). It is a contradiction of terms to speak of anyone holding *khamar* land as a ryot, unless a *bhag-jotedar* is considered such; and I have pointed out that he is not looked on as a ryot, but as another form of labourer.

Section 50 bestows a number of valuable privileges on the ryot: would it be too much to ask that one provision be added on behalf of the man at whose expense we are generous? viz. that the occupancy right be liable to be revoked for non-payment of the "fair and equitable rent" on the due date? We have taken great trouble to insure the ryot against exaction. We have gone so far as to interfere with the liberty of contract between him and his master, and it will surely be only just to the zemindar that we insist on punctual payment from the ryot, as we insist on his punctually paying the revenue. If the zemindar is liable to lose his estate for non-payment of revenue on a fixed date, there can be no injustice in holding this right and interest conferred on ryots liable to sale for the same reasons.

Section 61 is subversive of the laws of political economy and justice. If the land is capable of bearing a higher rent, why should the zemindar be compelled to let it at a lower rate (*to a middleman who may exact much more from the cultivating tenant*)?

B.—Admitting that rents are no longer to be fixed by consent, the next best thing is a table of rates. It is another question how such a table is to be prepared, and it pre-supposes a certain dead level in the out-turn of lands, as if improvement and industry were of no account.

Section 76.—I can see no reason for an arbitrary limit. The only recognised limit should be what is fair and equitable.

Section 89.—The ordinary ryot, who most requires protection, appears to get very little, and yet to be competent to make an agreement which his landlord will respect. Section 129 would be harmless as far as any class of improvements is concerned; but it will afford a spur to law-suits founded on imaginary improvements, and supported with all the wit and ingenuity shown on such occasions by a people prone to litigation.

CHAPTER XIII.—I think it must be allowed that the position of the zemindar under the Bill will be scarcely better than that of a mere rent-charger. Neither he nor his tenant could effect a compromise in future; they must be ranged in hostile camps, and the rules of the contest are rigidly fixed. A member of the Council has stated that 90 per cent. of the ryots in Bengal have occupancy rights. In another place I find it stated that "it is on all hands admitted to be the fact that, with or without right, the great peasant population of Bengal has long held the land at very low rates, far below the market rack-rent ": these are Sir G. Campbell's very words. If the above statements be correct, then the mere fact of a few disturbances in Pubna, due, perhaps, to an over-zealous officer, are not a sufficient plea for legislation.

I regard an Act which abolishes freedom of contract between landlord and tenant as a backward step in legislation.

I cannot help observing in conclusion that the zemindars suffer from a daily increasing difficulty in the collection of their rents and the Government cesses ; and I think that it behoves us to strengthen their hands to the utmost.

Consider the large arrear in Government estates, where the manager is armed with an exceptional procedure and the whole power of the Government; what must be the difficulties of a private individual whose only remedy is a civil suit, which is worthless as a resource, if his ryots combine against him ?

From HERBERT MOSLEY, Esq., Collector of Moorshedabad.

18th May 1883.

In my opinion, the new Rent Bill goes much too far, and will result in difficulties to zemindars, which may have a prejudicial effect on the Government revenue.

2. Generally, the effect left on my mind after reading the Bill is that it has been drawn up for the purpose of supporting an ignorant and easily-deluded peasantry against zemindars who are always trying to get the better of them. In some parts of the country it may be that the ryot is unable to look after himself, but it is certainly not the case everywhere. In this district, as in many others, the zemindars have by no means the best of it; and little more is wanted than a much cheaper and a very much more expeditious mode of deciding suits than exists at present.

4. CHAPTER I., Section 3 (5).—I would strike out the latter part of this clause. I do not see why, in a law for the protection of the cultivator, the same protection should be extended to him after he ceases to be one. He should, I think, cease to be a ryot when he ceases to cultivate, using the land for other purposes. In the same section, I would strike out everything relating to sub-letting, for reasons given further on.

17. There is, in Sections 45, 47 and 50, the same disabling of a certain class to make contracts which I think so objectionable throughout the Bill; this is likely often to inflict hardship. For instance, it is often highly advantageous to the ryot to hold certain lands for a year or two, and this may suit the zemindar too, except for this new law, which would void any contract to give it back after the term, and so the ryot will not get it.

18. Section 47 will cause injustice by handing over, as occupancy land, land which has expressly been let for a term only.

19. In Section 50 I would alter Clause A to one expressing that he may only use the land for cultivation, and Clause E I would eliminate. If, as I think is the case, this Bill is intended to protect ryots, I fail to see why it should allow sub-letting. A ryot ceases to be a ryot when he ceases to cultivate; and when he sub-lets he becomes the most oppressive of all landlords, a petty middleman. To protect the actual cultivator is well ; to put a man between him and the zemindar can only injure one or the other. If the sub-tenant only pays a fair and equitable rent to the middleman, it is very evident that the latter pays

a less than fair and equitable rent to the zemindar, which would be contrary to Clause C; and if the ryot turned middleman does pay a fair and equitable rent to the zemindar, then it is evident that the sub-tenant, the actual cultivator, pays an unfair and inequitable rent; and how does this improve the condition of the cultivating class?

22. As regards the sections providing for tables of rates, I can only say that I do not believe that such tables could possibly be prepared accurately. My experience in settlements shows that no two villages are alike, or can fairly have one table of rates assigned to them; and the Special Officer who was sent up here to inquire about this matter told me that his inquiries led to exactly the same result.

23. I also doubt very much whether such a list (of the market prices at harvest time) as that contemplated in Section 83 can ever possibly be prepared with any accuracy; and without accuracy the provision would be very mischievous.

24. Turning now to ordinary ryots, I see, by Section 90, that a zemindar cannot let land for a term at all, and Section 95 will effec-tually stop a zemindar from spending money on improvements whenever rents have been enhanced a short time previously.

25. And letting for a short term at a nominal rent to improve the land will be put a stop to, for the ryot, when he is called on for an enhanced rent, will refuse, and then, by Section 93, the landlord may have to pay compensation for improvements, and must have to pay compensation for disturbance, though all this was allowed for in the shape of nominal rent.

29. I think Section 171 (on the right to reap during distraint) should specifically declare how the cost of cutting, &c. (Clause 2) is to be met, and, as I remarked at the commencement of this letter, I should prefer to see a simpler and quicker procedure for suits. And I cannot but again say that I am afraid the Bill, if passed, will result in ruin to many zemindars, and I may add that the agitation among the ryots that, you may remember, occurred to the south of this district some time ago, when a Bill was being prepared, shadows forth pretty dis-tinctly what may be expected if this Bill passes.

From E. J. BARTON, Esq., Collector of Jessore.

31st May 1883.

3. I have doubts if it would be expedient to pass the Bill in its present shape. I think that a more speedy and cheaper means of realising rent is desirable, and that the Bill which secures this would do all that is necessary.

4. The parts of the Bill which are open to objection are those which introduce changes in the respective rights of landlord and tenant, and raise the tenant into the position of a co-partner at the expense of the landlord, without giving the latter any compensation for the property of which he is deprived.

5. Constant changes in legislation are greatly to be deprecated in this country, and should only be made when a clear and undoubted necessity arises. In the present case I do not think that any such necessity has arisen. I here speak of Lower Bengal. . . . The Bill, in important matters, deprives a landlord of liberty to contract with his ryots. I consider that some of its provisions, instead of conferring a benefit upon the cultivating ryots, as they seem intended to do, will injure them. I consider that the Legislature should interfere with the liberty of contract only in cases of most pressing necessity, and that no case of this kind has been established, so far as the landlords and tenants of Lower Bengal are concerned. In my opinion, the Bill will not improve

matters as regards the condition of the ryots, and there is grave reason to fear that it will aggravate the evils which it professes to remedy.

From F. WYER, Esq., Collector of Hooghly.

26th June 1883.

8. It seems to me that the right of occupancy should be acquired only by the actual cultivator, and that it should not be transferable, otherwise the right will, in all probability, pass in a few years into the hands of the money-lenders.

11. It is the general opinion that the table of rates cannot be prepared, and in that opinion I agree.

16. Sections 93 and 94, Clauses A and B, and Sub-section 2 should, I think, be struck out. If (under them) the ryot does not choose to pay a fair and equitable rent, the landlord has to suffer. He has to pay compensation for disturbance. Does he disturb when the ryot refuses to pay his just rent?

19. *Section* 166.—If the power of distraining crops for current arrears is continued the procedure should be very much less complex than that proposed in the Bill. The costs (under the Bill) would be very heavy, and would ultimately fall on the ryot.

22. The Bill excites great apprehensions in the minds of the zemindars, and will, I think, not effect any permanent settlement of the rent question.

From E. V. WESTMACOTT, Esq., Collector of Dacca.

23rd July 1883.

5. The action of the proposed law will only be to make the occupancy ryot the rack-renter instead of the present landlord, and the actual cultivator will not be the better for it.

9. I do not believe that the proposed law will have any effect whatever in raising the condition of the masses.

11. To speak of the wretchedness of Bengal ryots as notorious argues absolute ignorance of the facts of the case, and can only excite ridicule in those who know anything of the ryots of Dinagepore, Backergunge, Noakhaly, to say nothing of other Bengal districts.

27. *Section* 50 (*a*) appears to open the door to endless litigation.

35. *Section* 79 (*c*).—Why should a ryot be allowed to apply for a reduction year after year when a landlord cannot apply for enhancement, even on proved increase of area, oftener than once in ten years?

38. *Section* 91.—Any law fixing the rent of a ryot without a right of occupancy, will always be a dead letter.

40. *Section* 93 (*b*).—I think this compensation to a ryot, who has no right of occupancy, is iniquitous. If the ryot does not agree to pay the enhanced rent, and does not give up his holding, he is considered liable to pay the enhanced rent for the next year. I do not see why the law should change this.

45. *Section* 119.—I think it objectionable to pass a law which will, in practice, be evaded, as will certainly be the case with the limitation of the rent to $\frac{5}{16}$ of the gross produce. In Noakhaly there is a quantity of land which remains uncultivated for years, and is only taken up when the price of rice is exceptionally high. I think it impossible to interfere with the free contracts which they make. I have never had any trouble in the settlement of any question arising from such free contract. I think that any attempt at legislative interference with free contract in these cases will hinder cultivation, if not practically evaded.

48. If the zemindar has power enough to compel the ryot to pay illegal cesses against his will, I do not object to the interference of the State ; but where both landlord and tenant are content with the indefinite relations between them, understood and freely accepted by both parties, but indefinite when brought before the tribunal of the moonsif, I think that very serious economic evils are likely to ensue from any attempt at legal definition or limitation, however attractive to a theoretic and sentimental statesman. The result of such an attempt will be to set class against class where relations are now friendly, as following the cherished customs of the country and the natural economic laws.

55. I think the proposed Act will do generally more harm than good in the Bengal districts, with which I am well acquainted.

From W. V. G. Taylor, Esq., Collector of Nuddea.

7th June 1883.

Among all whom I have consulted, the consensus of opinion is against the Bill as being one-sided and tending to lower the status of the zemindar.

2. I consider that portions of it are unsuited to this district, that they would unnecessarily deprive zemindars of privileges which they have long enjoyed and to which they are entitled, without conferring on the old ryots any corresponding advantage, and only benefiting new comers who have no claims on the estate. On the other hand, some of the benefits conferred on the ryots appear to me of a very doubtful nature, notably the transfer of occupancy rights by sale.

3. *Sections 5 and 6* appear to me to be inapplicable to this district, in which the *utbandi* system prevails to a very great extent. Lands let out on this system have hitherto been considered to belong to the land-lords as their private property. Under the Bill such lands will become ryoti; and it seems questionable whether privileges so long enjoyed, and from which no injury to the ryots accrued, should be taken away.

Section 45.—Tho *utbandi* system will make almost every ryot a settled ryot, with a right of occupancy in the lands he may be holding since March. It cannot be the intention of the Bill to take advantage of a special system such as this.

Section 93.—I presume the Court has to decide whether the claim for enhancement is just and fair and in accordance to the law, before ejecting the ryot. In that case it seems hard that the landlord should have to grant compensation for disturbance which would never have occurred but for the obstinate rejection of such just claim by the ryot.

From Lord H. Ulick Brown, Commissioner of the Rajshahye and Cooch Behar Division.

22nd September 1883.

9. The Bill proposes to effect a violent revolution in the ownership of landed property, and to change the landed system over a large and important tract of country, affecting one way or the other the interests of above fifty-five millions of people. The magnitude and importance of the measure can hardly be over-rated.

10. I think that such important changes, affecting detrimentally the rights and interests of a large and important class, should only be made on very strong grounds ; such as, for instance, the grounds advanced by Mr. Gladstone when introducing a somewhat similar measure for Ireland in 1870. . . . The result of such a measure as this in that case might well make thinking men pause before introducing it into another

country, even if the circumstances under which the Irish measure was applied existed here. . . . The result of a similar measure in Ireland was almost disastrous, but it was tried to meet circumstances which seemed to the Government to require special treatment.

11. What are the circumstances under which it is proposed to introduce the present measure? They are about as different to those found in Ireland as it is possible to conceive. No special and strong grounds, political or other, exist in the present case, nor have any been asserted in support of this Bill. . . . It is well known that in Eastern Bengal the ryots are very much the stronger, and that if protection or assistance is required there, it is required by the zemindar.

In 1877, so far from any measure to assist the ryots being thought necessary or advisable, the Lieut.-Governor thought special legislation necessary to enable the zemindars all over Bengal to recover their rents in cases where there was no dispute, combinations among some ryots and a general disinclination to meet their undisputed liabilities having called for such legislation in aid of the weaker party—the zemindars. . . . Matters have in no way changed since then. There has been no general feeling of discontent among the ryots of the country as a body. I am sure that all Government officers will agree in this, and in thinking that the ryots of Bengal are, as a body, in a contented prosperous condition, nor will it be denied that there has been no general request on the part of the ryots for such legislation as is now proposed.

12. It is clear, then, that the present measure is proposed, not because it is necessary, but because, in the opinion of the Government, the land system of the Bill is preferable to the existing one. It seems to me that the passing of such a Bill would not be justified by the circumstances under which it is proposed, and that, even if there were no other objections, it would not be right to pass it.

13. But there are other, and, in my opinion, serious objections to the Bill. There is, first, the one, argued so universally and strongly by the zemindars, that it is an infringement of the rights guaranteed to them by the permanent settlement.

The representations of the zemindars on this point seem to me to be most reasonable, and entitled to the fullest consideration. I have always thought that the quotations from the writings of Mr. Francis, Sir John Shore, Lord Cornwallis, and others, as to whether the zemindars had proprietary rights or not before the permanent settlement, which quotations have been so often brought forward by both sides when discussing the question of the infringement of the permanent settlement by the passing of Act X. of 1859, and such Bills as this one, are not really much to the point, as the case of the zemindars rests on a much stronger ground, viz. the declaration of the Permanent Settlement Regulation that they are proprietors of their estates.

The zemindars do not stand alone in thinking that Act X. of 1859, and such bills as this are breaches of the conditions of the permanent settlement. The English barrister-judges of the High Court, and especially the chief justice of the year when Act X. of 1859 was passed, and the present chief justice, are entirely in accord on that question.

I do not deny that on grave grounds of public necessity, such as apprehensions of general disturbances, it may be necessary to depart from even such engagements as the permanent settlement; but no one says that they exist in the present case. Nor do I forget that the permanent settlement allows Government to interfere for the welfare and protection of the ryot. But if it had been intended that such interference could amount to the destruction of the proprietary rights then conferred, such rights would never have been conferred; and then I request reference to paragraph 11 of this letter, as it can scarcely be alleged that interference is necessary in the very slightest degree for the protection of the ryots who are in Bengal proper stronger than the zemindars.

14. Next, we have for ninety years treated the zemindars as real proprietors, making them discharge the duties of proprietors as regards matters connected with police, crime, furnishing, supplies to troops on the march, and, above all, the collection of public demands. Is it fair or just to deprive them now of several of the most important rights of a proprietor?

15. In what I have said as to the ryots being stronger than the zemindars, as to the former not requiring assistance against the latter, and as to the latter (as admitted by the Governments of Bengal and India in 1877) requiring assistance against the former, I have had principally in view the ryots of Bengal Proper. I know that in Behar the zemindars are, generally speaking, the stronger; but if any measures nearly approaching those in the Bill had been necessary in that province, some measure or other would assuredly have been proposed by Sir Richard Temple or Sir Ashley Eden in 1876 and 1877 to assist the ryots of Behar, who have not asked for this Bill any more than have the ryots of Bengal.

16. Another objection is, that it is a serious thing to create among the nobility and gentry of a population of fifty-five millions, a feeling that the Government have injured such an important class, and that without nearly sufficient cause, and without any demand for it on the part of the classes for whose sake the injury is done.

17. Another objection is the possibly disturbing effect the Bill might have on the ryots throughout the country. Though, happily, they are of a very different mould to the Irish, still when the ryots of Bengal and Behar see that, without any general representation on their part—without, so far as they know, any reason at all for the action of the Government—the zemindars are deprived of rights, while others are at the same time conferred on the ryots, I think it very possible that the idea may occur to the latter, that, as they have got so much without asking for it, Government must be actuated by a great desire to please them and to injure the zemindars who are sacrificed for their sake, and that by agitation further concessions may be obtained. Such agitation might before long grow and gain strength till it became a source of much trouble to the Government.

18. For these reasons I am opposed to the most important provisions of the Bill, and think that none of them should be applied to Bengal proper. But provisions for facilitating the recovery of rent should be enacted.

23. In conclusion, I hope that, after all that was said and done in 1877, and the unchanged circumstances since then, a provision will be made for the recovery of undisputed rents. It seems to me very unjust to omit such a provision in favour of the zemindar from a Bill which proposes to deprive him of so much. In 1877 the zemindar asked for bread; his claim to it was admitted by the Governments of Bengal and India; in 1883 he is refused a crumb and given a very large stone.

THE LATEST MEETING OF THE ZEMINDARS.

ONE of the largest meetings yet held in India, to express dissatisfaction with the Bengal Tenancy Bill, was held in the Town Hall of Calcutta on the 29th December 1883.

The chair was taken by the MAHARAJAH OF DURBHUNGA, and the MAHARAJAH OF DOOMROAN moved the first Resolution, to the effect that *the Government has entirely failed to show that any grounds exist for introducing into the Bengal Tenancy Bill revolutionary provisions which are a novel departure from the ancient custom and the existing law relating to landlord and tenant, and which will most injuriously affect all classes of the community who are in any way interested in land.*

The Maharajah, addressing the meeting in *Urdu*, made the following remarks : " You are aware of the revolutionary provisions embodied in the Bill. Nothing has been so clearly made out in recent discussions than that these revolutionary provisions are a departure from the ancient custom of the land. Under the worst of the Moguls your proprietary rights were always respected : he was extortionate, but never confiscated your proprietary rights. It has been said that the zemindars were then mere collectors of Government revenue. The histories of many of the families, whose representatives I see around me, give a flat contradiction to that statement. The zemindaries which have descended to me from a long line of ancestors, existed, as I learn from my family records, from a long time anterior to the Mahomedan conquest of the country, and my ancestors possessed greater rights and privileges than I have come to enjoy under the permanent settlement. The rights recognized by that settlement have never, before this, been questioned by the Government or the Courts of Law.

" Gentlemen, it has been said that the tenants under you had greater rights before the introduction of the permanent settlement than they enjoy at present ; and that it is the duty of the Legislature to rehabilitate them in their old rights. The assertion as to such rights having existed, is refuted by the two highest judicial authorities in the land.

" The advocates of the Bill admit that its provisions will sweep away your vested rights guaranteed under the permanent settlement; but they add that the Government reserved the power to enact laws for the protection and welfare of your ryots, and that the Legislature is simply exercising that power. It cannot be denied that, in certain contingencies, under certain political necessities, the Government of a country would be justified in trenching on vested rights. But no such grave political necessity exists in the present instance. If the reservation is held to justify the Government in taking away your proprietary rights guaranteed by the permanent settlement, then that settlement would have no meaning.

" It has been said, Gentlemen, that you, zemindars in Bengal Proper, are weak and your ryots are strong ; and that we in Behar are strong and our ryots are low and depressed. Why is then the same nostrum prescribed for two evils which are so entirely opposed to each other in their nature ? The provision intended to make the Behar ryots strong would necessarily, if also applied to ryots of Bengal, aggravate the evil, by making the strength of the latter excessive. But what is the actual condition of things in our much-maligned province of Behar ? I need only quote in answer what the Lieut.-Governor said on the subject."

The Maharajah, after citing passages in Sir Ashley Eden's speeches in 1881 and 1882 testifying to the growing prosperity of the cultivators, said : " This opinion must have been available to the Government when it indited its despatch to the Secretary of State on the Rent Bill in March 1882, and to the members of the Legislative Council when they made their furious denunciations of our zemindari system in March 1883. But it did not suit their purpose to give place, in their speeches, to Sir Ashley Eden's publicly-expressed opinions on the question.

" You have heard it said that a drowning man catches at a straw, and you may, therefore, understand why our mighty legislators caught at a straw like the opinion of a Government pleader at Gya, in defence of the position they had taken up in the Council. They could find nothing better. Why was not an inquiry instituted before we were so ruth-lessly denounced in Council? The Government despatch relies on certain figures taken from the Road Cess returns. Those figures go on the assumption that all lands in a district are equally cultivated. This is an error ; besides, the figures do not show that higher rents prevail in Behar than in Bengal. The despatch quotes the opinions of Messrs. Metcalfe, Geddes and McDonnel; but it forgets that these opinions, which, as far as I know, never before were deemed worthy of facing the light, were followed by the Behar Rent Commission ; and that that body, composed of experienced officials and non-officials, never recommended the violent and radical changes which have been embodied in the Bengal Tenancy Bill. Then, two officers, Messrs. Tobin and Finucane, were appointed to determine what was called equitable rents, the former being deputed to Shahabad and the latter to a selected tract in the North Gangetic districts. What was the result of the inquiry? Mr. Tobin found that the rents had not been changed for the last forty years and were exceptionally low. When this result was made known to the authorities, the inquiry in the Southern districts was immediately stopped, because the result militated against opinions pronounced in certain quarters. Mr. Finucane's report, on the other hand, was exten-sively quoted in Council. The rent-rates found by Mr. Finucane in the Mozufferpore district, are not, however, higher than those found to prevail in Bengal Proper, as will appear when the larger size and the greater productiveness of the tract selected for Mr. Finucane's examination is considered. These, Gentlemen, are the sum and substance of the evidence on which a whole class of zemindars has been condemned. A great portion of Behar consists of lands occupied by indigo-planters, of Crown estates and of escheated estates. If you compare the position and condition of our ryots with those of the ryots in the Crown and escheated estates, you will find, as you well know, that our ryots are far better off. The reason is obvious. The ryots belong to the same castes as the zemindars ; they are Brahmins, Rajputs, Palhuns, Kaysts, Gowalas and Kurmis ; and Mahomedans likewise are represented in both classes. Indeed, zemindars have often many of their own kith and kin among their ryots. Woe, therefore, to the zemindars who would disregard the voice of the community among whom they live, and try to play the part of the rapacious or tyrannical landlord. All these are facts which a little inquiry would have brought out; but no inquiry was instituted, we were condemned unheard, and it is now proposed to confiscate our rights by this revolutionary measure. I ask you, Gentlemen, to record your emphatic opinion that the measure has no justification in the actual condition of things. A common danger has brought us together from distant parts of the country. We have come, respectfully and loyally, to submit this our last appeal to the Government, in the metropolis of India. We have come to ask the Government to have regard for its plighted faith, and to protect the vested rights of an important section of its subjects ; to show to the Government that the revolutionary changes, which it proposes to effect by the Bengal Tenancy Bill, have neither been asked for by the ryots nor are calculated to do them good. The alarm and consternation that have come on the zemindars throughout the country can hardly be described. Our mighty Government may afford to disregard that alarm and consternation; but it should not forget that the foundation of the British rule in India is justice—justice to all alike ; and that all cases of injustice, of broken faith, tend directly or indirectly to sap that foundation. It is the duty of all loyal subjects to speak out on an occasion like this; and I would deem myself unworthy of that character of loyalty which has always distinguished the family to which I have the honour to belong, if I had not spoken out as I have done."

Mr. J. J. J. KESWICK, in seconding the Resolution, said : " Maharajahs, Rajahs, and Gentlemen,—It is unnecessary for me to trouble you with a speech, as I spoke on the subject on a former occasion, and my views against the Bill are well known. I would much rather listen to those gentlemen who have not spoken before, and I am glad to see this great meeting of influential zemindars, as it shows the earnestness of your protest against this uncalled-for and unnecessary measure."

Baboo DWARKANATH CHUCKERBUTTY supported the Resolution, and observed, in the course of his speech, that the Government of the late Viceroy had been taunted for his aggressive policy. " We have been told," he said, " of the wickedness and folly of the wars it carried on, and of the perpetual unrest in which it kept the Empire; but the Government of the present Viceroy seems actuated by the same spirit, only the scene is changed : we had war with foreign nations, and now we have a war of races at home. Lord Lytton fought with gunpowder and cannon. Lord Ripon delights in legislative explosives ; and, if this Bill becomes law, it will cause a fearful upheaval of society."

The MAHARAJAH OF DINAGEPORE moved the second Resolution to the effect that *the Bill, if passed into law, will be detrimental to the peace and tranquillity of the country, by fostering disputes and litigation between all classes of the agricultural population, and thereby interfere with the general welfare of the community.*

Mr. BELL, in seconding the Resolution, made the following observations in a clear and forcible speech, which could not be condensed without detriment, and should, therefore, be read in a full report of the meeting: " I was struck with what my friend said when he contrasted the aggressive policy of Lord Ripon with the aggressive policy of Lord Lytton ; but he omitted to say that Lord Lytton's arms were directed against the enemies of his country, while Lord Ripon is attacking those who have always been the support of the British Government. . . . It is proposed in the Bill that no agreement between the landlord and his tenant shall be valid, unless it receives the sanction of a revenue officer. It seems to me that a landlord and his tenant can agree about the rates of rent, considering that they know the land and the produce that it grows, far better than any revenue officer can do. It is simply preposterous to press a proposition that no engagement shall be made between landlord and tenant except with the sanction of a Government officer." Then, referring to the approval which the Bengal Tenancy Bill received from the Lieutenant-Governor, Mr. Bell said : " Although I am opposed to the Lieutenant-Governor on this Bill, he is a gentleman for whom I entertain profound respect, and whose opinion I would not oppose were I not supported by the almost unanimous opinion of the officials and non-officials throughout the country. . . . What I complain of and deeply deplore, is the injudicious indifference with which this unanimous consensus of opinion has been received. At the same time, though the odds are against us, I do not despair, for I feel we are fighting a righteous cause. I feel that it is impossible for Lord Ripon, if he regards his reputation as a statesman, to turn a deaf ear to the almost unanimous voice—both official and non-official—of India. I myself have confidence that the settlement to which my friend, the Maharajah, alludes—of Lord Cornwallis—will not be permitted to be torn to shreds, and I am sure that you will agree with me that the name of Cornwallis ought never to be mentioned without exciting in your breasts the profoundest feelings of gratitude. I read the other day the epitaph on his monument, and I think that the words upon it correctly describe our feelings, that *after the monument is crumbled into dust, millions will still attest the wisdom of his conduct and the virtue of his life."*

RAJAH HURBULLUB NARAINSING moved the third Resolution to the effect that *if the deprivation of the landlords of their just rights, inherited from generation to generation, confirmed by the permanent settlement and consecrated by a century of British rule, be deemed essential to the welfare of the tenantry, the Government be solicited to consider the justice of allowing the zemindars to surrender their estates on receiving such compensation in money as will, when invested in Government securities, produce a permanent return equal to their present income.*

Mr. GREGOR GRANT, from whose speech a passage has already been quoted, made also the following statement: " About nine years ago, Sir George Campbell, *for the sake of peace and good government of the Sonthal Pergunnahs,* deprived the zemindars of the power to settle their own lands with the ryots, and appointed Government officials to grant leases to them instead. The effect has been that, whereas suits for the recovery of rent were formerly almost unknown when the zemindar made his own settlement, they have, under the Government settlements, multiplied a hundredfold."

The HONOURABLE HARBANS SAHAI, in supporting the Resolution, said : " There can be no two opinions as to the justice of our demand. There is no revolution in the land; and if unfortunately there were one, a settled Government would confiscate the rights only of the guilty; and if it became necessary to trench on the vested rights of the innocent, it would, in honour and justice, deem itself bound to offer compensation. The state of things in Ireland does not exist in India; your ryots have not complained of you, have not sought relief against you, nor have they asked for additional rights. You have heard from preceding speakers the overwhelming testimony there is, that the condition of our tenantry is improving from year to year under the existing conditions. Were the Bill to become law, your zemindari office would have to be transferred to the Revenue officer's *cutcherry* or to the Civil Court, with, at every step, a law-suit or some legal proceeding, fines, harassment from surveys, records of rights, settlements, and the like. You know what law-suits mean—simply ruin to those engaged in them. The visit of a Common Court peon to a village is justly dreaded by those on whom it is inflicted: under the Tenancy Bill you will have no end of such visits."

RAJAH SHYAMA SUNKER RAI CHOWDHREE, in moving the fourth Resolution, went into the origin and history of the rights of the zemindars, and added the following remarks: " Among the fifty thousand or more proprietors of land in Bengal and Behar, about a thousand are descendants of persons who were proprietors at the time of the permanent settlement; the rest derive their title from purchase at Government revenue sales, or at other public or private sales. The one thousand original proprietors and their descendants have spent a large amount of capital on their estates since 1793: therefore, the whole of the fifty thousand proprietors have invested capital in land, in good faith and perfect reliance on the guarantee of rights afforded by the permanent settlement Regulations. Surely they are entitled to compensation for any of those rights which may be taken from them." The resolution was to the effect that, *as thousand of estates have been made of waste and other lands upon the faith of the zemindars being entitled to their present rights, suitable clauses may be introduced into the Bill for providing compensation to the zemindars for the loss of their rights.*

Mr. J. G. APCAR, in seconding the Resolution, made the following observations in the course of his speech: "When an injustice is perpetrated to any class, it is an injury to the whole State ; and the Tenancy Bill is a measure that certainly calls for the active sympathy with the zemindars of all who are interested in the welfare of India. The zemindars are a class on whom the stability of the Empire greatly rests ; and when we find legislation proposed that has offended the officials, angered the European community, and is beginning to alienate the zemindars, I think it is time for us to take alarm. In what manner has this Bill come before us ? It has been brought forward, not merely on insufficient evidence, but on no evidence at all. It has been framed upon assumption: it is pressed forward by men selected for the purpose. I would ask, why is it and how is it that those who have ripe experience, and could form a correct judgment on the subject, have been studiously kept from dealing with it ? Why has the assistance of Mr. Dampier, of Mr. Monro, and of our learned Advocate-General not been called in ? In our opposition to this measure there is no question of party politics. Liberals oppose it. I would instance my friend, Mr. Keswick, who is a strong Liberal, or at least was so, until the definition of that term came to be a person who is generous at other persons' expense. But this is not all ; there have been reasonable representations made, and they have been treated with contempt ; there have been opinions given—official opinions—and I would ask the Government how it is that that most able minute of our honoured Chief Justice has not had place given to it in the opinions published by the Government ?

"Is it for the sake of the ryot that this measure has been brought out ? We shall find that, if passed into law, it will reduce him to a worse state than that which he now occupies. For whose good, then, is the measure proposed ? Government takes no heed that the value of property is being reduced thirty per cent. ; it ignores the fact that people have been dealing with the property in the belief that it had been permanently settled, and on the faith of the British Government. Is it not paying too heavy a price for a policy by which the Government forfeits the confidence of all who have anything to lose. and imperils the peace and prosperity of the country ? I ask you, Gentlemen, is not that too heavy a cost ? "

Baboo SOORJ NARAIN SING, of Bhangulpore, in a long speech supporting the Resolution, observed : "Government has, for a long series of years, from the Permanent Settlement to the present day, sold estates on the understanding that the purchasers would have in them the rights which the existing law gives to landed proprietors. I have seen documents in which the authorised officers of the Government stated that certain zemindaris purchased from the State were free from *mourosi* and other tenant rights. Is it just that those who have invested their capital in such estates should be deprived of the rights they bought, without receiving any compensation for the same ? "

Nawab VELAYET ALI KHAN, who spoke in Urdu, proposed the fifth Resolution, to the effect that *in view of the provisions of the Bengal Tenancy Bill, which will deprive the landlords of their legitimate prestige and influence, and reduce them to a state of helplessness, the Government should be requested to relieve the zemindars of the duty of collecting the road and public works cesses, and of such other services and obligations as are now cast upon them by law or custom.*

Baboo SALIGRAM SING, in seconding the Resolution, referred to the many important duties which now devolve upon zemindars, such as aiding in the demarcation of land, assisting the police in the apprehension of offenders, supplying provisions to the troops that pass through their lands, collecting the Government cesses, and furnishing information on various matters. He also recalled the eminent services which the zemindars had rendered to the Government in critical times ; and argued that their altered position under the Bill, and the loss of prestige which would ensue, would deprive them of the power of duly fulfilling such duties.

The MAHARAJAH OF GHIDORE moved the sixth Resolution, which was that *the Viceroy in Council be moved to publish for general information, in English and in the vernaculars, the Bengal Tenancy Bill as it may be amended by the Select Committee, and to grant sufficient time to the public for the consideration of the amended Bill.*

Baboo PROSONNO CHUNDER ROY, Zemindar of Nuddea, in seconding the Resolution, explained that, according to the custom prevailing in his district, lands were not let out on lease, but that the cultivators were each year allowed to plough and sow such lands as they pleased, the zemindar's agent being afterwards sent to see what land each had cultivated, and to compute the rent according to customary rules mutually accepted. The Bill would convert these casual cultivators, and even trespassers, into middlemen of the class it proposes to create, giving them the right to sub-let their zemindar's land, and to sell their new rights to outsiders.

Baboo TROYLUCKO NATH MITTER, in supporting the Resolution, observed that the changes which the Bill had undergone were so numerous, and some of them so important and so novel in their character, that, unless the Bill was before the public for a reasonable period, it would be impossible for those whose interests are affected by it, to consider its provisions and express their opinion on them. He added : "To justify hasty legislation, necessity for the same must be made out. It must be shown that the circumstances of the country had attained a critical position ; that the relations of the different classes were strained ; that their attitude was menacing, and that conflict and calamity would ensue without immediate legislative interference. But can this be said of the present relations between the rent-paying and the rent-receiving classes? Is it not a fact that, two months before the Bill was introduced, their relations were perfectly amicable? I may add, without fear of contradiction, that even its introduction has not yet excited any general bitterness of feeling between the two classes. Why, then, force this legislative measure with undue speed ? "

Baboo SHEO PROTAB NARAIN, Delegate for the MAHARAJAH OF HUTWA, who had been prevented from attending the meeting by a heavy domestic affliction, said, in supporting the sixth Resolution : "The history of the Bill shows what great changes it has undergone, not always at the hands of the Select Committee, but also at those of certain gentlemen who have been charged ever and anon with the making of the Bill ; how, with its many revolutionary changes, we find in it but little of Sir Ashley Eden's original Bill for the speedy realisation of rents. The dwarf has grown into the monster which threatens to swallow up all our rights. In the Select Committee, Gentlemen, the public has no access, and its few members are left to re-arrange things according to their idiosyncrasies, without any light from outside. It is nothing but just, therefore, that the fullest opportunity of discussing its recommendations should be given to the public. But while those acquainted with the English language will thus be in a position to know and discuss the changes recommended, there is an infinitely more numerous class who, on account of their ignorance of that language, will not be able to form any idea of those changes, and the ryots come in this category. We ask, therefore, the Government not to proceed with this Bill until accurate translations of it in the vernaculars, embodying the recommendations of the Select Committee, have been for some time before the public.

Baboo CHUCKEN LALL SING, Zemindar of Chuckdiggee, proposed, and Baboo HUROCHUNDER ROY CHOWDHREE, Zemindar of Mymemsing, seconded the seventh Resolution, that *a memorial be presented to the Viceroy in Council embodying the Resolutions passed at the meeting, and that it be forwarded with the signature of the Chairman.*

A vote of thanks to His Highness the Chairman was proposed by Maharajah JOTENDRO MOHUN TAGORE, and seconded by Baboo JOY KISSEN MOOKERJEE, and unanimously carried, as were the seven preceding Resolutions.

The meeting then separated.

London: Printed by W. H. Allen & Co., 13 Waterloo Place, Pall Mall. S.W.

*Maharaja Sir Jotendra Mn
Sahad*

Paper
K.C.S.I

A PROTEST

TO THE

PROPOSED CADASTRAL SURVEY

IN

BEHAR.

Behar Cadastral Survey.

MONSTER MEETING AT SONEPORE AGAINST THE PROPOSED CADASTRAL SURVEY IN BEHAR.

A MONSTER MEETING of landholders, tenureholders and ryots was held at Sonepore on the 15th November 1891 at 3 P. M. in the Camp of H. H. the Maharaja Bahadur of Durbhanga. This big *shamiana* in front of the Camp was literally crowded to suffocation. It is estimated that there were at least 2,000 persons present in the *shamiana*, while outside the crowd must have been more than six times that number.

The proceedings commenced by Rai Jai Prakash Lal, Dewan of H. H. the Maharaja of Domraon, moving that H. H. the Maharaja Bahadur of Durbhanga do take the chair. This was seconded by Rai Kashi Prasad of Patna. The Maharaja Bahadur in opening the meeting read out the names of those who were unavoidably absent but fully sympathised with the objects of the meeting by letters and telegrams, and he proceeded to say :—

Maharajas and Gentlemen,—At the earnest request of many Zemindars of other Districts, who have already held meetings in Purneah, Bhaugulpore, Patna, Shahabad, Tikari, Chupra, Mozufferpore, and various other places, we have met here to-day to discuss a subject which is of deep interest to us all. The Lieutenant-Governor, as you are aware, sometime ago submitted to the Government of India the proposal for a cadastral survey of Behar, and he is naturally anxious to learn the views, which the landholders of the province entertain regarding the proposal. I have not seen the correspondence which passed between the Lieutenant-Governor and the Government of India on the subject; but I understand that it is proposed that a cadastral survey with a record of rights, shall be made of whole Behar, and that the expenses of this survey shall be met by a cess upon the land, to be paid in equal proportions by the Zemindars and Ryots. An additional cess will, of course be a very severe burden upon both the Zemindars and Ryots, and the question which we, as landholders, have to consider, is whether the expense and harassment, which this survey will entail upon us all, will be counter-balanced by the advantages which may eventually be expected to result from it. This is a question which I ask you calmly and temperately to consider. The Lieutenant-Governor, no doubt, believes that the proposed cadastral survey will be of great benefit to the country, that it will settle all disputes regarding the holdings and rents of the ryots, and furnish Government with a vast amount of statistical information regarding the rural population which at present is not procurable. As you are aware, in all temporarily settled Provinces, cadastral survey has been effected, and in all permanently settled Districts of the N. W. Provinces, cadastral survey has also been carried out. But neither in the temporarily nor in the permanently settled Districts of the N. W. Provinces, was any survey cess imposed upon the landholders. The whole expense of the survey operations was borne by Government. It therefore seems to me that if a cadastral survey is decided upon the Behar Zemindars and Ryots may fairly look to be treated with the same consideration as was shown to the Zemindars and Ryots of the permanently settled Districts of the N. W. Provinces. If a cadastral survey is made in Behar, it will certainly not be at the request of either the Zemindars or Ryots (loud applause). Zemindars or Ryots, wishing for a survey and record of rights of their respective estates and holdings can have the survey effected under the provisions of the Bengal Tenancy Act (loud applause). But when a survey is made at the instance of Government, and for objects which the Government have in view, it seems to me only reasonable that Government should pay the expenses of such survey, as in the case of the permanently settled Districts of the N. W. Provinces. The Zemindars and Ryots of Behar may fairly claim to be treated as Zemindars and Ryots of the permanently settled estates in the Benares Division. In these cases all expenses of survey were borne by Government, and there seems to be no reason why a different rule should be laid down for Behar, as neither the Zemindars nor Ryots of Behar have asked for the survey (Loud Applause). I think, therefore, that if it is decided that there shall be a cadastral survey for Behar, we may reasonably ask Government to bear the expenses. I am not, I am sorry to say, in a position to tell you what the actual expense of the cadastral survey will be. It is, I understand, estimated that it will cost about 8 annas an acre, but upon this point I am not competent to give any opinion. The Lieutenant-Governor having great experience in settlement matters considers, I believe, that it should not exceed this amount. Possibly this may have been the cost to Government of the cadastral survey in the North-West Provinces, but what I fear is that His Honour may not have had attention called to the fact that the cadastral survey in Behar will cost more than the one in the North-West Provinces, and will be attended with much greater difficulties. The Ryots of Behar are not in a position to pay this new cess or tax without ruin to many, impoverishment of more ; and even assuming that the Zemindars could afford to pay the cess, it is obvious that they would suffer still further through the impoverishment of their Ryots. (Applause.) In Behar, there will not only be the actual expenses incurred by Government in making the survey, but in addition there will be crushing expenses of litigation to which the survey will give rise, and I need hardly say that both Zemindars and Ryots contemplate the litigation with horror. It is quite certain that the Ryots cannot, in the present state of the District, afford to enter into litigation without impoverishing themselves, and yet it is equally certain they will litigate to the utmost, as shown by experience in other Districts where cadastral survey has been made. I am told that in the present survey of a portion of the Purneah District over 2,400 cases were filed by the Zemindars and Ryots against the survey proceedings. Purneah, you all know is the most thinly populated District of Behar. A great portion of the land is either a jungle or under water. In the densely-populated Districts of Behar there will be infinitely more cases and with appeals to higher Courts, which this litigation will involve it will be years before the settlement of a District is completed. I can imagine the confusion that will result, while this litigation is pending, and cannot help thinking that the Lieutenant-Governor has not had his attention directed to this view of the subject. If we could have a cadastral survey effected without litigation and without harassment and expense to which this litigation will give rise, both Zemindars and Ryots would accept it with pleasure (hear, hear. and cheers), but we, zemindars, know that this is impossible. A cadastral survey with its record of rights means years of litigation and this litigation will be equally ruinous to both Zemindars and Ryots. Such are my views of the cadastral survey and you will now have an opportunity of hearing the views of the other gennlemen, who will address the meeting. I wish only to say that it is with great reluctance I have come forward to oppose Sir Charles Elliot's proposal for the cadastral survey. The Lieutenant Governor has no object to gain by the survey. On the contrary, it will impose upon him and the Government officers under him great additional labour, and he certainly would not care to propose a measure which in the time of his predecessor had to be abandoned, unless he believed that it was for the benefit of the country. (Cheers.) Unfortunately we, ladholders, are of a diffrent opinion. All we have now to do is to place temperately before the Lieutenant-Governor our objections to the proposed measure, and we feel sure that he will give every consideration to them. (Hear, hear.) Moreover, it is well known to most of you that should the cadastral survey be actually started, it is more than likely that the officer, placed at the head of affairs, would be a gentleman who, however estimable, holds one-sided views on the relations between landlords and tenant, and his appointment would be most dangerous to the interests of all concerned in such a momentous question. I may mention that when Mr. Finucane was deputed by the Government of Bengal to make enquiries into the average outturn per biggah in Behar, he went to the Nurhun estate and merely had a sanding crop of rice thrashed out before him and took that as the actual produce of the area the crop was cut from, without bringing into calculation the value of the straw and the second crop of *khesari* and sometimes *mung* which almost are always obtained. We also propose at the suggestion of the different meetings, to form a branch of our Association at Calcutta so as to be able to place ourselves on any grave necessity in direct and immediate communication with the heads of Government. The advantage of it is so manifest that it is scarcely necessary for me to dwell upon the fact. Our branch being in Calcutta and in direct touch with Government would be much better able to let us know what the real ideas of Government are, so as to be able to protect our interests to the utmost. Moreover, there is always a difficulty in the Mofussil, owing to the poorness of communication in getting up such meeting as this to express publicly our views and grievances ; whereas if we had strong representatives in Calcutta they could, and would, be most valuable aids to us when required. It is an absolute impossibility for the Government to carry out this survey with a trustworthy staff of subordinates; for men poorly paid as the amins would be, simply prey alike upon Zemindar and Ryot, and the hardest part of it is oppression which would naturally fall upon the Ryot who is quite incapable, priticularly during these trying times, to bear such a burden, so that in every way this atempt to ameliorate the condition of the Ryot is bound to end in being a most bitter curse to him (Tremendous applause.)

His Highness explained the purport of his speech in vernacular and then asked the gentlemen in charge of the resolution to proceed. The first resolution was as follows:—

That considering that the proposal for the Cadastral Survey and General Record of Rights is much exercising and agitating the mind of the people of Behar interested in land, the Behar landholders assembled at this meeting think it imperative duty to approach the Government with a respectful representation bringing to the notice of Government the fact of the widespread anxiety, and submitting that all correspondence and reports referring to it be published, and the public should be given a fair and full opportunity of discussing the question on its merits before any action is taken, especially as they are of opinion that there is no urgency about the matter and the present year of distress is an inopportune one for the commencement of an undertaking of this kind.

It was moved by the Maharajah Bahadur of Gidhur and seconded by Babu Sheetul Prasad, representative of seven annas of the Tikari Raj, who in doing so spoke in Urdoo, the following being a translation of his speech :—

Gentlemen—I do not understand why in such an important matter as this, affecting all classes interested in land in Behar, the Behar Landholders as a body, through their accredited channels of communication should not have been consulted. We have heard from vague reports that landholders here and there, who often times choose to appear agreeable to officials by not running counter to their opinions, even at the sacrifice of their interests and the interests of their countrymen have been asked in an offhand way in the course of conversation about this important matter. If such opinions have been asked and given favouring the reported official view in this matter the best we should say of it is that this is not the view of Behar landholders assembled at this grand and august assembly I see before me, or of any landholder in Behar. I shall go further and say that it is not the view of tho great body of tenure-holders or ryots. The vaguest reports about these matters have created serious apprehensions and dismay and it is time and I shall say that it is the duty of the Behar Landholders' Association to approach Government for the fullest information on the matter. No false delicacy should keep them back from doing their duty. It is true that it is considered in some quarters that when the zemindars agitate on any matter it is thought that that measure must be conducive to the welfare of the Ryots ; with such false logic and assumptions we must bear to put up and must not forget our duty either to ourselves or to our Ryots whose interests are intimately bound up with ours specially in the present question. Gentlemen.—You know how dfficult it is to alter an opinion once formed, specially in our bureaucratic India. If you can prove by facts and figures and inexhorable logic, that an official opinion is wrong, you can never expect a change out of consideration to a fact which is besides the question and what they call in India prestige, so when an opinion has been once formed, do what you may say, what you say your arguments will be set at naught and you will be descried as you have been more than once decried, as rack renting landlords, who like to continue the old abuses and treat their Ryots as serfs. It is therefore of the utmost importance that you should approach Government all at once before any opinion has been formed simply on *exparte* reports of officials.

The resolution was supported by Rai Radhe Kishen, also of Patna who spoke as follows :—

Gentlemen,—So far as there is any proposal before Government as to the Cadastral Survey and general record of rights, we have only the vaguest sorts of reports. The Behar Landholders through their accredited channels of communication have not yet been consulted on the matter, and so far as I know there is yet no public declaration of any kind that such a thing is contemplated. We came to learn only yesterday that an important Government Resolution on the subject is shortly to be published in the Gazette. Yet these vague reports of sorts have created a degree of anxiety in the mind of those interested in land which is only equal in intensity to the anxiety we felt when the Bengal Tenancy Act was before the legislature, with this difference that whereas in the matter of the Bengal Tenancy Act, the ryots knowing that Government was to take away from your rights and to give it to them, did think the measure conducive to their interests, in the present instance their anxiety on account of these reports from what is coming on, is, I have reason to believe, equal to ours. Meetings, as you must have read in the newspapers, have already been held in all the districts and important centres of Patna and Bhagulpore Divisions largely attended by Zamindars and tenure holders and Ryots, and in all these meetings unanimous resolutions to the effect that the proposed cadastral survey and general record of rights was unnecessary, would be disastrous and would lead to expensive and ruinous litigation, have been passed and Behar Landholders' Association appealed to, to bring these resolutions to the notice of Government at an early date. This alarm and anxiety should not be allowed to prevail and the Behar Landholders think it their duty to approach Government with a humble representation that the true state of facts regarding the question should be fully known and all correspondence and reports regarding it published, and the public given a fair and full opportunity of discussing the question on its merits before any action is taken. There is no urgency in the matter at the present, a season of distress is not an opportune year for the commencement of an undertaking of this kind. This is our first resolution which I ask you to adopt.

' The resolution was put to the vote and carried unanimously. The 2nd resolution was as follows :—

That in the opinion of this meeting regard being had to the provisions of clause II Section 101 and Section 158, as also Section 56 of the Bengal Tenancy Act, the exercise of the power vested in Government under clause I Section 101 appears wholly unnecssary and to be an unwise interference with the rights and discretions vested in the parties interested in the question. That considering the fact that there is no evidence of any agrarian dispute or any general rise of rent so as to show that illegal enhancements have been resorted to, and it is yet premature to pronounce an opinion as to the ultimate effect of the experimental survey caused in a very small area and not yet in a whole district as promised at the time of the enactment of the Bengal Tenancy Act, and the Behar Landholders' Association having before them reliable information that the immediate effect of that experimen_ tal proceeding has been disastrous to the parties concerned ; and knowing as they do know that it is not a fact that the ryots have not yet in hand a trustworthy record of their rights and that every right regarding their tenures is uncertain, there does not appear any ground whatsoever for the exercise of the extraordinary powers vested in Govern ment under clause I Section 101.

This was moved by Babu Sheo Pratap Narayan, representative of H. H. the Maharajah Bahadur of Hutwa who in doing so said :—

Gentldmen—You are all aware of the provisions of section 56, under it you have to give receipts of rents to your tenants. These are now to be in counterfoils, and the particulars that are to be stated in these receipts are the following ;—

1. Serial number of Receipt.
2. Estate ; Village, Thana.
3. Tenant's name, son of
4. Particulars of the holding.

Nukdi, Bighas ; rent Rs.

Bauli, Bighas ; Maunds ; or Rs.

$$\left\{\begin{array}{l}\text{Jalkur Rs.}\\ \text{Bunkur Rs.}\\ \text{Phulkur Rs.}\end{array}\right.$$

Govt. Cesses $\left\{\begin{array}{l}\text{Road Cess Rs.}\\ \text{Public Works Cess, Rs.}\end{array}\right.$

5 Signature of the Landholder or his authorized Agent.

Most of the Behar Landholders had introduced this system of counterfoil receipts in their Zemindaries even before the passing of the Bengal Tenancy Act, and their system of counterfoil receipts. was,

I believe, originally suggested by the Behar Landholders themselves·
These receipts would contain from year to year, almost all the particulars,
that aje sought to be recorded with regard to holding. Then we have
section 158, under which either the landlord or the tenant can apply
to the Court having jurisdiction to try a case for the possession of the
land for the determination of the following particulars.

(a) The situation, quantity and boundaries of the land
(b) The name and description of the tenant there-of.
(c) The class to which they belong *i.e.,* to say whether he is a
tenure-holder, ryot holding at fixed rates, occupancy ryot, non-
occupancy ryot or under-ryot, and if he is a tenure-holder
whether he is a permanent tenure holder or not, and whether
his rent is liable to enhancement during the contribution of
tenure
(d) And the rent payable by him at the time of the application.

We have then section 101, Clause 2 under which the Local Government, on being moved thereto by the landlord, or a body of Ryots and
on their depositing the costs can order a survey and record of rights, and
under which the Local Government on its own motion can order survey when there is an agrarian dispute and when it thinks that the
measure is calculated to avert it, unless even the extraordinary power
reserved to Government under section 112 may be exercised, if necessity for the exercise of that power arises under clause 2 section 101·
There is no conceivable case, put it on any ground whatever, that is
not clearly covered by these sections ; where is then the necessity for
the exercise of the extraordinary power under clause 1 of section 101
and are not the parties interested, the landlords, the ryot or the tenure-holder the best judges of their own affairs ? The option and
discretion to apply for survey and measurement is now given to landlords as well as to ryots. If necessity arises they will apply under
the section, as they do even now apply, even an individual ryot can
apply under Section 158 and apply to Court for the adjudication of all
these matters, and who will deny that our Munsiffs and Sub-Judges are
better trained to form more accurate decision on these matters than
the Sub-Divisional Collectors and Collectors who are to be appointed
for the purposes of a general survey and record of rights under Section
158. Even the aid of a revenue officer can be availed of in cases where
it is deemed necessary to call such aid. The grounds on which the
Government of Bengal could apply to the Government of India for
sanction to order a general survey and record of rights though these
are not specifically mentioned in Section 101, are, we suppose the
following;—

1st. That there exists serious agrarain dispute

2nd. That a general rise of rents has been such as to show that illegal enhancements have been resorted to.

3rd. That the experimental survey to which the Government was plunged has proved a success.

4th. That without it the ryots cannot know for certain what is the demand of landlords.

Now is there any evidence of any one of these statements? The affirmative of each of these propositions have to be shown, and so long as they are not shown, where is the necessity for the exercise of the extraordinary powers under Clause 1 Section 101?

Babu Ramdhary Sahay, Secretary to the Tirhoot Landholders' Association, seconded the resolution in an eloquent vernacular speech and it was supported by Babu Parameshwar Narayan Mahta and Babu Nandan Lal of Mozufferpore and by Babu Gajadhur Prasad of Patna, whose speech was interrupted by frequent cheers. Babu Nandan Lal showed by reference to facts and figures that the cost of the survey and of the maintenance of the record will come up to a higher figure than the value of the property itself. While Babu Gajadhar Prasad said that if the survey was calculated to do good to any class, it was to the class of which he was a representative, namely, the lawyers; because he was confident as a lawyer that there would be an immense increase in litigation. In concluding, he said that the survey would bring down a host of locusts in the shape of Ameens who will eat up the ryot's substance. On being put to the vote the Resolution was carried.

The 3rd Resolution was as follows :—

"That the total outlay on the survey and general record of rights of this Province, the Behar londholders estimate at two crores or thereabouts, and the annual expenditure for the preservation and continuance of the record will be not less than 15 lacs ; while even this estimate only represents a fraction of the actual cost which parties will have to incur ; that if under the powers vested in the Local Government under Section 114 of the Bengal Tenancy Act, the expenses or any portion of the expenses of the survey and general record of rights be ordered to be defrayed by the landlords and tenants whose lands are surveyed and rights recorded, it will be a heavy burden of taxation which neither landlords nor tenants will be able to bear ; and if any cess be proposed to be levied for the preservation and continuance of the records, it will impoverish the landlords and ryots, who, all cesses added, will have to pay indirect taxes in cesses alone double the amount of the tax that is leviable on incomes other than those on land, and in whose case even the lowest minimum income is not exempt from taxation. The Behar landholders also respectfully submit that the addition of these cesses is an indirect, even if not direct, infringement of the rights, vested in them by the Permanent Settlement."

In moving this Resolution Babu Gouri Shunker, representative of Rajah Rameshwar Sing of Ramnugar spoke as follows :—

I rise to speak on behalf of Raja Rameshwar Singh Bahadur. The present measure has his hearty sympathy, According to Mr. Finucane the cost in the experimental tract for the survey and general record of rights, need not exceed 8½ annas per acre, or about a tenth part of one year's rental.

Turning however to total figures, in tracts other than experimental we find that the cost of surveying 1,209,680 acres in 1889-90 was Rs. 8,32,836-12 ans. or about 12 ans. per acre.

Calculating at 12 annas, the expenses for surveying and recording rights in Behar can hardly be less than 2 crores of rupees. This however represent a mere fraction of the expenses, legitimate and illegtimate which the parties shall have to bear. There are the legitimate cost of litigation and constantly dancing attendance from office to office and there is no good concealing the fact, a good deal of illegitimate expense which the parties shall have to incur in feeding the Amins and people of that sort. You have heard from a previous speaker, that all expenses added, the sum total was near enough to the value of the property itself, so you see under the circumstances, you don't profit by the measure but people who will come by your place as purchasers.

Then the amount that will be needed for the preservation and continuance of the record, will according to our estimate come up to 15 lakhs. Where will all this money come from ? Section 114 of the Bengal Tenancy Act gives the Lieutenant Governor the power to apportion the expenses between the parties ; but the question is will they be able to bear the burden ? I shall not speak for the Ze_mindars ; but I shall tell you what our sentimentalists are doing for the Ryots. According to Mr. Finucane, the average holding in the experimental tract is about 3 acres on the produce of which have to *live 5 or 6 individuals.* Already, you know, as a *result* from the Salt Administration Report that the average ration of salt in Behar is 9 annas, which is 12 annas in Bengal ; it could not be otherwise *than that* the Behar Ryots should have stint themselves in that necessary article of consumption, the salt ; for let us calculate what is the produce of 3 acres on which 5 or 6 individuals have to live. Under the most favorable circumstances, the produce will be 60 maunds of paddy plus say 20 maunds of *khesari* the price of which will be in average year about Rs. 80, out of that shall have to be deducted charges for cultivation ; say Rs. 16 and rents about 15 total 30. There remain Rs. 50. on which the burden of taxation is as follows :—

	Rs.	As.
On Salt one maund about ...	2	8
On Clothes &c. import duty	1	0
On Road Cess and Public cess	0	8
Total	4	0

No account is taken of the excise duty on the above, though we all know that a part of the ryot's income go to the head ; but taking 4 rupees as the amount payble out of an income of rupees 15, the ryots have already to pay rupees 4 as taxation out of an income of rupees 50 or 8 per cent, which is treble as much as the rate fixed under the Incometax Act and in the present instance not even the lowest maximum is exempt from taxation.

After being seconded by Babu Harndar Singh representive of Raja of Seohur, the resolution was put to the vote and carried. The fourth rasolution was as follows :—

"That it is too well known that the Government have not a trustworthy staff to carry out the proposed survey, and the Amins would harass to an infinite extent, and whatever safeguard the Government might propose would be futile to stay the oppression ; that the measure is calculated to give rise to ill-feelings and unfounded claims which will lead to very heavy and expensive litigation, as already has been the case in Purneah and Sriuuggur with respect to the boundaries, and with respect to the nature of holding and rates of rents ; that this will be ruinous to the parties concerned ; and that whatever certainty will be gained by this expensive measures, and harassing costly litigation, will be existing nowhere even after the lapse of the shortest period."

Nawab Sarfraz Husain Khan of Patna, moved and

being seconded by Babu Ambica Prashad Singh of Chainpur and Salemgurh and put to the vote it was carried unanimously.

The 5th Resolution was as follows :—

"That a Memorial be drafted and submitted to His Honour the Lieutenant–Governor, containing these Resolutions, and also containing such representations with regard to them, as may be deemed necessary and proper.''

It was moved by Babu Nandan Lal and seconded by Babu Parmeswari Lal of Patna and carried.

The 6th Resolution was as follows ·—

"That an Executive Committee, consisting of the following Behar landholders, be formed for the purpose of determining what steps ought to be taken to fully represent the views of the people interested in the land to Government regarding the matter, and generally to take measures to protect the people from this and similar proceedings, which, though intended for their good, are calculated to be ruinous both to landlords and ryots, and also to decide upon the formation of a Head Branch Association in Calcutta."

This was moved by Babu Drighoal Lal Haswa of Gya and being supported by Mr. Seppe representative of the Maharajah of Chota Nagpur was put to the vote and carried.

A vote of thanks to the Chair was proposed by Babu Ramdhary Sabay and being carried with acclamation brought the proceedings to a close.

MEETING OF THE BRITISH INDIAN ASSOCIATION.

THERE was a large and influential gathering of the zemindars of Bengal in the hall of the British Indian Association rooms, on Saturday the 12 December 1891, to consider the propriety of submitting a Representation to the Government of Bengal, regarding the Cadastral Survey of Behar recently ordered by the Government of Bengal. Among the noblemen and gentlemen present we noticed the following :—H. H., Maharaja Luchmiswar Singh, Bahadur, K. C, I. E., Durbhanga—*in the Chair*. Maharaja Bahadur Sir Jotendra Mohan Tagore, K, C. S. I., Maharaja Bahadur Sir Narendra Krishna, K. C. I. E., Maharaja Durga Charan Law, C. I. E., Raja Peary Mohan Mukerjea, C. S. I., Raja Dilawar Reza, Maharaj Kumar Benoy Krishna, Maharaj Kumar Prodyat Kumar Tagore, Moulvi Mahamad Yusuff Khan Bahadur, Rai Tej Narain Singh Bahadur, Rai Shib Chunder Banerjea Bahadur, Rai Raj Kumar Sarvadhikari Bahadur, Babus Chandilal Singh, Damodardas Burma, Sital Prosad Singh, Kiran Chandra Roy, Janakinath Roy, Sitanath Roy, Narendranath Mukerjea Jodhu Kumar Mukerjea, Matilal Ghose, Saligram Singh, Mahabir Prasad, Devaprasad Sarvadhikari, Mr. J. Ghosal, Pandit Prannath Saraswati, Syed Moulvi Ali, Syed Mahamad Tahir, Babus Haro Mohan Roy Chowdhuri, Bolaki Lal, Nanuu Singh, Gopal Narain Singh, Ugramohan Tagore, Jaladhinath Mukerjea, Nalin Vihari Mukerjea, Jotendranath Mukerjea, Sarat Kumar Banerjea, Kissen Sahai, Bhubaneswar Misra, Pran Kristo Bagchi, Jogesh Chandra Bhattacharjea, Benaik Chandra Chatterjea; Radhasyam Mozumdar, Mathura Nath Ghose, Kasiswar Mukerjea, Kalidas Banerjea, Sarat Kumar Lahiri, Sivapratap Banerjea, Raghunath Singh, Raghunandan Prasad, Rama Prasad, Surendranath Mukerjea and others.

Maharaja Bahadur Sir Jotendra Mohan Tagore, the president of the British Indian Association, proposed his Highness the Maharaja of Durbhanga as Chairman, and in doing so he said that in consequence of ill-health he (the mover) was unable to take an active part in the proceedings, but the objects of the meeting had his hearty sympathy. There was no fitter person among them, both on account of his position and the closeness of the effect which the proposed measure had upon him, to preside over their deliberations on the matter for discussion; than His Highness the Maharaja of Durbhanga, and he felt sure that the Resolution would meet with their unanimous support. Maharaja Bahadur Sir Narendra Krishna seconded the resolution which was carried by acclamation.

His Highness the Maharaja of Durbhanga on taking the chair said that he was grateful for the honor which the meeting had done him in electing him their chairman. Of course he was expected to make a speech ; but that would mean simply a repetition of what he had already said on the subject at Sonepur, at a meeting held there three weeks ago, and attended by over 2,000 zemindars of that part of the province. He would not therefore inflict a speech on them, for he felt sure that most of those present were acquainted with his remarks, but this he would say, that the Behar zemindars were unanimous in condemning the proposed cadastral survey, and to a man believed that instead of working good it would do incalculable harm. As a Behar land-holder he was glad to see so many influential Bengal zemindars willing to join their brother zemindars in a protest against the measure. He felt sure that the Government would give their protest a respectful hearing. - The proposed measure had been conceived on a misconception, and it was their duty to respectfully represent in what direction that misconception lay ; and he would be mistaken in his estimate of the justice of the Government if their representation failed. He had said enough, and he would leave it to others to discuss the question.

The first resolution was moved by Maharaja Bahadur Sir Narendra Krishna, and seconded by Moulvi Mahomed Yusuff Khan Bahadur. Rai Shib Chandra Banerjea Bahadur, in supporting the resolution said :—

Maharajas, Rajas and gentlemen,—You have done me a great honor by calling on me to support the first resolution. I feel I am unable to do full justice to the subject to consider which we have met here to-day. I mean the proposed cadastral survey and settlement of a part of Behar. I shall however try to deal with it in the best way I can. I shall consider the subject under six different heads :—1st, I shall show you that the measure is unnecessary and uncalled for ; 2nd, that it will lead to expensive litigation ; 3rd that it will be ruinously expensive ; 4th, that there are many difficulties attending it ; 5th, that it will disturb the peaceful relations between landlords and tenants ; and 6th, that it is inopportune.

The survey and settlement proposed is not necessary. The conditions under which such proceedings ought ordinarily to be undertaken according to law are set forth in clauses *a* to *d* of Section 101 of the Bengal Tenancy Act ; none of those conditions however exist in the present case. (1) Neither the Landlords nor the Tenants ask for it. (2) No serious dispute likely to arise is to be averted by the preparation of a record of rights. (3) The estates to be surveyed are neither the property of Government nor managed by the Court of Wards and lastly no settlement of Government revenue is being made in respect of the local area to be surveyed. Under such circumstances it is difficult to justify the measure without an exposition of the cause (not vouchsafed to the public) which has induced the Government of India to sanction the proceedings. Almost all the material information to be collected by the survey and settlement, so far as the interests of the ryots even are concerned, is available in the records of the Zamindars, and if there are exceptional defects in solitary cases, that affords no reasonable grounds for ignoring the existence of better records in the province at large ; and cannot justify the levy of heavy and in some instances of ruinous costs for a new set of papers in slightly modified forms.

The particulars required to be recorded among others, to be added to or left out, under Section 102 of the Tenancy Act relating to the names of tenants ; the class to which he belongs either permanent or temporary, the situation, quantity and boundaries of the land, the rent payable and whether it is liable to enhancement or not and similar matters of detail are ordinarily available in all well-managed Zamindaries. It is therefore hard that what has answered the legitimate wants of both landlords and tenants for ages and never been contested as a rule as insufficient or unsatisfactory should be ignored by Government and in attempting to replace them by another set of records apparently varying only in shape and not in substance, opportunity should be given to raise contentions not subsisting or long lost sight of and forgotten. The issue of Rent receipts

in the form prescribed in Schedule II of the Tenancy Act, has con-
tributed to make many points connected with rents and tenures so
clear that what defects if any, did exist in the old Zemindary papers
has been essentially rectified. Over and above this, Section 158 of
the Act gives power to every aggrieved ryot to enforce the survey
and settlement of his tenure in the way a general survey and settlement is calculated to do. But the material difference in the procedure is significantly great. In the one case only the ryot suffering
a hardship applies for its removal and incurs the liability of paying
the needful costs if awarded against him ; in the other case wronged
or not wronged, seeking or not seeking redress—all must be
exposed to the annoyance and expense incident to extensive
survey and settlement operations conducted at the first stage by
Ameens and Amlahs not above temptation and not sparing or
scrupulous in their dealings with ignorant and illiterate ryots.

With due deference to the present rulers of the country, I have
satisfied myself by a careful enquiry, the result of which accords with
very long experience of the affairs of zemindars and ryots, that the proposed survey and settlement is unnecessary and uncalled for, so far as
the real needs thereof are concerned and that the expense and annoyance concerned therewith will be quite disproportionate to the extra
advantages to be derived from it and that in the interests alike of the
Zemindars and ryots it will be judicious and kind for Government to
spare the country from the effects of the measure contemplated.

It goes without saying that the proposed measure will be attended with an increase of litigation unprecedented in its character. The
landlords and the ryots will both be involved in law suits, the cost
of which it will take them years to recoup, if it does not prove
altogether ruinous to many of them. In the thinly inhabited district
of Purneah filled with jungle and water in several parts there
were 2400 cases in courts in connection with the survey and settlement undertaken of only a small part of that district. In the
Bhagulpore tract which forms also a small fraction of the entire district
the number of contested cases in court aggregated to several thousands.

There are many zemindars and ryots who are unable punctually
  pay the Government revenue and landlords' rent without raising
loans at usurious rates of interest, for them to be saddled with the
cost of the proposed survey and settlement operations means clear
ruin ; and if I may be allowed to say so I would add that the

parties in whose interests it is to be undertaken will be fleeced to enrich the village mooktear and the members of law above him.

The cost estimate at 8 annas per acre is believed to be much below the mark and does not include many items of expense legal and illegal which are unavoidable. It is estimated by people who possess practical experience of all the details of the business that the cost of the contemplated operations will amount to two crores of rupees in round numbers over and above the annual expenditure of thousands required for the maintenance and preservation of the elaborate and voluminous records which to be useful will have to be kept in order and efficiency.

The difficulties of the undertaking are undoubtedly great. I cannot do better than quote the opinions of some of the high officers of Government who were consulted on the subject.

Mr. Beames, who was then Commissioner of the Burdwan Division, and who is known to be a great authority in revenue matters was of opinion that " to introduce the system into an old and permanently settled province will not only be very expensive but will stir up agitation and litigation on all sides. The officers whom I have consulted agree with me in thinking that the whole procedure is objectionable, and in hoping that the country is not about to be plunged into a state of confusion, unparalleled since the days of Native rule, merely for the purpose of endeavouring to arrive at a result which can never be attained."

Mr. Bailow, Commissioner of the Bhagulpore Division, and all the Collectors under him, objected to a cadastral survey, on the ground that the whole of its effect "will be lost unless arrangements are made for the mutation of names, &c., after the record is complete." Mr. Oldham Deputy Commissioner of the Sonthal Pergunnahs, where a cadastral survey was made, acknowledged the difficulties of the operation and candidly confessed that it would be useful for a certain period, having proved so for nine years only in the Sonthal Pergunnahs. He would not attempt to keep up the records by entering mutations in consideration of the vastness of the work.

Mr. Wilson, Collector of Midnapore said :—

" The proposed operations would be of no permanent value without the means of correcting the records by keeping them up to date, and I do not think it would be wise to enter upon a project, involving the expenditure of nearly four crores of rupees [the estimate here is four for the whole of the territories under the Lieutenant-Governor-ship of Bengal, and is undoubtedly an underestimate] without cousi-dering how the record of rights is to be kept up, and what the annual cost of keeping it up would be. This is the more necessary, and as to prevent the confusion which must result from the accumulation of arrears, the process of correction should follow closely on the prepara-tion of the original." Mr. Wilson then proceeded to point out that "the amount of work in respect of transfer and leases alone may be to some extent estimated by referring to the statistical return of the Registration Department, 134,250 transfer, and 19,519 leases were registered in the year 1882-83. If the survey of any district were complete it might be possible to require the survey number to be given in all leases and transfer deeds. The Registry Office could then furnish the Survey Office with needful particulars regarding all registered transactions. This would be troublesome and expensive, and a considerable permanent staff would be required in the Survey Office. It must be remembered, however, long before the survey and record of rights of any district was complete, and before, therefore, the mention of survey numbers in documents relating to land could be made compulsory, a considerable number of changes would have occurred, and consequently there would be much difficulty in bring-ing the entries up to date. With regard to the numerous transactions which are not registered including enhancements, it would probably be suggested that the necessary information should be collected by means of patwaris. But the cost of this would be very great. If any reliance is to be placed on a patwari's papers he must have a decent salary, and it can be hardly thought that Rs. 10 a month—the lowest pay of a mohurir—would be too large an amount to give in order to raise him above the temptation, which surround him. Now there are in Bengal 2,48,706 villages, and if the odd 48,706 be omitted as uninhabited, a patwari on Rs. 10 a month, in each of the remaining 200,000 would cost in all Rs. 2,4000,000 a year, or nearly two and a half crores of rupees. I take no account of the cost of the estab-lishment which would be required in each district for the purpose of arranging and entering in the records the information supplied by patwaris, nor is it necessary to discuss here the percentage of dis-honest or otherwise erroneous entries likely to be found in a patwari's papers. Who would bear the cost I know not but whether the money is to come from Government or the zemindars, I would suggest that this large income, if really available from any source should be devoted to the rapid construction of railways, canals and roads, as large public works of this class are in my judgment, likely to be more useful than patwaris."

Lord Ulick Browne said :—

"A record made in 1885 that A is an occupancy holder of holding B may be quite useless in 1988 owing to A leaving it, and to its being split into three holdings given to three non-occupancy ryots, or split into four bits, two of which are given to non-occupancy ryots and two to adjacent occupancy holdings thus also affecting the record of this holding made in 1885 . . . I do not think it would be possible by any legal provision to obtain correct information of the numerous changes in permanently settled estates and if it were possible the business of recording changes would be so vast that it does not seem advisable to undertake it. I think therefore, that it is not worthwhile undertaking an operation of such magnitude in order to secure such limited advantages as could be expected from it, while much forgery and perjury would be inevitable."

"Every one concerned being hostile to the whole proceeding no one would be very ready to give correct information. The general feeling in such cases is that if there must be a survey it is advisable to cripple its power of evil by supplying as many erroneous or distorted facts as may be. The statements of landlords and tenants regarding rents and rights would not be found to agree, and it will not always be easy to decide which is right......and I fear that when all is said and done any such general record will contain a very considerable percentage of erroneous entries."

The Commissioner of the Chittagang Division was equally pronounced in his opinion. Admitting the want of authoritative agricultural records in Bengal, he proceeded to say that "the work of effecting a remedy is truly a gigantic task, and if attempted on the proposed lines an impossible one." He apprehended that "almost every single entry" with regard to rent would lead to a "protracted dispute," and then went on to observe : "It would be possible to make out a record which will show only the status and position of the tenant, though even that would be a task of no mean magnitude but once we attempt to touch the question of rent we enter on an enquiry that covers the whole dispute which is at present agitating the agricultural community in Lower Bengal and putting such a strain on the relations existing between landlords and tenants. It may be necessary to enter on a work of such magnitude for the preservation of the public peace, but I do not consider that anything short of a grave crisis will be held to justify our taking in hand so intricate and difficult an undertaking."

I will conclude by quoting the opinion of Mr. Cotton then an officiating Commissioner, now the Chief Secretary to the Government of Bengal, whose sympathies with the people of this province are well known to all. Mr Cotton was "constrained" to say that he looked with "anxiety" on the provisions of the Bill which empowered the local Government to undertake a cadastral survey "in any case with the previous sanction of the Governor General in Council." "The proposal to introduce a survey and record of rights over the whole of Bengal," wrote Mr. Cotton "is by no means the panacea which some seem to consider it." He did not dwell so much on the difficulties of the proposal, but he objected to it "on the very ground on which it was generally supported." Mr. Cotton then went on in his own expressive and eloquent way to say : "It is well, no doubt that an independent agricultural record should exist which neither zemindar nor zemindar's amla could transfer. [Para. 103 of Government of India's Despatch No. 6, dated 21st March, 1882.] Such a record is very desirable on many grounds, but I see no reason for supposing that it will bring with it a general agricultural settlement or any material increase of rural prosperity. And a similar result has not ensued in those provinces in India in which a survey and record of rights has been accomplished. It is not fair to compare the North-West Provinces with Bengal, as other causes have led to the accumulation of wealth in our favoured province ; but I certainly do not find any evidence to show that the record of rights has led to the enrichment of the peasantry of Upper India.

And I am sure of this that in Bengal, where owing partly to the accident of the Permanent Settlement, it has hitherto been the policy of Government to interfere as little as possible with the people, the attempt to make a survey and record of rights will give rise to great local opposition and to excessive litigation, by which many persons who are now welloff will be impoverished. A survey and records of rights is necessary where disputes exist, where oppression prevails, and where the peasantry are poor and need protection.

For this reason, the provisions of the Bill are likely to prove useful, if they are judiciously enforced. But over most parts of Bengal it cannot be alleged that there are disputes, oppression or poverty ; to introduce a settlement of rents and record of rights in Bengal generally will merely excite disputes and kindle litigation. The normal relation of landlord and tenant in these provinces is one of compromise ; it is true that rights are unadjusted, the balance of rent is undetermined ; the current demand of rent is not fixed ; the area of cultivation is often unknown ; it is for the convenience of both parties that the claims of either are not put to the test, and yet it is not the case that the ordinary relations between landlord and tenant are unfriendly. The narrow induction drawn by local officials from occasional disturbances which come to their notice misleads them and has misled Government into the delusion that general disaffection exists. The one or two cases of disturbance come prominently to notice, the thousands and thousands of instances in which order and contentment prevail pass by unobserved. But the existing state of things, which is satisfactory because it is in accordance with the custom of the country and not objected to by any, will certainly not continue after the appearance of the 'Revenue Officer' in the districts

All that was elastic and unsettled will, under the new procedure, be stereotyped and fixed, and both parties will struggle with one another to the utmost in the Civil Courts in order that disputes may be decided which would never have arisen if the Surveyor's rod and the Settlement Officer's Registers had not galvanised them into life. It is difficult to over-estimate the bitterness of feelings which a survey and record of rights will thus provoke. The evil, I think will outweigh any administrative advantages derived from it. I venture also to think that most persons who are competent from their experience and knowledge of these provinces to form an opinion on the subject will be found to agree with me in this deliberate conclusion, that a survey and record of rights, if it is calculated to settle disputes where they already exist, is equally calculated, where they do not, to call them into existence.

The statements of such distinguished officers supported by the officers of the Maharajas and Rajas and other leading Zemindars who are present here to-day ought in such matters certainly to outweigh the contrary opinions of one or two officers of Government who re-

commended the measure. Its proceedings will certainly lead to bad feeling between zemindars and tenants. It is only five years since the
Bengal Tenancy Act was enforced and just as the differences between
the zemindars and ryots are settling down and peace and good feeling
are being restored it is to be regretted that any thing should be done
which is calculated to foster hostile feeelings between the parties. The
comfort of a ryot depends to some extent as much upon the good
will of his zemindar as that of the zemindar more or less on his ryot.

Gentlemen, last but certainly not the least is the question whether
the Government should have selected this as the proper time for
carrying out the measure demands serious consideration. It is
admitted on all hands that there is a scarcity, if not actual famine,
in Behar brought on by a partial failure of the crops. The ryots are
at present entirely at the mercy of the landlords for the maintenance
of themselves and their families. At such a time one can easily
guess what the effect of a hostile feeling between the two parties
will be and considering that many of the zemindars in Behar are
indebted and that it is not easy to raise fresh loans, it will be impossible to be lenient in the recovery of rents and afford any relief to
their distressed ryots if they are required to bear the enormous cost
of the survey and settlement operations even if they are allowed to
pay instalments.

The time is certainly inopportune to carry out the measure. Sir
Steuart Baley abandoned it for a time at least as there was scarcity in
Behar in 1889 and scarcely have the zemindars and ryots got over
the bad effects of bad years, when they have to face another calamity
of the like kind this year. If notwithstanding our respectful representations the measure is carried out the result will be, many of the
old landed classes in Behar who are heavily involved now, will be
sold up and before the good effects of the survey are felt by them
they will have to make room for the Bunnia Mahajans who buy
their property in execution of their decrees and so with ryots. The
village Bunnia, crafter than the town Bunnia, will sell the ryot out and
the old peasantry of the soil will disappear. If Government has
really any money to spare at this time for the good of the landlords
and ryots, I would beg most respectfully to suggest that measures be
adopted to preserve old families of zemindars from ruin and as a
measure calculated to afford relief to ryots whose amelioration it is
the humane object of Government to achieve, agricultural banks in

the mofussil like the Montsde-picta of France should be started. In-calculable good will be done to the ryots if money is advanced to them on low rates of interest instead of the 24 per cent. which they now pay to the village *Bunnia*. It is a known fact that for genera-tions together these poor ryots can never get out of the books of the village *Bunnia*. A scheme to carry out the system of agricultural banks can easily be drawn out to be worked through the agency of the District Boards. On these grounds Government ought to be implored to withdraw its sanction to the commencement of the survey and settlement proceedings in Behar.

. Gentlemen, I have heard, some of you say that the Government of Bengal having, without letting the persons interested know obtained the sanction of the Government of India and of the Secretary of State is determined to proceed with the survey and will not give any heed to our representation. I must tell you that you are entirely mistaken. We have in Sir Charles Elliott a very just Lieutenant-Governor. If a good case is made out he is sure to listen to us and postpone the measure at least for some years if he be not inclined altogether to withdraw it. Then we have Lord Lansdowne as our Viceroy, a states-man of great experience and soundness of judgment and of wide sympathies with the people of India over whom he rules. Such being the case we need not despair of obtaining just consideration at his hands if he is convinced of the strength and justice of our case.

. Gentlemen, justice is the key-stone of the British Government and you may depend upon it that justice will be done to you if you have a righteous cause. None of us need be under any apprehen sion of incurring the displeasure of the officials, for none wish more than they to know the opinions and feelings of people interested in any measure which the Government is going to introduce. It will be an insult to their sense of justice to think otherwise.

, I have detained you too long and must now sit down to make room for other eloquent and learned speakers who are to follow me. I beg therefore to support the first resolution which has been so ably moved by Maharaja Sir Narendra Krishna Bahadur and seconded by Moulvi Mohammed Yasoof Khan Bahadur and which runs as follows : "That in the opinion of this Meeting the Cadastral Survey of Behar recently ordered by the Government of Bengal will prove disastrous in its effects to both landlords and tenants in the Province, and is calculated to seriously disturb the peaceful relations which exist between them at present". The resolution was put to the meeting and carried unanimously.

Maharajah Durga Churn Law, C. I. E, in moving the second resolutiou, which ran thus:—"That a Representation be submitted to Governmant respectfully showing the evil consequences which are likely to result from the proposed Survey operation as well as from the preparation of a Record of Rights, and humbly praying that the recent orders in connection therewith be withdrawu, especially in view of the general scarcity with which the Province is threatened,"—said :—

The speech you have just heard is so full and to the point that there remains but little for me to add, without having to repeat most of what has already been so well said. It is difficult to understand why the Government is so very pressing in the matter of a Cadastral survey when the principal parties concerned in the affair, namely landlords and ryots are both strongly opposed to the measure. It is said that their interests will be promoted by it. But in what manner such a result would be achieved they fail to perceive. The landed proprietors cannot be so blind as not to be able to recognise their own advantages. Their experience leads them more to look to the other side of the picture and they feel keenly the difficulties which surround the question. The trouble and annoyance as well as the endless litigation which is sure to ensue will outweigh any trifling advantage which might be expected from the measure. The result to my mind will be a serious disturbance of the harmony among the landed classes which exists at present. It is no wonder therefore that there should be a wide-spread alarm among them. When the chief parties concerned, as I have already mentioned, do not want a measure of this kind, there is no reason why it should be forced upon them. If, however, Government passes the matter for purposes of its owu, then it is quite clear that Government should pay all the expense attending the operations, and no attempt should be made to saddle landlords and tenants with it. There is another circumstance which perhaps is not generally known to you ; it appears that Behar is not the only part of the Province which will be affected by the orders issued by Government. From the information which has reached me I find that survey operations have already commenced in a certain permanently settled estate in Orissa and it is quite possible that such operations are going on in other per-

manently settled estates as well   Thus the mischief that is appre
hended in Behar, and to avert which we have met here to-day, has
already taken effect in Orissa.   The survey operations, it will thus
be seen have been undertaken in Orissa, in spite of the present
miserable condition of the ryots on account of the late cyclone which
passed over the land—and this has been done notwithstanding, from
every enquiry that has been made, no trace could be found of any
Government order authorising such operations in that part of the,
Province.   I hope that the proceedings of this meeting will merit the,
attention of his Honor the Lieutenant-Governor so as to induce him to
reconsider the position taken by Government. With this view a
respectful representation should be submitted to his Honor, and let,
us earnestly trust that this may have the effect of persuading the,
Government to withdraw its orders.   Having nothing further to say
I have much pleasure in moving the Resolution which has been
placed in my hand.

Raja Peary Mohun Mookerjee seconded the resolution, and in,
doing so said :—I beg to second the proposition. From the history
of the measure which his Honor the Lieutenant-Governor has given
to the public, there cannot be the slightest doubt that the measure
has been resolved upon after much anxious consideration and after,
Government have satisfied themselves by the ;experimental survey
of a portion of Mozuffurpur that the proposed survey and record of,
rights would benefit both landholders and ryots.   In the face of this
determination deliberately come to and of the sanction which the
measure has received from the Government of India and the Secre-,
tary of State, we shall have to fight a lost battle if we go up to Government with a representation praying that the orders for the survey of
the four districts of Behar be cancelled.   I am nevertheless strong in
the opinion that such a representation should be made.   All that has
been ordered to be immediately done is a tranverse or skeleton, survey of the districts at the public expense.   The cadastral survey and,
record of rights won't be taken in hand till November next. We
have therefore nearly a year before us to show that the orders of
Government are based simply on official data : that the parties most
concerned in the matter have neither been consulted nor allowed an
opportunity to submit their views on the subject, and that whereas
the public are allowed to have their say before any measure of taxation is introduced, here is a measure involving heavy taxation which

has come as a thunderbolt, all of a sudden, upon landholders and ryots. The noblemen and gentlemen who have spoken before me have dwelt on the ruinous expenditure and the crop of lawsuits which the proposed cadastral survey involves. But what appears to me the most telling argument against the measure is that after all that expenditure and trouble has been undergone, the result will be far from adequate to the sacrifice which we are required to make. A complete record of the respective rights and delegations of landholders and ryots in respect of all the tenures and holdings in a district is no doubt a very desirable thing, but those acquainted with our rural economy should at once see that such a record would be practically valueless in this country unless it is annually corrected. The changes which are constantly occurring in the ownership and occupancy of land by transfers, relinquishments, inheritance, and by decrees of Courts are enormous. You will have some idea of the extent of these changes if you examine the figures regarding any one of these causes. You will find that in a single year, 1889-90 the number of sales and exchanges registered in these Provinces amounted to 206,703, and the number of permanent leases granted amounted to 76,390. You will see therefore that taking into account all the causes which contribute to changes of ownership and occupation of land, and to the creation of new rights, the record of rights, to be at all useful, would require correction every year in several hundreds of thousands of different particulars. I think all these facts and arguments should be respectfully submitted to Government and that his Honor the Lieutenant-Governor should be prayed to reconsider the whole question.

The resolution, which was supported by Rai Taj Naryan Singh Bahadur of Bhagulpore, was carried unanimously.

The third resolution was to this effect :—"That the Committee of the British Indian Association be requested to draw up the representation for submission to Government and to do all other acts which may be necessary in connection therewith" It was proposed by Babu Saligram Singh, seconded by Babu Ugra Mohun Tagore, and supported by Syed Delawar Reza, and was carried unanimously.

Before the proceedings of the meeting were brought to a close, Maharaj Kumar Benoy Krishna proposed a vote of thanks to the' chair and said :—

I rise to do a very pleasant duty, and that is to propose a vote of' thanks to the chair, but one thing that strikes me most forcibly is the manner in which our distinguished chairman has conducted the pro-ceedings of the meeting to-day, He has placed completely at the hands of the Bengal Zemindars the case of the Behar landholders in the full hope that the leaders of the British Indian Association will do all they can to lay the case before the Government. This is very gratifying and I am sure the Committee of our Association will justi-fy the confidence reposed in them. With these few observations I beg to move a vote of thanks to the chair.

The proposal was seconded by Babu Damodardas Barmah.

The proceding then came to a close.

RESOLUTION

BY THE

GOVERNMENT OF BENGAL, REVENUE DEPARTMENT.

Dated 9th November 1891.

The Government of India having sanctioned the resumption of survey and settlement operations in Behar, the Lieutenant-Governor considers that it will be to the advantage of all parties concerned that he should take an early opportunity of stating publicly the objects and intentions of Government in carrying out this under-taking.

2.   Soon after the Bengal Tenancy Act, VIII of 1885, came into force, Mr. E. W. Collin, C. S., was appointed to carry out the survey and settlement of a portion of the Mozufferpore district. These operations were initiated with the object of gaining some experience of the difficulties to be met with, and of the best and most economi-cal methods of dealing with them, as well as of gauging their pro-bable cost. They were avowedly intended to be of an experimental character, in the hope that if successfully accomplished, they might be generally extended. The experiment lasted about a year, during which about 400 square miles were cadastrally surveyed and a record of rights was prepared for about 150 square miles.

3.   The Lieutenant-Governor, Sir S. C. Bayley, in submitting the final report of this work to the Government of India, expressed himself satisfied with the rcsults of the experimental survey, and stated his opinion that there was good reason for desiring to extend the process to other tracts in the position of that dealt with in

Mozufferpore. He also intimated his view that, should the experiment which had been tried at the expense of the State be extended, the cost must be paid by the zemindars and ryots concerned, and that a charge of 8 annas an acre would be by no means excessive for the benefits conferred. The Government of India in reviewing this report concurred in Sir S. C. Bayley's view that it was desirable to extend the measure to other tracts. They regarded Mr. Collin's report as throwing much light on existing agricultural condition in Behar, and as a valuable addition to the evidence already collected of the depressed state of the cultivating classes in that part of the country. They particularly noticed the fact that the Tenancy Act had defined and enlarged the rights of the tenants, and that in tracts like Behar an authoritative survey and record appeared to be indispensable to give reality to the provisions of the act. In the review of this correspondence the Secretary of State wrote as follows ·—

The Settlement Officer, who appears to have conducted his operations with skill and judgment, is careful to say that, for statistical purposes, generalisations cannot be safely based on the facts ascertained over a limited area of 56,588 acres. Still, so far as the proceedings went, they show—

(1) That the work of survey and of recording rights in Behar was smoother than had been expected ; that it was satisfactory to the ryots and not disliked by the zemindars.

(2) That the whole operation can probably be carried out at a cost of not more than Rs. 320 per square mile.

(3) That the work had not given rise to litigation or class enmities, while it has safeguarded the position of the ryots and increased the value of their rights.

His lordship went on to say that he noted the opinion expressed by the Government of India that, even if the continuous maintenance of the village record cannot be fully secured, still an accurate knowledge of existing facts would be of great advantage as affording a basis on which a better state of things might grow up under the Tenancy Act, and that a survey and record of rights ought to be attempted in other parmanently settled tracts, where doubts prevail as to existing tenures and rents. He laid weight on the conclusion that the cost of the survey and of the subsequent maintenance of the village record must be kept within the narrowest possible limits, as the expenses will have to be defrayed by the classes and localities concerned, and said he would await with interest further information and proposals on these most important matters.

4. In march 1889, Mr. Boxwell, Commissioner of Patna, submitted a report on the question of extending the survey and settlement operations in his division. His conclusions were stated in the following words :—

(a) The evidence produced from many different places prove that all over the division there is a general uncertainty differing in intensity.

(b) Both the complaints of landlords and the attitude of the ryots prove that the ryots are beginning to appreciate their widespread right of occupancy.

(c) Transactions between zemindars, indigo-planters, and ryots prove that there is uncertainty with respect to tenure.

(d) And that individual ryots are not strong enough to deal commercially with either of the other two parties.

(e) The effect of the Tenancy Act in diminishing uncertainty about both rent and tenure is already felt.

(f) The effect of the Mozufferpore survey and record is universally acknowledged.

When this report and other papers connected with the subject came before Sir Steuart Bayley, in September 1889, he reviewed the question as a whole, and, with full knowledge of the condition of Behar, recorded his deliberate opinion that the considerations in favour of the proposed resumption of the Mozufferpore experimental survey-settlement proceedings decidedly preponderated. He asked the Government of India to accord sanction under the Tenancy Act to a survey and settlement of rights of the Patna Division with power to exempt particular tracts for special cause shown : and he explained the delay in making this application by a reference to proceedings which had been undertaken to gain further experience in lands under the control of Government, and to the survey of estates the proprietors of which had voluntarily offered to pay the necessary expenses

5. Sir Steuart Bayley considered that the effects of a survey-settlement would be to define the holdings and rents of each ryot, to place in the landlord's hands means which very few now have of proving without difficulty what they are entitled to claim, and to

give the ryots the power of resisting illegal and improper claims. He foresaw that such a measure would be unfavourably received by the zemindar's employers, as it would put an end to the large profits made by those who collect rent for the proprietors, a numerous and powerful class divided into various grades, from the farmers of many villages to the patwari or gomashta. After giving all such considera. tions their full weight, the late Lieutenant Governor, as has been said, recommended the adoption of the measure in question. At the same time, having regard to the partial failure in the Patna Division of the autumn and winter harvests of 1888-89, and to the serious injuries caused by the floods of 1889 to the autumn crops in Chumparun, Mozufferpore and Durbhunga, he proposed to postpone the commen. cement of the work until the effects of these calamities of season had disappeared.

6. The Government of India in reply stated that survey parties would be provisionally reserved for employment in Bengal upon the supposition that the Behar Survey would be commenced in 1891-92 ; though, it was added, no final decision could be given authorizing the survey until the question of cost and the share which it was proposed to accept on the part of Government was more precisely determined. In reviewing this correspondence, the Secretary of State for India wrote on the 20th February 1890 :—"I am glad to learn that it is proposed to carry on this important work as soon as the people re-cover from the loss caused by the scarcity of 1889. It is satisfactory that the Government of Bengal expect the cost of the work to fall below the sum, eight annas per acre, first estimated. I have no doubt that your Government will arrange for the diligent prosecution of the undertaking as soon as the circumstances of the country permit."

7. The outline of the correspondence as above presented is suffi-cient to show the progress made with the project up to the time when the late Lieutenant-Governor had to abandon it temporarily on account of the scarcity of 1888-89. The question reserved by the Govern-ment of India for more precise determination has been·fully examined and settled in the usual course ; and as a direct result of the Secre-tary of State's orders last quoted, the whole subject has again recently been laid before the Government of India and proposals have been submitted for carrying out the survey and settlement of the four dis-tricts of the Patna Division which lie north of the river Ganges.

8. The Government of Bengal did not fail to represent, as clearly

as possible, the difficulty of the work in prospect, and the fact that the scheme will not in the commencement commend itself favourably to the landed interests concerned. But Sir Charles Elliot expressed his compléte concurrence with the views expressed by his predecessor that the advantages which will accrue to the people from the survey and settlement proceedings outweigh thc inconveniences and difficulties that may arise, and that they justify the undertaking. His Honor entirely agrees with all that has been said during the course of the discussion as to the advantage, and, indeed the absolute necessity, of such a survey settlement and if administration is to be conducted with complete and accurate knowledge of economic facts, if famine is to be successfully combated when it comes, and if the relations of landlords and tenants are to be put on a secure and definite basis by the authoritative registration of areas held and rents fixed. He regards such a measure as a necessary corollary to the Permanent Settlement, and as the only way in which Government can give full effect to the principles laid down by the Bengal Tenancy Act as to the rights of the different classes of ryots, by creating the accurate record of those rights, and establishing a system for registering them in future.

9. In reply to this communication, his Excellency the Governor-General in Council has been pleased to issue orders sanctioning the proposed operations. In view of the partial failure of the late rains and the prospecis of some degree of scarcity, it is not proposed to bcgin the survey this year, but arrangements are being matured for making a commencement of the work this season by demarcating the village boundaries and starting the skeleton or traverse survey (the cost of which will be borne by Government), while the field-to-field survey will be put in hand in Nevember 1092. The reasons why it is in contemplation to confine the survey and settlement to the districts of North Behar are that the evils arising from the uncertainties of tenures and want of a record of rights have been felt there more than elsewhere, on account of the poverty and density of the population.

10. Sir Charles Elliot has not failed to notice indications of uneasiness felt by the classes interested, especially the zemindars, and there can be little doubt that much of this uneasiness is due to misconception on the part of those classes of the objects of the survey-settlement proceedings, and of the spirit in which they will be,

carried out. He has therefore deemed it disirable, besides recapitu‑ lating briefly the official history of the measure in hand, to give some explanation of its scope and character.

11. The objects of the cadastral survey and settlement of Behar are to obtain an accurate record (1) of the area and situation of all villages and estates, of each tenure and of each ryot's holding within an estate, and (2) of the status of everyone who has rights in the land and of the rent paid by each ryot and tenure-holder. In other words, the intention is to carry out accurately what every zemindar is understood to attempt to carry out more or less accurately, but often fails in doing. On every estate, zemindari accounts are kept up, which correspond in all but accuracy to the khasra and khatian of the settlement, and it is incredible that the zemindars should really wish not to have the opportunity of making these accounts correct. The Lieutenant-Governor has recently ascertained by personal enquiry the value which gentlemen of such experience as Messrs. Burrows, Thomson and Mylne of Beheea in Shahabad attach to the information collected in the cadastral survey which was effected for the canal-irrigated villages in that district. His Highness the Maha‑ raja of Tipperah is so convinced of the utility of a cadastral survey that he has recently made application to the Government to have such a survey carried out in all his estates which lie in British territory. It is within the knowledge of the Court of Wards and of Government that, in the zemindaries which have come under the temporary management of the Court, there is generally an ignorance on the part of the late proprietors' officials of the rights and interests appertaining to the estate which is altogether incompatible with successful administration.. In one important estate still under the Court whole mehals had been lost sight of and had paid nothing to the proprietors for many years, in other estates, where survey settle‑ ments had to be undertaken, it came to light that managers were ignorant whether the estates were compact or scattered, or where the lands were situated. It is a fact also, of which zemindars must be fully cognizant, that purchasers of estates are often unable to find out what are the boundaries of the property they have bought, or to obtain any records showing who the ryots are, where their lands lie, or what their rents are. These are instances of the inconvenience and defects which would all be removed by a field-to-field survey and an accurate record of rights.

12. On the other hand, the gain to the ryot of having his rights recorded and his status and rent determined is incontestable. The law has bestowed on him certain rights, and the Government has decided that it is the duty of the administration to provide him with the means of knowing precisely wherein they consist. This knowledge will benefit him in his dealings with his zemindar in any dispute as to the rent due to him, with indigo-planters when he wishes to lease his fields to them, and with the Opium Department officers when he applies for an advance for growing opium on his land.

13. Putting aside the fear of the unknown, which will be dissipated as the work of survey goes on, and the fear of increased litigation, which the experience of Mr. Collin's experimented survey shows not to be probable, it appears to the Lieutenant-Governor that the main reason for which the contemplated cadastral survey of Behar will not be welcomed, in the first instance, by the landowners of the division, is their fear of the cost of the proceedings. The Lieutenant-Governor can not hope altogether to dispel this fear, but he believes that explanations will do a good deal to diminish it. After carefully examining all that has been written on this subject, the Bengal Government has come to the conclusion that, as an estimate based on the actual cost hitherto incurred elsewhere, the entire charge cannot be safely taken at less than eight annas an acre, though it is hoped that there will be some reduction in the expenditure when the operations are undertaken on a wider scale than they have hitherto been carried out anywhere. Of this estimated cost of of 8 annas an acre, the Govenment of India has accepted the charge of one-eighth of the total expenditure as representing the cost of traverse surveys. Of the rest the Lieutenant-Governor has decided that half, or three and-a-half annas an acre, should be paid by the zemindars, and the other half divided among the subordinate interests. Thus a ryot holding an area of 3 or 4 acres may have to pay 10½ or 14 annas, an amount which certainly cannot be considered excessive, since it ensures him security in the possession of those rights which the Tenancy Act has declared to belong to him. The lowest charge for a copy of an extract from the Jamabandi excceeds one rupee, and his Honor understands that cultivators often pay even larger sums for documents or considerations of much less real value than the extracts from the khasras and khatians will be to them. The zemindars who own large properties will necessarily have larger total sums, but not

proportionately larger charges, to pay : but in return, though no general increase in the rents of ryots can be contemplated, they will reap some return from the discovery of concealed holdings and of tenures in which a large increase of area has taken place without any corresponding rise in rent, which will go some way towards compensating them for the outlay entailed upon them. Moreover, the survey itself will, it has been calculated, take about five years for two parties at the rate of 2,500 square miles a year, so that the total sum payable by the general body of zemindars each year will be distributed over a considerable period. In some cases, no doubt, the aggregate amounts which will fall upon single zemindars in any one year will be large ; and to meet this difficulty, the Government intends to facilitate payments by allowing them to be liquidated by instalments. Sir Charles Elliot has no doubt whatever that in the end the zemindars will find the results well worth the money they will have, under the law, to pay for the survey and settlement operations. He feels sure that the zemindars of the large estates in which such proceedings have recently been completed would agree in the view that they have received, by an accurate and a well-ordered rent-roll which has been generally accompanied by a slight increase in rents, good value for their expenditure. It is the Lieutenant-Governor's intention to have published shortly an account of what the surveys and records of rights in those large estates have costed and the returns they have produced to the landlords, so that the zemindars of North Behar will be in a position to judge for themselves of the advantageous results which they may anticipate.

14. His Honor need hardly notice the suspicion, if any such exists, that the survey and settlement operations are intended to restrict just rights. There is no intention whatever on the part of Government to restrict the just rights of a single individual or of a class : nor would Government have the power to do so if it so desired.

15. The Lieutenant-Governor's object, in making the statements contained in this Resolution, has been to dispel the prevailing ignorance of the real objects of a survey-settlement and the intentions of Government and to make known the truth ; and he trusts that the effect of what he has ordered to be published will be to show that some of the suspicions which may have obtained credence are unfounded and some are exaggerated ; and that in the minds of those who

are best able to judge, the convinction will be established that the settlement-survey of Behar is likely to produce great benefits to all classes who are interested in the land.

Ordered—That a copy of this resolution be published in the *Calcutta Gazette* for general information.

By order of the Lieutenant-Governor of Bengal.

C. E. BUCKLAND
Off. Secretary to the Goverment of Bengal.

RESOLUTION

BY THE

GOVERNMENT OF BENGAL, REVENUE DEPARTMENT.

No. 3745 L.R., dated 10th December 1891.

In paragraph 13 of the Government Resolution No. 1243 L.R., dated the 9th November 1891, published at pages 1895-99 of the Supplement to the *Calcutta Gazette* of the 18th idem, on the subject of the resumption of survey and settlement operations in North Behar, it was declared that an account would shortly be published of what the surveys and records-of-rights in some large estates had cost, and the returns which they had produced to the landlords. Four such estates have recently been surveyed and settled, viz., the Churaman, Maldwar, Shankarpur and Srinagar-Banaili Wards' Estates, and the following paragraphs contain the main results of the operations.

2. *Churaman Estate*—The mehals comprised in this estate are situated entirely within the Dinajpur district. They do not form a compact tract of country, but contain villages which lie scattered about the district and are interlaced with other estates. The survey and settlement operations were undertaken while the estate was under the Court of Wards. The total area of the estate, as ascertained by the survey, is 169,936 acres, of which 114,802 acres were surveyed by non-professional agency under the procedure, and the remaining 55,134 acres, which were held by the late ward jointly with other co-sharer landlords, were surveyed and settled under the provisions of .Chapter X of the Bengal Tenancy Act. The financial result of the operations was that a considerable area was recovered from the wrongful possession of other zemindars, and an additional

rental of Rs. 4,621, or about 3·8 per cent. of the entire rental, was obtained chiefly from the rental of lands recovered from other proprietors. The cost of the operations amounted to Rs. 89,154 or 8 annas and 4 pies per acre, the rather high rate per acre being due to the scattered nature of the estate. As to apportionment of cost, a report is awaited from the local officers in respect to the area surveyed under the old rules.

The benefits of the operations to the zemindar and to the ryots are thus summarised by the Settlement Officer :—

" I have mentioned what increase in the rental has been effected by the settlement. But an increased rental is not the only gain to the landlord. That is, indeed, a trifling gain compared with others. There was no such thing as a complete rent-roll for any of the mehals previous to the survey ; and in the landlord's books and papers the areas of tenants' holdings were conspicuous by their absence. The landlords had no idea of the quantity of waste land, and how much of that again was culturable and how much unculturable. All these details have now been definitely ascertained and recorded ; the amount of the rentals can no longer be a matter of speculation, and peculation of portions of the realizations by the patwaris will no longer be easy. It is impossible now for the zemindars' amin to quarrel with the ryots over the local *rassi*, and put down the areas of the holdings in accordance with his caprices ; for the local standard bigha in each village has been definitely ascertained and authoritatively recorded. The record of rights will give the landlords every facility for effecting a legal enhancement of rent in the future, in accordance with rise in prices, and the boundaries, as demarcated and plotted in the maps, will, it is hoped, be effectual in preventing future litigation with neighbouring landlords. The amounts respectively payable by the landlords and tenants towards meeting the cost of the survey and settlement have not yet been declared by the Government under section 114 of the Tenancy Act, but a settlement has been submitted showing the amounts for which the landlords and tenants are severally liable. In that statement the sum of 5 annas 3 pie to the acre is shown to be the share of cost chargeable to the landlords, and this sum I consider to be a very cheap price for the advantages gained by them."

" As regards the tenants who will have to bear a share of the costs of survey and settlement, it is hardly necessary to point out in detail the manifold advantages the survey has effected on their behalf. The settlement may be said to have opened their eyes. They have, I believe, for the first time undertsood what their legal rights and status are, and now these have been safe-guarded by the settlement. All of them, except the lower strata of the two unintelligent classes, the Palis and the Dessis, have eagerly sought their khatians, and asked whether these would be binding on the landlords. Was it true that the settled and occupancy ryots could not be' rejected by the landlords at their will ? Could they, under any circumstances, legally refuse to pay enhanced rental ? Would the question of their local *rassi* crop up when the landlord shall send an amin to measure their holdings, or was it settled for good ? Should they pay to the patwaris anything more than the amounts recorded in their khatians ? These and several other questions which they have asked show that they have taken a keen and intelligent interest in the settlement proceedings. A large number of tenants of each village attended the amin during the measurements, and they have all more or less understood the process of measuring their holdings and the calculation of their areas. The awakening of this intelligence, and the greater interest and attachment to their holdings which this must necessarily cause, not to mention the legal protection which the khatians afford them, are benefits for which the sum of four annas to the acre—the amount of cost shown in the apportionment statement as chargeable to the ryots—does not appear to be at all too high.

As regards the litigation created by the survey, it is reported that 105 petitions were registered in the Settlement Officer's Office 84 were disposed of summarily and 21 were tried as suits under section 107 of the Act ; of these six were uncontested. No appeals were presented against the Settlement Officer's decision.

3. *Maldwar Estate.*—The survey-settlement was undertaken by the Court of Wards. The mehals constituting this estate are situated in the two districts—Dinajpur and Purneah. They do not form a compact block, but contain several villages which lie scattered widely apart from each other. As ascertained by the survey, the estate contains an area of 93,082 acres, of which 58,267 acres are cultivated, 15.942 acres cultivable, and 18,873 acres waste. The total cost of the survey and record of rights was Rs, 60,751, of which Rs. 36,113 were incurred on survey and Rs 24,638 on settlement, the rates per acre being 5 annas 10 pies for survey and 4 annas 2 pies for settle-

ment. The high cost of the survey was due partly to the scattered positions of the villages, and partly to the irregular supply of cooli labour, the obstruction of ryots, the passive opposition of neighbouring zemindars, the inexperience of newly-trained amins, and the insufficient support accorded to the latter by the officials of the estate. The total cost has been apportioned as follows:—

		Rs.
Landlords	..,	38,149
Tenure-holders		492
Ryots		22,110
Total	...	60,751

There are in the estate 13,163 rent-paying holdings, occupied by 9,421 ryots. Fair rents were settled in 6,217 cases by the mutual consent of the landlord and tenant, the result being an enhancement of Rs. 4,508, which was obtained by assessing excess land found in the possession of the ryots, after deducting 20 per cent. from the area resulting from the present survey, on the ground of close measurements. The assessment of this excess land was made at the average rate for land of the same class in the village. As regards the remaining 6,946 holdings, the existing rents were recorded. Thus for the entire estate the total new rental is Rs. 95,714, so that the enhancement is 4·71 per cent. on the previous rental (Rs. 91,206), 7·6 per cent. on the total cost of the work, and 11·8 per cent. on the proprietors' outlay.

" The following account of the attitude of the tenantry is given by the Settlement Officer :—

The settlement operations were conducted without any friction or difficulty. During the early part of the operations the tenantry showed indifference by their absence from the scene of operations. The attitude shortly, however, changed from indifference and obstruction to one of eagerness and hearty co-operation. It has been stated that the impression had got abroad among the tenantry that the Settlement office was a branch of the manager's office, and that the rents were to be enchanced unusually high, and that they would gain no advantage in any way from the effects of the settlement. But when the erroneous nature of the impression was fully explained to them, they took great interest in the work. One application only was made by the tenants of lot Senua to the Commissioner of the Division in his executive capacity, stating that the manager was doing " zulum " in order to make them agree to pay enhancements. The application was sent to me for disposal. Their rents have not been enhanced in this settlement, although the manager pressed for enhancement, as I found that the ryots of this particular lot Senua had paid a high enhancement a few years ago during the time of the late proprietor, Baboo Budhi Nath Chaudhuri. "

There were altogether 1,243 suits and objections. Of these, 495 were disposed of summarily, and the rest were tried by the Settlement Officer in accordance with the procedure of a Civil Court. There were six appeals preferred before the Special Judge, of which three were dismissed, two allowed, and one was still pending when the Settlement Officer's report was submitted.

4. *Shankarpur Estate.*—The Shankarpur Estate consists of villages and parts of villages widely scattered over the districts of Dinajpur, Bogra, Rajshahye, and Maldah, the principal portion being in Dinajpur, and has been under the management of the Court of Wards since 1873.

The aggregate area of the estate, as ascertained by the survey, is 157,802 acres, and the total cost of the survey-settlement was Rs. 1,31,729, of which Rs. 89,611 were for survey and Rs. 42,118 for settlement, the rates per acre being 7 annas and 3 pies and 3 annas and 6 pies respectively. The high cost of the survey is attributed to the scattered nature of the property, the necessity for measuring lands of other estates interlaced with those belonging to the ward, and the sickness which prevailed among the establishment. The cost has been apportioned as follows :—

	Rs.	A.	P.
Ward	60,485	0	0
Co-sharer landlords and their patnidars	47,522	8	0
Ryots	23,721	8	0
Total	1,31,729	0	0

The total number of holdings in the estate is 32,607, the average size of a holding being 3 acres. The Board reported that rents were settled mainly by amicable arrangement between the management and the tenants, an allowance of 20 or 25 per cent. of the excess areas found in their possession being made to the tenants on account of the closer measurement of the professional survey, and the rest of the excess lands being assessed at the rates paid for similar lands in the village. The result has been an enhancement of the rental of the estate from Rs. 90,573-5-6 to Rs. 1,07,619-12-2, or nearly 19 per cent. on the previous rental, 13 per cent. on the total outlay, and 16 per cent. on the landlord's outlay, the increase on the ward's share being from Rs. 49,305 to Rs. 59,022. The average rate of rent on the cultivated area is stated to be Rs. 1-9-3 per acre.

The following extract from the Settlement Officer's report sums up the result of the operations :—

" No obstruction or friction was met with in carrying out the settle ment operations. The adoption of the English standard bigha for assessment in the estate Jehangirpore created dissatisfaction among the tenants, but it was removed by the granting of a larger allowance arranged amicably between the tenants and manager. The manager of the estate had taken an active part in conducting the demarcation, and rendered me assistance in the work of settlement generally.

Soon after the commencement of the present survey all the ryots appeared to have been frightened on seeing their lands measured by chain instead of *rassi*, which was used in the previous settlements, and to think of the probable enhancement that might result from the new mode of survey and settlement under the Tenancy Act, and under that impression several tenants filed *istafanama* of their holdings in the Munsif's Court of Balughat and were willing to run away. To remove such sensation among the illiterate tenants, I had to take much trouble to explain to them the provisions of the law whenever I visited the villages to test the amin's work. I gave them assurance that their due claims would by no means be overlooked. But at last when they came to understand, after the settlement of a few *tarafs* had been completed, that the intention of Government by the present settlement was to protect the tenants from the exercise of the illegal proceedings of their zemindars of depriving the ryots of their legal rights to hold the lands, and to prevent further litigation between the tenants respecting their holdings—at the same time to prepare correct records to enable the landlords to realize their just dues—they began to appreciate and take interest in the matter by attending the amins regularly to point out their lands and to clear up the errors that crept in the records during the khanapuri. They appear now to have been satisfied with the concessions allowed to them for different systems of measurement. The fact that the tenants have appreciated the benefit of the present survey and settlement is apparent from the earnestness with which they came forward with applications to have their lands measured that came under cultivation since the survey. The reduction of *istafanamas* and increase of transfer of holdings smce the completion of settlement of villages clearly shows how the tenants· liked the proceedings. * * * * * * The cost-rate of the Shankarpur settlement cannot be considered as an index to the probable cost for such operation in· a healthy district, in which the estates are compact and the survey records are properly prepared.

Of 2,265 petitions filed, 918 were summarily settled, and the remaining 1,347 objections were tried as civil suits by the Settlement Officer. Of the latter, 467 suits were amicably settled ; in 14 cases the plaintiffs were permitted to withdraw the suits, and 866 objections were regularly contested. Twenty-one appeals were preferred against the decision of the Settlement Officer, of which 6 were dismissed, 3 decreed, and 2 remanded for retrial ; and the remaining 10 were pending when the settlement report was submitted.

5. *Srinagar-Banaili Estates*—These estates are situated in the districts of Bhagalpur, Monghyr, Purneah, Maldah and Darbhanga, and are owned jointly by the Srinagar Ward and Raja Pudmanand Singh of Banaili. The villages in Bhagalpur and Monghyr lie in comparatively compact blocks, but the estates in the three other districts are much scattered. Proceedings were initiated, with the object of ascertaining and recording existing rents, on an application from the Court of Wards, in which Raja Pudmanand Singh, the co-sharer in the geater part of the property, joined. The total area surveyed was 447,189 acres, but the total area settled was only· 426,652 acres, the remainder having been excluded from settlement on account of lands belonging to other proprietors having been found interlaced with the surveyed area, and for other reasons. The cost of survey was Rs. 1,32,328, and that of settlement is estimated to be Rs. 1,62,000, the total cost of the operations thus being Rs. 2,94,328 or annas 10-6 on the total area surveyed. The causes which have rendered the settlement expensive and protracted are reported to be the scattered nature of the estates, disputes as to the standards of measurement and as to existing rents, the large number of·

objection petitions filed, the necessity of making a fresh copy of the records for the proprietors, and the remand during 1890 of 14 boundary disputes for retrial. As regards apportionment of the cost, it has been decided that the ryots should pay 2 annas an acre on the area of their holdings, the balance being paid by the landlords according to their several interests, but as the operations are not yet quite concluded, it is not possible to state the exact sum payable by the parties concerned.

The following extracts from the Settlement Officer's report show the results of the survey-settlement :—

Excluding the pergunnah of Akbarabad and a small area in the Kotwalli pergunnah, in the Maldah district, the records of which are not yet complete, the result of the record and settlement of rentals shows that the nominal rent-roll has increased from a demand of Rs. 4,68,328 to Rs. 4,69,498, or an increase of Rs. 1,170, equal to an increase of 23 per cent. There has been an increase of rental in Bhagalpur and Maldah, and decrease in Monghyr, Purneah, and Darbhanga. The decrease is a decrease in the rent-demand, and is due not to any arbitrary reduction of rent or rates of rent, but to the settlement of disputes as to existing rates. There has been a real increase of Rs. 22, 020, that is to say, the total rental, after striking out the disputed claims, has been increased by that sum in conseqnence of the settlement. The record and settlement of rents has performed two functions : firstly, the rent-roll has been cleared of disputes, and, secondly, an increase of Rs· 22, 020, equal to 4·7 per cent has been obtained. With regard to the first point it is to be remembered that the landlords' rent-roll was known to be in confusion, and the rent demand was never collected in full. The object of the settlement was to clear up these disputes and not to effect an enhancement of rents. I have noted some of the causes of the confusion which was greatest in the Nohatta tehsil of the Bhagalpur district. It arose chiefly from the system of letting out villages in lease, under which the lessees' endeavoured to enhance the rates or, at least, to gain an addition to the rental during the period of their leases.

*   *   *   *   *.   *.   *   *

. The value of the settlement is not to be tested by the increase of rent obtained. This increase is small, amounting to 4·7 of the ascertained rent demand. It gives a return of a little over 7 per cent on the outlay. The object of the settlement was, however, not to enhance rents, but to clear up the confusion in the rent-roll and to enable the rent to be punctually collected. The effect of the decision of disputes as to rents may be judged by the fact that in 1886-87 the rent collections of the Srinagar Estate were only 63 per cent. of the demand, whereas in 1889 90 112 per cent. of the demand, and in 1890-91 125 per cent. was collected. Apart from the adjustment of the rent demand, the records will enable the estates to prevent unauthorised encroachments and additions to holdings. The result will be especially valuable in the Purneah district, where in the absence of any records or measurement papers, the raiyats had taken possession of large areas without payment of rent and in many cases had converted lands into rent-free tenures supported by deeds of sale and other documents which the landlords were unable to disprove. In future, the proprietors will be in a position to prevent any further accretions to such rent-free tenures as now exist."

As regards the attitude of the parties concerned the Settlement Officer reports as follows :—

" The attitude of the landlords and tenants towards the survey and settlement was varied. At first there was considerable opposition from both sides. The local agents of the estates gave little help, and the raiyats were naturally afraid of the proceedings. Matters improved when the present manager was appointed but a great deal had of necessity to be left to the inferior agents who often appeared unreasonable in their claims and disposed to press demands which they were unable to prove. The fact that the landlords only gained decrees in 59 per cent. of the contested cases shows that the claims of the landlords were in many cases unreasonable. The raiyats as a rule showed no disposition to hold aloof from the proceedings. They readily came to the Settlement Officer's camp to have the entries explained, and appeared to take great pains to have their records correctly prepared. The large number of objections filed is a proof of the interest taken in the proceedings. The Collector of Bhagalpur who is responsible for the Court of Wards estate has throughout the operations rendered me much assistance. The only instance of organized opposition has occurred in the Akbarabad pergunnah of the Maldah district where the proceedings are still delayed in consequence of the refusal of the raiyats to have the entries in the records tested. The dispute arose over the standard of measurement, and when this was judicially decided after an appeal to the Special

Judge, the raiyats still held aloof and claimed that all should be recorded without proof as raiyats at fixed rents. It has been pointed out to them that if they can prove such rights, they will be registered, but few of them are able to do so and hence they have adopted an attitude of sullen opposition. Measures are being taken by the officer left in charge of the operations to complete the records of the area in dispute, which consists of 22 villages and about 12 square miles.

There was a considerable amount of litigation in this estate, due to long pending disputes and confusion in the landlord's records. The case-work of the Settlement Officer was as follows ;—

(1) Objection suits under section 106 of the Bengal Tenancy Act 2,852
(2) Suits under section 104(2) for settlement of fair rents ... 632
(3) Boundary disputes 368

Total ... 3,852

Of the suits under section 106, 1,743 were brought to trial and decided, and of the 632 suits for fair rents, 477 eventually came to trial. There were also about 20,000 petitions of objection against entries in the record, and these were all heard and the entries corrected, if necessary, on the spot.

The following is a statement of the appeals preferred against the decision of the Settlement Officers :—

CLASS.	Total number.	Decision upheld.	Modified.	Reversed.	Remanded.	Struck off.	Pending.
Appeals to the Commissioner in boundary disputes cases ...	67	39	2	7	14	4	1
Appeals to the Special Judge against decisions under section 104(2) and section 106 of the Bengal Tenancy Act	271	123	34	68	13	18	15

By order of the Lieutenant-Governor of Bengal,

C. E. BUCKLAND,

Secretary to the Government of Bengal.

To

HIS HONOR THE LIEUTENANT-GOVERNOR OF BENGAL.

> THE humble memorial of the Behar
> Landholders' Association and
> others at a Public Meeting
> assembled at Sonepur on the
> 15th November 1891.

MOST RESPECTFULLY SHEWETH,

1. THAT Your Memorialists have learnt with concern that Your Honor has been pleased to pass orders for a Cadastral Survey and Settlement of a part of Behar which will lead to the imposition upon the people of these Provinces heavy expenses and additional taxation.

2. That they are vitally interested in this matter and are persuaded that if the true nature of the proposed proceedings had been placed before Your Honor such orders could not have been passed.

3. That Your Memorialists beg to urge that the additional taxation which the measure will lead to, is a direct infringement of the rights as vested in the landlords under the Permanent Settlement. It is universally known that a solemn promise was given to the Zemindars by Lord Cornwallis that no demand would ever be made upon them and their heirs and successors by the present or any future Government for an augmentation of the Public Assessment in consequence of the improvement of their estates. That notwithstanding the fact that the Zemindars and tenants have been made to pay other taxes, they beg to urge that this is another infringement of their vested rights and a direct violation of British faith.

4. The covenant of the Permanent Settlement was distinct, solemn and unambiguous and any breach of it, in whatever shape, is regarded by your memorialists as a serious violation of their just rights.

5. Your Memorialists beg to urge that irrespective of the land tax they have to pay most of the local taxes raised in Bengal, the Road Cess, the Public Cess, Zemindari Dak Cess, the Embankment Cess, the Municipal taxes, the Chowkedaree tax, the Rural Police Cess, Irrigation Cess besides other indirect taxes, and any additional expense or taxation will be severely felt by them.

6. Your Memorialists beg to say that although under the rules, your Memorialists are required to pay 3½ annas per acre, but as a matter of fact, your Memorialists fear they shall have to pay much more than that, and the burden of paying the whole cost of the survey will be thrown upon them, leaving them to realize as best as they can, the share which the ryots will be required by the Government order, to pay towards the cost.

7. That Your Memorialists beg to urge, that from the experience they have of the difficulties and delays in realizing the road cess and public cess from ryots, they feel it a great hardship to have to pay the whole cost at first.

8. That Your Memorialists also beg to observe that in a very large number of cases, there are defaults made by Zemindars in the payments of road and public cesses and that in those instances there have been sales of their estates at very inadequate prices.

9. That Your Memorialists beg to urge that the proceeding if not necessary, for neither the Zemindars nor the ryots, as far as they are aware, have asked for it. The conditions mentioned in Section 101 of the Bengal Tenancy Act have not occurred to necessitate the introduction of such measure. Further, the materials now available with the Zemindars and ryots are amply sufficient for statistical and other purposes. The rent receipts which under Section 56 of the Rent Act are now issued to tenants contain almost all the informations which are required to be entered in a record of rights under the Tenancy Act. The Road Cess papers filed by the Zemindars in the Collector's Office are, as regards the jumma of lands, conclusive evidence against the Landlords, and under the law no higher rents could be claimed by any Zemindar unless there has been a decree for enhancement subsequently. The Luggits, Khusrahs, Siahas, Khutians, Jummabundis, Hustbuds and Wasil-bakies contain correct descriptions of the holdings o each ryot. The estates in Behar having come under the operation of the Butwarah Law, have been measured and adopted by the Revenue officers. These Butwarah Khusrahs described correctly the boundaries of the holding of each ryot, together with a specification of their rights.

10. That Your Memorialists beg further to urge that under Section 158 of the Tenancy Act, any aggrieved ryot can enforce the Survey and Settlement of his tenure, and the procedure to be

applied on his application is the same as will have to be applied to a general survey and settlement. The material difference in the procedure however is very great. In the one case only the ryot suffering a hardship applies for its removal and incurs the liability of paying costs if awarded against him, whereas in the other case, all are exposed to the annoyance and expense incident to extensive survey operations.

11. That the ameens who are generally employed to make measurements are not above temptation and are not scrupulous in their dealings with illiterate tenants and hence there is a great risk of the papers being untrustworthy records of the actual state of things.

12. That your Memorialists beg also to urge that under the present circumstances if there are any mistakes or incorrect statements in the Zemindary records they could be corrected on a representation properly made, but in the case of settlement records, if any incorrect items are entered and the records are confirmed by settlement officers without any knowledge of the mistakes the mischief thereby committed is kept up and there is no chance of its being ever set aside, or corrected by the Civil Courts (*Vide* I. L. R. Vol. XVII Cal. p. Gokul Saw *vs*. Govind Saw.)

13. That Your Memorialists also beg to observe that the measure will be attended with an increase of litigation, which will be very expensive to both Landlords and tenants, and in a good many cases will be ruinous to both. The results of the experimental survey in Mozufferpur and those of the surveys of the Srinaggar, Benalli and other estates show there was a very large number of applications and suits. The Zemindars and royts have over and above the sum they have to pay Government to engage special pleaders and mooktears for the whole period of time the estate were under survey and settlement besides incurring other expenses, legal and illegal, incidental to litigation. During the period surveys and settlements were made in those estates no proper collections could be made from tenants and it took in the Srinugger and Benelli estates full 3 or 4 years to complete the whole thing. Even now a part still remains to be completed on account of the opposition and obstruction of the royts.

14. That Your Memorialists beg to urge further that from practical experience of the details of the business, the cost of the contemplated operations will be two crores of Rupees in round number,

that the estimate of the cost at 8 annas per acre is a low estimate. In the Srinugger, Benelli and other estates the cost has been 10 annas 6 pie an acre, out of which the ryots will have to pay only 2 annas although the whole cost of about 3 lacs of rupees has been realized from the Zemindars ; besides there will be an annual expenditure of several thousands for the maintenance and preservation of the records, which would be otherwise useless. Considering the general indebtedness of the Zemindars and ryots in Behar, your Memorialists apprehend that they will not be able to pay the enormous cost of the survey and settlement operations besides the cost of litigation, and will be obliged to borrow money which will eventually lead to their interests being sold up.

15. That Your Memorialists beg in the third place to urge that the difficulties attending the measure are very great. Many of the high officers of Government having a great experience of the Province who were consulted by the Government regarding the Cadastral Survey have in very clear terms laid down that the measure should not be introduced in those Provinces and that it is beset with very great difficulties, and that it will create disputes where none existed.

16. That Your Memorialists also beg to urge that the settlement of permanently as well as temporarily settled estates in the North-West Provinces has been made at the cost of Government alone. Neither the Zemindars nor the tenants there have had to pay a pice towards the expenses. If Government requires informations for its own purposes, which statistical informations neither the Zemindars nor the tenants desire to have, it is but just and reasonable that Government should pay the whole cost of the survey and settlement operations.

17. That Your Memorialists apprehend that the measure, if introduced, will lead to bad feeling between Zemindars and tenants and will seriously disturb the peaceful relations which now exist between them.

18. Lastly, Your Memorialists beg Your Honor's consideration to the fact that the time selected for carrying out the measure is most inopportune. There is a great scarcity in Behar, in consequence of a partial failure of the crops. The rains having failed this year the prospects in the whole of Behar are very gloomy and your memorialists apprehend there may be another famine in Behar like the one of 1874, and that the opening of famine relief measures in some

Districts has become absolutely necessary. The years previous to this were also bad years, and neither the Zemindars nor the tenants will now be in a position to bear the enormous costs of the survey and settlement and the heavy litigation which will attend it.

19. Your Memorialists feel sure that the proposed Cadastral Survey and Settlement will be disastrous in its effects, and will certainly lead to the impoverishment, if not to the total extinction, of the landed classes in Behar.

20. That your Memorialists therefore respectfully beg to approach Your Honor with the prayer that Your Honor will be graciously pleased to withdraw the orders recently passed for a Cadastral Survey and Settlement of a part of Behar, or should Your Honor deem fit to postpone the carrying out of the measure for some years to come.

And Your Memorialists as in duty bound shall ever pray.

To

C. E. BUCKLAND, Esq,

Secretary to the Government of Bengal,

Revenue Department.

Sir,

I HAVE the honor to inform you that at a public meeting of the landholders of Bengal and Behar and of other persons interested in land, held on Saturday the 12th December 1891, at the British Indian Association Rooms, to consider the propriety of submitting a Representation to Government in regard to the proposed Cadastral Survey and Settlement of Behar recently ordered by the Government of Bengal, it was resolved that the Committee of the British Indian Association be requested to draw up a memorial to Government respectfully pointing out the evil consequences of the proposed Survey and Settlement, and humbly praying that the orders passed by His Honor regarding the proposed measure be withdrawn.

2. In compliance with this request, the Managing Committee of the British Indian Association venture to approach His Honor the Lieutenant-Governor with a memorial praying that on a consideration of the circumstances herein mentioned, His Honor will be graciously pleased to withdraw the orders for a Survey and Settlement of Behar, or at least to postpone the measure for some years.

3. The Committee beg to urge in the first place that it will lead to additional taxation, which will be a direct violation of the just rights of land-holders under the Permanent Settlement. They beg to refer your Honor to the solemn promise made by Lord Cornwallis "that no demand shall ever be made on the Zemindars, their heirs and representatives by this or by any future Government on any grounds."

4. The Committee beg to say that the reasons given for having a Cadastral Survey and Settlement in Behar are not such as would justify Government in introducing the measure, when the consequences will be very serious to the interests of all classes interested in land—The condition of the ryots of Behar is not such as will necessitate any other action after the passing of the Tenancy act. The experimental survey and record of rights which was made in Mozufferpur was not even of a whole District, but of only 413 square miles out of 3004 square miles of that District. The Committee beg also to urge that from what they have come to know, the

results of the survey of even that small portion was not successful. There has not been a general increase of rents in Behar since the passing of the Tenancy act as to lead to a presumption of illegal enhancements having been made. They beg to say that there have been no agrarian dispute there. The Committee beg to urge on your Honor that no grounds of a substantial and practical character exist for the introduction of the proposed measure.

5. The Committee beg to urge that the results of survey and settlement of a part of the Benaili and Srinagar and other small estates which were under the Court of Wards, were unsuccessful. The Benaili Zemindar who was heavily indebted at the time the Survey was started had to incur an additional expense of one lac and a half which was paid to Government besides Rs. 50,000 which he incurred as litigation expenses leaving other expenditure which was not legal, and similarly with the Srinagar Zemindars.

6. The Committee submit that although under the rules, the Zemindars will have to pay $3\frac{1}{2}$ annas per acre, but as a matter of fact they will have to pay much more than that and the Benaili and Srinagar Zemindars had to pay the whole amount to Government in the first instance with the prospect of realizing 2 annas per acre only from the ryots as best as they can.

7. The Committee beg to urge that the measure is wholly unnecessary and uncalled for. Neither the Zemindars nor the ryots ask for it, and the conditions mentioned in Sec. 101 of the Tenancy Act have not occurred to necessitate the introduction of such a measure. The materials now available in the Zemindari records being amply sufficient for State and other purposes.

8. Further, the measure is calculated to increase litigation which will last for years and which will be very expensive to both landlords and tenants.

9. The expense of the survey and settlement which will have to be paid by the landlords and tenants, the Committee have after a careful calculation found, will not be less than two crores of Rupees, besides other expenses which both landlords and tenants will have to bear.

10. Considering the general indebtedness of the zemindars and tenants of Behar, they can ill-afford to pay the costs which will be saddled on them for the survey and settlement; and what with the costs of litigation and the enormous costs of the survey and set-

tlement, the Committee fear that many of the Zemindars and tenants will be sold up.

11. That besides the costs mentioned above they apprehend there will be an annual expense of several lakhs of Rupees to maintain and preserve the records, which otherwise would be wholly useless, and that would be an additional burden on the people of Behar.

12. All the influential and leading Zemindars are almost unanimous in considering that the measure if introduced will be fraught with incalculable mischief.

13. The measure if adopted will seriously disturb the peaceful relations which now exist between the landholders and tenants of these Provinces.

14. The Committee beg His Honor seriously to consider that the present time is most inopportune for carrying out the measure contemplated. There is a famine in some parts of Behar and a great scarcity in others caused by partial failure of the crops. This will seriously tell upon the landlords and tenants, and it will take them some years before they will be able to get over the ruinous effects of several successive bad seasons. The Committee submit, that the proposed Cadastral Survey and Settlement will be disastrous in its effects, and will certainly lead to the impoverishment, if not total extinction of the landed classes in Behar.

15. The Committee respectfully pray that His Honor will be graciously pleased to withdraw his orders for the proposed Cadastral Survey and Settlement of Behar, or at least to postpone the measure for some time to come.

16. The Committee beg to refer your Honor to the report of the Behar Rent Commission. They did not think it wise and judicious to suggest a hazardous and ruinous undertaking like the Cadastral Survey Settlement of Behar, but they suggested that in order to secure a trustworthy record, that the zemindars should be bound to file in a public office their accounts, which might well be verified and tested by Revenue officers. These returns might be made to include boundaries of each holding and other essential particulars which the Government might think necessary to have for Statistical purposes.

CALCUTTA,

The   February 1892.

I have the honor to be

SIR,

Your most obedient Servant.

A PROTEST

TO THE

PROPOSED CADASTRAL SURVEY

IN

BEHAR.

PART II.

PROPOSED BEHAR ᵢ CADASTRAL SURVEY.

BEHAR HERALD, 31ST OCTOBER 1891.

THERE is a good deal of alarm amongst the zemindary body, as also the knowing section of tenure-holders and ryots of Behar at the prospect of an order for the general survey of the districts of these provinces. Meetings have already been held at the towns of Purneah, Gya, Arrah, Mozufferpore and Motihari in which large numbers of zamindars, tenure holders and ryots attended, and in all these meetings resolutions unanimously protesting against the proposed Cadastral Survey, as needlessly harassing to the landlords and tenants, and leading to endless litigations, have been carried, and in all these meetings, the Behar Landholders' Association have been asked to early memorialize Government against the proposed Survey. Such meetings have not been confined to the districts alone, but important village centres as Tikari in Gya and Kulharia in Shahabad have taken up the agitation, and we hear more meetings are coming on shortly in the districts of Sarun and Patna.

When the Bengal Tenancy Act was before the Legislative Council of India a ready way of deprecating the agitation then going on was to say that the agitation was being kept on by the Behar Lanholders Association wherein the smaller zemindars and tenure holders were not, it used to be said, properly represented. In the present instance therefore the Association, though aware from vague sorts of reports what was coming on, thought fit to hold its hands until the alarm had permeated the zemindary body as a whole and to go up to Government only when it would be its imperative duty to bring to the notice of Government that the proposal of a Cadastral Survey in Behar is much exercising and agitating the public mind in Behar,

It is much to be regretted that the Government of Bengal even for once did not think it proper to consult those whose interests were thus to be directly touched, through their properly accredited channels, in a matter of such vital importance, before asking for the sanction of the Government of India to the proposed Cadastral Survey. It rested its decision possibly on the facts brought before it by Mr. Finucane, and his officials belonging to a Department of work the maintenance of which had to be justified by a show of work. If the people were consulted they might have told the Government of Bengal and through it, the Government of India (1st) that there was no necessity whatever of putting in force clause 1 of section 101 of the Bengal Tenancy Act, specially when Government was not in a solvent condition to meet the enormous charges of a general survey and record of rights; that (2ndly) it was entirely optional either with the landlord or a large class of ryots to apply for such survey and record of rights to the Local Government under clause 2 of that section; and wherever necessity would exist, and there cannot be the least doubt that landlords and te_ nants collectively and severally were better judges of such necessity than Mr. Finucane and his Department, such applications would be made.

Well, it will be likely said, that the ryots of Behar—the dumb millions of the philanthropists—are not possibly aware of the exis‑tence of the provisions of the Bengal Tenancy Act, and the bureau of Agriculture and its Director represent them; but the Government of Bengal need not have provided on an *exparte* statement. The grounds on which it could apply for sanction to the Government of India, under section 101, though these grounds are not specifically given in the law, would be we presume these.

1st. A general rise of rents, leading to a presumption that illegal enhancements have been resorted to.

2nd. A general increase of agrarian disputes.

3rd. A successful experimental survey of a definite tract.

4th. Such solvency of its own exchequer, as would justify it to allot some of its surplus revenue to, at best, an experiment of problematical good.

We opine none of these grounds and conditions are existing at the present moment.

The Bengal Tenancy Act commenced in 1885, since then as the figures below will show the zemindary rental of this Province have stood at the same figure, with such variations as can only be due to difficulty of realization in one year, and increase of collections in the next.

	Total Road Cess in Behar in rupees.	Total Public Works Cess in Behar in rupees.
1885-86	14,87,233	14,72,912
1887-88	14,63,259	14,63,259
1888-89	14,33,353	14,33,353
1889-90	14,80,843	14,80,844

As for agrarian disputes, the number of cases under the Rent law as given in the Administration Reports will show that there is not much evidence of any. Excepting the suits for rents, disputes under other heads are merely nominal : and suits for rents and speedy disposals thereof are the only points which the Bengal Tenancy Act did not properly provide for.

As to the third point a somewhat distinct pledge was given at the time of the passing of the Bengal Tenancy Act, that the operation of Chapter X was to depend on the success of an experimental survey of a small tract of land.

During the debates on this Chapter, His Honor the Lieutenant-Governor. (Sir Rivers Thompson) said :—

"With the sanction of the Secretary of State, and of the Government of India, the utmost we should attempt in the first instance would be one single district and we shall be guided much by the success we meet within that district before providing further."

The Viceroy said :—"At the same time, His Excellency could assure the Hon'ble Member that, not only in deference to the suggestions made to them by the Secretary of State but also from their own appreciation of the exigencies of the case, the Government of India would be indisposed to consent to the application of the section referred to, otherwise than in the sense and spirit recommended by Lord Kimberley.

Now it will perhaps be said that such an experimental survey was held in a certain tract in the district of Mozufferpur and the result is before Government, though not before the public. We respectfully submit that the Government pronouncement of the success or otherwise of the measure, ought to have been delayed till the public have an opportunity of saying what it had to say as to such results, and that such pronouncement should have been delayed for some years to wait events that might come and have not yet come. From the imperfect glimpse of these proceedings which cannot be gathered from some meagre reports it is impossible to say that the result has proved to be a success, and even if it were, the circumstances of this vast province are so varied in its different parts, that an experiment in one district, can hardly be said to hold good for another; nothing was clearer than this, when during the Bengal Tenancy Act, certain tracts in Shahabad and Mozufferpur were measured and rates determined. However, considering the result of the experimental survey at Mozufferpur, from such imperfect glimpse as we get from meagre sources published we find that the only thing on which the Director exultingly pronounces his operation to be a success, is the low rate of expense, and the small number of suits that up to the period of his survey had come on.

The cost the Director finds to be 9 annas per acre. This however we presume to include lands from which rents are received and the lands fallow and waste. Therefore the avarage cost on arable lands from which rents are received would be much more than 9 annas per acre.

Again, this would represent only the legitimate cost to Government. But the actual cost to the parties, legitimate and illegitimate, would be considerably high. Calculating even at 9 annas per acre, the total outlay necessary for the survey of 44,192 square miles of Behar would come up to the amount of 1½ millions (not 84 lakhs of rupees) as the *Indian Mirror* says is the Government estimate, while the total rental of these Provinces is a little above 44 millions.

Thus the legitimate cost, even at the lowest figure of 9 annas per acre, would be a full third of the rental of this Province for one year— not a tenth part of one year's rental, which the Director of Agricultural Department in his Report calculated for his given tract.

As to litigation we are told that in surveying 413 square miles, there were 326 boundary disputes—and though some of the cases were amicably settled there have been appeals in other cases. Each of these boundary disputes means at least an expenditure of 500 rupees to the party-litigants. But boundary disputes form only one item of litigation. Not even an imperfect glimpse is afforded to us in this report, as to the disputes between landlords and tenants, as to the nature of the holdings and as to rates of rent they do pay. Then as between the ryots themselves, quarrels would often arise as to the title and possession of lands.

As to the 4th ground, we are not at all aware that the Government of Bengal is so solvent, that it would be justified in applying a crore of its revenues for a measure of at best, questionable utility.

There is a general complaint in India as to scarcity of rains. The Hattia rains in Behar were very scanty and actual distress is apprehended. We urgently appeal to His Honor the Leutenant-Governor, who is now in our midst, to consider and to pause.

BEHAR HERLD 14TH NOVEMBER 1891.

WE have seen that Section 101, clause 2 provides for all cases and power is given to the landlord, or a body of landlords, or tenants to apply for survey and record of rights when necessary. This refers to the survey and general record of rights of an estate, or of a whole area comprised in the estates of a landlord, or body of landlords, and to survey and record of rights of such an estate or area by *Revenue Officers*. But power is also vested to individual ryot under the Act to have a survey and record of his rights of his own holding by a proceeding in court under Section 158 of the Bengal Tenancy Act. That section provides: "(1) The Court, having jurisdiction to determine a suit for the possession of land may, on the application of either the landlord or the tenant of the land, determine all or any of the following matters, namely :—

(a) The situation, quantity and boundaries of the land ;

(b) The name and description of the tenant there-of if any ;

(c) The class to which he belongs, that is to say, whe her he is a tenure-holder, ryot holding at fixed rates, occupancy ryot, non-occupancy ryot, or under-ryot, and if he is a tenure-holder, whether he is a permanent tenure-holder or not, and whether his rent is liable to enhancement during the continuance of his tenure ; and

(d) The rent payable by him at the time of the application.

(2) If, in the opinion of the court, any of these matters cannot be satisfactorily determined without a local enquiry the court may direct that a local enquiry be held under Chapter XXV of the Code of Civil Procedure by such Revenue Officers as the Local Government may authorize in that behalf by rule made under Section 392 of the said Code.

(3) The order on any application under this section shall have the effect of, and be subject to the like appeal as, a decree."

Now it is difficult to see, why parties, landlords and ryots should not themselves be left to act on the provisions of this section which is full in all its details. It empowers either of them to apply to the Court having jurisdiction, to declare the nature of the holdings, and the rights of the parties thereon, with all details regarding the boundaries and rates of rent. The proceedings being by an *application*, and not by a suit, no court-fees would be needed, the trial is to be either by a Munsiff, or a Sub Judge more experienced and better trained officers than the Settlement Deputy Collectors of Mr. Finucane's Department. The case is to be decided on such legal evidence, as the parties and their legal advisers would choose to bring before the court, and there is further more a provision for local enquiry by a Revenue Officer.

Then the order has the effect of a decree, and is subject to appeal.

While there can be no doubt that the parties will get better justice by the procedure here laid down, if they were left to their own choice, there are reasons to suppose that it would be cheaper. To instance a few items : (1) the services of a legal adviser, the parties will get much cheaper at the sudder stations where our courts are situated, than in the distant muffusil, where the settlement officer will be recording the rights. (2) The temporary Amin, or whatever else you may call him, will be more rapacious than the regular amlahs of our permanently constituted courts. (3) As a flood-gate of litigation will be opened, every man, who will have to produce any copy of any document or record as a piece of evidence, shall, we are afraid, have to pay much more as expedition-money, than under ordinary circumstances, where each man bides his own time. (4) And in all these matters the ryots will suffer much more than the landlords, who are more accustomed to laws and law's ways.

BEHAR HERALD, 5TH DECEMBER 1891.

THE PROPOSED CADASTRAL SURVEY OF BEHAR—We beg to draw the attention of the landlords and tenants to a part of the Government Resolution on the Cadastral Survey, wherein it is proposed that for *reasons shown* estates are to be exempted from the general operation. They have a year before them to be ready with their applications showing such reasons. We believe the rent roll is now well-known in all estates. Several big Zemindaries of the Province have been under the management of Government, as Courts of Wards. It can not be said that the rent-roll is uncertain and unknown in these cases. In most of these cases not a pice has been since added by the owners to the rent-roll of these estates. In several cases again, the estates have been surveyed and tenures and rates recorded under Section 38 of the Law of Landlord and Tenant (Bengal Council Act VIII of 1868) by the Collector and Civil Courts. In these cases too, a fresh survey and record of rights would be perfectly unnecessary. Then, in the cases of many estates Jamabandis have been prepared at the time the Thackbust adopted these as showing the extent of the lands and rates and Jumas. There is no uncertainty in these cases, nor in cases where the Raibundi made at the partition of estates has been adopted by the ryots.

In all cases, Jamabundis have been filed under the order of the Board of Revenue for a series of years in the Collectorate. If the present Government would only enquire why the practice had to be discontinued and many of these Jamabundis destroyed a state of facts will be disclosed, which we are sure, will make it less zealous for the preparation of Jamabundis of estates and arranging for the record of changes.

However that may be, wherever both landlords and ryots agree to the rent-roll given in these Jamabundis, there can hardly be any further need for the record of rights. So in case were Jamabundis have been filed at the valuation and re-valuation of estates for Road Cess and Public Works Cess. In some cases, there have been litigations between landlords and tenants and areas and Jamas determined by the Civil Courts. There have been either decrees for all lands in the estates, or on the determination of some test cases both landlords and tenants *enmasse* have acquiesced in a rent-roll prepared on the basis of such test-decrees. In our opinion, it will be found that these exhaust all estates, and that there is no uncertainty about these rent-rolls; but should any bad case be found in which the Jamabandi is yet uncertain, applications for exemption ought to be based with a rent roll to which both landlords and tenants agree. In all cases applications for exemption ought to come both from landlords and tenants on the basis of a common Jamabundi. Now as counter-foil printed receipts have as a rule been given in all cases, and accepted by ryots there can be no hesitation on the part both of landlords and tenants to agree to a common Jamabundi, and to ward off a common evil they should do so even in cases, where some amount of ill-feeling and disagreement exist. The argument that if no uncertainty exists the record of rights will be plain-sailing for the settlement officials, and so there ought to be no objection to the Government Resolution and order based thereon is the worst kind of fallacious arguing in a circle. It amounts to this: There ought to be a general record of rights because there is *uncertainty*. There ought to be a general record of rights because there is no *uncertainty*, and so the thing to be done is easy and unattended with difficulties.

We say, that if the experimental survey was, as is unfortunately, however, not the case, unattended with difficulties, frictions, litigations, that would have shown that in the experimental tract no necessity whatever existed for the expensive experiment.

ENGLISHMAN, 19TH DECEMBER 1891.

A Sequel of Surveying.

HIS HONOR THE LIEUTENANT-GOVERNOR has lost no time in giving effect to the promise made in his recent Resolution regarding the servey and settlement operations in No th Behar, that "an account would shortly be published of what the surveys and records of rights in some large estates had cost and the returns which they had produced to the land-lord." The last *Calcutta Gazette* gives this information for the Churaman, Maldwar, Shenkerpur, and Srinagar-Banaili Estates, and, although we have every sympathy with Sir Charles Elliott's motives in pushing forward the Behar Settlement, we must say that the facts now laid before the public more than bear out everything that has been said against that undertaking. Of the four estates dealt with, only one, the Srinagar-Banaili, is situated in Behar, and the first fact that strikes one is the immense amount of litigation its settlement gave rise to. As many as 20,000 "petitions of objection" were laid, and 3,852 suits of sorts instituted . Of objection suits 1,743 actually came to trial, and these were suplemented by 447 "fair rent" suits, and 368 boundary disputes. This return represents in any case a very heavy outlay in legal costs, but when it appears that of the 447 decisions in four rent cases 271 were carried to an Appellate Court, its amount must have been large indeed. An unpleasant fact is that the decision of the Settlement Officer was reversed in 68 cases and modified in 34. That in all these cases trained and expensive pleaders were employed there can be little doubt. Besides these, 67 boundary cases were carried upon appeal before the Divisional Commissioner. It is very probable that the costs in stamps may have been small, but it is equally certain that hardly one of the 20,000 objections was made without its being submitted to a village lawyer of opinion, accompanied by an appropriate fee.

The total outlay on the survey and settlement operations in Srinagar-Banaili was Rs. 294,323, or 10½ annas an acre, which is appreciably more than the eight annas an acre, on which the Government estimate is based. It must, however, be remembered that the area on which the average is based contains much waste land in the Srinagar-Banaili report; it does not appear how much waste the survey covered, but in the Maldwar Estate, in which an average cost of 10 annas an acre is estimated, only 58,267 acres are cultivated out of 93,082 surveyed, so that the Rs. 60,750 expended on their settlement really represents a charge of 17 annas on each acre on cultivated land in the possession of ryots. All through the published papers there is an attempt to overcome the known opposition of the Behar landlords by a very broad suggestion that a ' survey will result in a considerable enhancement of rent. It is prominently stated that in the Churaman Estate the rental was increased during settlement by 3·8 per cent. in the Maldwar Estate by 4·7 per cent. in the Shanker-pur Estae by 19 per cent. and in the Srinagar-Banaili Estate by 4·7 per cent. These enhancements may have been entirely justifiable, and in the estates situated in Bengal Proper this was most probably the case, but a very large section of the Civil Service of the Lower Provinces hold the opinion that a further increase of rents in North Behar is to be urgently deprecated. Another promise seems to be held out to the landlords by the proposal to require the tenantry to pay half the cost of settlement or, at the Government calculation, four annas an acre. Such a division of the cyst may be entirely equi-table, but it is to be observed that in practice Government exacted only two annas an acre in Srinagar-Banaili. In the large estate of Shan-kerpur the ryots paid only Rs. 23,721 out of Rs. 1,31,729, the balance of Rs. 1,08,008 being debited to the proprietors. The settlement Officers report considerable recalcitrancy among the tenantry even under these favourable conditions. It seems more than probable that much increased exactions will not be welcomed by the far poorer pea-santry of North Behar. We are quite prepared to admit that there may be certaiu advantages attainable by the ryots from such a survey and settlement as the Government of Bengal proposes, but we fear that the attendant litigation and expenditure will more than counter-vail such benefits. A still stronger objection is that, as it is not in-tended to maintain any machinery for the continuous correction of the settlement, its records obtained with so much labour and cost will be nearly worthless a quarter of a century hence if not in ten years.

ART. IX.—THE PROPOSED CADASTRAL SURVEY OF BEHAR.

I

IN view of the interest which the question of the Cadastral Survey and Record of Rights has evoked in Bengal, and the agitation and alarm it is causing in Behar, it may not be amiss to bring together all that is known of the subject, and to examine the question in the light of what is known.

2. Section 101 of the Bengal Tenancy Act, on which, we suppose, action is intended to be taken, provides :

" *Clause* (1).—The Local Government may in any case, with the previous sanction of the Governor-General in Council, and may, if it thinks fit, without such sanction in any of the cases next hereinafter mentioned, make an order directing that a survey be made, and record of rights be prepared, in respect of the lands in a local area by a Revenue officer.

" *Clause* 2.—The cases in which an order may be made under this section, without the previous sanction of the Governor-General in Council, are the following (namely) :—

    ' (a)—Where the landlord, or *a large portion of the landlords* or *of the tenants*, applies for such an order, and deposits or gives security for such amount, for the payment of expenses, as the Local Government directs ;

    " (b)—Where the preparation of such a record is calculated to settle or avert a serious dispute existing, or likely to arise, between the tenants and their landlords generally.

    " (c)—Where the local area is comprised in an estate or tenure which belongs to, or is managed by, the Government or the Court of Wards ; and

    " (d)—Where a settlement of revenue is being made in respect of the local area."

3. There are two clauses of this section under which an order for a survey and record of rights can be made :—

    1st.—Where the previous sanction of the Governor-General in Council is needed.

2nd.—Where it is not needed.

Cases under the second clause are :—

(*a*)—When the Local Government is moved thereto by *a landlord* or *a large portion of the landlords* or *of the tenants,* and deposits of costs are made ;

(*b*)—Without being thus moved, where the Local Government is of opinion that the measure is calculated to avert a serious agrarian dispute ;

(*c*)—With respect to estates which belong to Government or are managed by the Court of Wards ; and

(*d*)—Where a settlement of revenue has to be made.

Clause (1) is new, that is, it did not exist in the previous laws of landlord and tenant in Bengal. Clause (2) brings together the provisions of section 27 of Act X of 1859 and section 38 of Act VIII of 1868 (B C.), and the law for the settlement of agrarian disputes, with this difference, that, in (*a*), it gives the power of moving the Local Government to a large body of landlords in a co-parcenary body, or a large proportion of tenants ; all tenure-holders and all classes of rayots coming under these terms according to the definitions.

4. Scarcely a case of real exigency can be conceived where clause 1 should operate, which is not covered by clause 2, and clause 2 (*a*) gives the option of moving the Local Government for a survey and record to the *landlords* and *tenants* alike. There cannot be any doubt that they are the best judges of their own affair, except, perhaps in a case of agrarian disputes, where they may be said for the time being to be blind to their interests, and in such a case the Local Government has the power to order a survey and record of rights of its own motion, if it thinks the measure calculated to avert serious disputes.

5. But a sound policy of *laissez faire,* where interference is absolutely uncalled for, and is calculated, as we shall show as we proceed further, to be mischievous, is at a discount in India. In the present instance the rayots are thought to be not sufficiently alive to their own interests and to be ignorant of the provisions of the law ; and the Bureau of Agriculture, and, after it, the Government, as their natural guardians, proper parties to move.

6. The action of the Local Government and the Government of India, so far as their power· extends under clause 1 of section 101, is found absolutely unfettered by any Legislative provisions; but there can be no doubt that the Local Goverument can move the Government of India only on reasons shown, and the Government of India in Council can accord such sanction only on sufficient grounds shown.

7. What all parties interested have a right to complain of is that, up to the present moment, the Local Government has simply proceeded on *ex-parte* statements, and it has obtained the sanction of the Government of India on such *ex-parte* statements. Even granting that the Bureau of Agriculture represents the rayots, the alleged dumb millions of.India, and we may perhaps have to say a few words hereafter to dispel the illusion, there was and is another party to the question, and there were recognized accredited channels of communication with that party ; but we know, as a fact, that they have not been taken into confidence in regard to this matter.

8. In the absence of all information regarding the grounds on which the Local Government asked for and obtained the sanction of the Government of India, we are left only to conjectures and surmises. We shall take all possible grounds that suggest themselves to us, and examine them, to see whether they are of sufficient weight to induce Government to launch into such a vast undertaking.

9. The possible grounds which suggest themselves to us are these :—

> 1st.—That the experimental survey and record of rights *promised* has proved a fair success.
>
> 2nd.—That the rayats have not yet in hand a trustworthy re cord of demands, and that such a trustworthy record of demands cannot be obtained without an expenditure of a crore-and-half of rupees.
>
> 3rd.—That there has been such a general increase of rents in the province since the passing of the Bengal Tenancy Act as to lead to a presumption of illegal enhancements having been made.
>
> 4th.—That agrarian disputes of a serious nature have arisen, or are likely to arise, and a general survey and record of rights is the best administrative reform to avert it.

5th.—That the exchequer of the Provincial Government is in such a solvent condition that it can apply its surplus revenue to this reform, and the surplus revenue, if any, cannot be better utilized.

6th.—That it can maintain the large establishment needed for preserving and continuing the record out of the current revenue.

We shall proceed to examine these grounds *seriatim*,

10. As to the first ground, the enactment of the whole of Chapter X., in which comes section 101, having been objected to in the debates on the Bengal Tenancy Bill, His Honour (Sir Rivers Thompson), the then Lieutenant-Governor, said : "With the sanction of the Secretary of State and the Government of India, the utmost we should attempt in the first instance would be one *single district,* and we shall be guided much by the success we meet within *that district* before proceeding further."

Sir Steuart Bayley said : "You have just now heard from His Honour the Lieutenant-Governor that this order of the Secretary of State is still in full force" (we shall refer to the order hereafter), "and that at present he has no intention of going beyond it. Certain provisions of this chapter are, of course, applicable everywhere. A landlord in Bengal Proper may apply to have these settlement operations brought into effect in regard to his estate, or a portion of his estates or, on a *riot taking place* in any *single landlord's estates, the Local Government may apply to the Government of India for permission to put it in force in that estate.* But with regard to a general record of rights, not only is it distinctly understood that the Lieutenant-Governor will apply it only in *some one 'selected district* in Behar and abide by the results of that experiment, *but it is also certain that, as the Secretary of State has not sanctioned anything beyond that, nothing beyond it will be carried out until the Secretary of State does sanction it.'*

His Excellency the President (Lord Dufferin) observed that no one, he imagined, could, in theory, be opposed to the introduction of this chapter. At the same time His Excellency could assure the Hon'ble Members that, not only in deference to the suggestions made to them by the Secretary of State, but also from their own appreciation of the exigencies of the case, the Government of India would be indisposed to consent to the application of the sections referred to otherwise than in the sense and spirit recommended by Lord Kimberley. By applying the machinery of the chapter *to a small and limited area in a tentative way, they would be* able to observe how the clauses were likely to work, and there was every hope that, by that cautious method of procedure, they would be able to obviate the objections to which the Hon'ble Members had referred.

11. Now the only experiment tried in Behar, so far as we are aware of, has been not of a *whole dtstrict*, but of an area of 413 square miles out of 3,004 square miles of that district.

12. Was it a success that would justify the general survey and record of rights of all the districts of this province at an enormous expense ?

13. The pronouncement, so far as the main object ;—the rayat having in hand a trustworthy record of his rights with any amount of certainty, unaffected by changes (transfers, successive partitions) can only be made after a certain number of years have passed, and time must also elapse to show whether any record obtained on a sufficiently comprehensive area would lead to the cessation of litigation and ill-feeling between what are alleged to be two antagonistic interests, and bring on that millennium which is now, on academic grounds alone, sanguinely anticipated as the result of an undertaking of this kind.

14. Now these prospective results are the only results that are to be looked for from such a great undertaking, and the experiment before it can be pronounced a success, must bide time. Even Mr. Finucane, in a meagre Report (First Annual Report of the Director of the Agricultural Department 1886) which, after some enquiry on the subject, we hear is the only report on the subject available to the public, sees this and says :—

Para. 20.—" It would be *premature*, with the information now available, to pronounce a final opinion on the benefits which may be expected from these operations to the landlords and rayats concerned; but if the success of the work may be judged by the absence of friction and of those difficulties which were anticipated in connection with the proceedings, the experiment may be said to have been so far eminently successful." The absence of friction and the absence of difficulties, even if these conditions were found existent in an experiment on the large scale to which the Bengal Government was pledged, would not in any way afford adequate means of judging of the benefits that would be conferred by a general survey and record of rights. There is, therefore, no experiment yet which would justify an undertaking of the sort (pledged or no pledge), and all that we have yet to go by is the old academic arguments and hasty generalizations on the point.

15. Apart from what Mr. Finucane himself says as to its being premature, with the information now available to pronounce a final opinion on the benefits which may be expected from these operations (Experimental Survey of a Tract of 413 square miles in the District of Muzafarpur) to the "landlords and rayats concerned," and the undertaking being expedient only in case of the experiment proving a pronounced success, we have some facts which do not much tend to show that the results arrived at elsewhere by similar operations of the kind give any great hope of success of the kind anticipated.

Turning to the report of Professional Survey of Season 1889-90, District Julpaiguri, p. XIII , Statistical Returns, administration Report for Bengal, 1889-90, we find in the column of Remarks by Executive Officers—Head 'Maps of Previous Surveys' used as a guide to boundaries, the following remarks : " The comparison of the boundaries of the 'time-expired jotes' was not quite so satisfactory owing to the encroachments on 'khas mehals ' in a large number of jotes ' the extreme difficulty in identifying them owing to the change of units, and the faulty character of the information as to towji numbers, &c. obtained in the field from the jotedars. With the ' arable waste land jotes,' however, the greatest trouble has been experienced— very few of the boundaries agree in shape, and from the change in the name of the jotedars, encroachments, want of distinguishing numbers, and various other causes, the comparison with the former records is very tedious and the progress slow."

This bodes ill for the " certainty " that we aim at the future.

16. As for the cessation of litigation, the number of suits of all kinds, in Orissa, Chota. Nagpur and the district of Chittagong, where periodical surveys have been made, does not give evidence of that happy and gradual diminution which is sought for from the general survey and record of rights. They are on the increase, and prove, perhaps, that the increase of litigation is due to other causes than the absence of a general survey and record of rights.

17. Then as to Mr. Finucane's statement regarding absence of friction and difficulties overcome, which, we again say, affords no ade-

quate means of estimating the benefits of the measure, if any, the only points touched on in the meagre Report of the Experimental Survey without sufficient details are these :—

(1). Cheapness of cost ; (2) Small number of suits ; (3) Absence of active opposition.

18. Referring to cost, Mr. Finucane says (para 19 of the Report) : The total cost of the operation of both survey and settlement to the end of July was Rs 1,44,032, or nearly 9 annas per acre on the area which had been cadastrally surveyed ;" and further on he says that the cost need not exceed 8½ annas per area, or about a tenth part of one year's rental.

Turning, however, to the later figures, not in any experimental tract but elsewhere we find that, in 1889-90, 12,08,680 acres were surveyed at a total cost of Rs. 8,32,836-12-0 (*vide* p. 23, Administration Report, Bengal, 1889-90,) *i. e.*, at an expense of 11 annas per acre, and, instead of the figure of expense per acre coming down as Mr. Finucane expects, it is likely to rise, and perhaps, too, this expense of 11 annas per acre does not include the expenditure for the records of rights ; but the point is not sufficiently clear.

19. The average expenditure per acre, calculated as above, is on all kinds of lands,—arable, fallow and waste—lands from which rents, are received, and lands from which no rents are received. Therefore the average, if calculated on arable lands from wich alone rents were received, would be much more. Calculating even at 9 annas per acre, the total outlay necessary for the survey of 44,,192 square miles of Behar would come up to the enormous amount of 1½ million, while the total rental of this province is a little above 4½ millions. Thus the legitimate cost (whoever pays it), even at the lowest figure of 9 annas per acre, would be a third of the rental of this province, for one year—not a tenth part of one year's rental, as the Director of Agricultural Department in his Report calculates.

20. But whether the actual expentiture to Government be at the rate of 9 annas, or 11 annas, per acre or more, this item would, we think, bear a small proportion to the expenditure to be actually incurred by the parties concerned. Mr. Finucane would, perhaps, say that under his model rules, no Amin finds a place in his establishment ; but the rose, without the name, smells as sweet. Would he be able to do without the employment of a subordinate agency on small pay unless he were to add enormously to the expense of the opera-

tions ? Now this individual, call him an Amin or by any other name, would expect to be sumptuously fed, and to retire with a good neat sum from the victimized villages at the end of his tempo-rary service. The rayats will bid, the zemindary amlahs will bid, for the good graces of this mighty official, and for incorrect records, unless the millennium has already come, or is near at hand.

21. Perhaps Mr. Finucane will tell us to trust to him and to his able assistants in the matter. But will not the actual cost be made up of such legitimate expense as these—

(1).—Expense of journey to and from the survey and record offices, both for landlords and tenants, and of witnesses, touters, *et hoc genus omne*, and loss of time.

(2).—Expense of placing a case before the Revenue officers and proving it (dispute or no dispute ; very heavy indeed where dispute arises).

22. Then, as to absence of friction, as evidenced by the small number of suits instituted in connection with the proceedings in the experimental tract. The glimpse given to the public of the experimental survey holds out no very hopeful prospect for the general survey and record of rights. In surveying 413 square miles, there appear to have been 326 boundary disputes. Though we are told that some of these disputes have been amicably settled, we are also told that appeals have been preferred in several cases. The costs to the parties in this litigation it is not easy to calculate. But boundary disputes form only one item of litigation. Mr. Finucane does not tell us how many cases arose in his experimental tract between landlords and tenants as to the nature of the tenants' holdings and the rates of rent, and how many cases there were between rayats as to the title and possession of lands. And even if he had told us this, some amount of assurance would also be necessary as to the competency of the officials engaged under him to try the various and complicated questions that had arisen.

One fact however, is clear from the meagre Report. Out of 26,123 tenants, whose holdings were recorded, in the cases of 7,520 tenants, or about one-third, applications had been made, on behalf either of landlords or tenants, to determine the fair rates, and though the fair rate settled under the rules was the rent actually paid, a fact which Mr. Finucane deprecates, the absence of friction, on which

Mr. Finucane congratulates himself, is not very evident ; for, whatever might have been the actual result, the cost to the parties could
not have been at all small. This is very much the state of things
which would necessarily arise and which makes the people so
anxious ; the experiment, imperfect as it is, shows that there will be
dispute in one out of three cases of rayats' holdings, measured and
recorded. Perhaps if real disputes actually existed and they were
settled in any way—bad, good or indifferent—there would not be
much to complain of ; but what is apprehended is that, with the
advent of the survey party and party for record of rights, disputes
would arise where none previously existed, and the idiosyncracies
of officials would be seized on by designing men, as inducement to
the setting-up of claims without any foundation in fact.

23. The second possible ground on which the sanction of the
Government of India for a general survey and record of rights could
be applied for by the Local Government, is, as we supposed, that the
rayats have not yet in hand a trustworthy record of demands, and
that such trustworthy record of demands cannot be obtained without
an expenditure of a crore-and-half of rupees.

Now, nobody has ever chosen to examine the correctness or
otherwise of the statement that has obtained currency since 1878,
that the Behar rayats have not in hand a trustworthy record of
demands, and that in this matter they are differently and less ad-
vantageously circumstanced than the great body of rayats of Bengal
Proper Let us weigh the facts. A great portion of the whole
area of Behar is comprised in a few Rajes. Two of these big
Rajes, comprising a great portion of the districts of Durbhangah,
Muzafarpur, and Saran, were, within the last twenty years, under the
management of the Court of Wards, and we believe not a pice has
been added to the rent-roll since the proprietors themselves assumed
direct charge of their estates. The whole Durbhangah Raj and a
good portion of the Hutwa Raj was surveyed by the Court of Wards.
A good portion of the Tikari Raj in the district of Gya, and the
Narhan Raj estates in the district of Muzafarpur, are still under the
Court of Wards. The Deo Raj in the district of Gya is being
managed under the supervision of the Collector, under a special Act,
and the Banelly Raj, comprising a good portion of the districts of
Purneah and Bhagulpur, has been for some years under the management of a special officer lent to the Raj by Government.

Other zemindaries not so large as the above, but the total area of which must bear a perceptible ratio to the whole area of the province, have been from time to time under the Collector's management. A small portion of the area of the whole district is also held by Government as khas mehals. Now can, it be said that the statement that the rayats have not a trustworthy record of demands in hand applies to these estates? The rayats, if they were to want it, could get at any time extract copies of rent-roll of their respective holdings from the Collectors' jamabandis, or Government can at any time, by an executive order, cause such copies to be furnished to them.

The Doomraon Raj, comprising a good part of Shahabad, has been extolled by successive Lieutenant-Governors for its good management, and the Betiah Raj, comprising a good part of the District of Champaran, is under the management of a European gentleman enjoying the confidence of Government. Can it be said that the rayats of these estates have not in hand a trustworthy record of demands? If they have not, they have simply to apply to get copies of extracts of jamabandies from these landlords. Then we have records the probative force of which is as good as the probative force of the proposed records will be after a certain lapse of time in cases of estates as follows :—

(1).—Where a measurement and record of rights have been made under section 27 of Act X of 1859 and section 38 of Act VIII of 1868 (B. C.).

(2).—Where a cadastral survey has been made within the last few years in tracts bordering on the irrigation canals.

(3).—Where a thak and survey were made in 1842-43 and settlement thereon. Many estates in this province will be found to come under this category.

(4). Where a partition of estates has taken place, and jamabandies have been filed on the basis of which the raibandi has been made.

(5). Where the jamabandi papers were filed and have been preserved under the orders of the Board of Revenue, uutil the time when such filing was put a stop to by further orders.

(6).—Where a *Teish*-khana, or 23 column Return, under the executive order of the Board of Revenue, has been filed, as in almost all the districts of Behar, showing the nature of holdings and the rates of rent paid.

(7)—In the road-cess returns and valuation statements.

(8).—In the decrees of courts. It will be, perhaps, said that some of these are *ex-parte* proceedings on the part of the landlord ; but they are good evidence in the hands of the rayats to contradict any extract of rent roll filed or tendered to the rayats by the zemindars in excess thereof.

24. The big Behar landholders introduced the system of counter-foil printed receipts some years before the amendment of the Law of landlord and tenant, and it was, we believe, at the suggestion of their organs that the system of receipts, undoubtedly a real improvement, was introduced into the Bengal Tenancy Act. Every rayat ought now to have in hand his counterfoil receipt and annual statement of account ; and section 56 of the Bengal Tenancy Act, and the form of receipt as given in the Act, prescribe the insertion of the particulars of the holding, particulars of the demands, and all details of payment. The annual account, while it prescribes the insertion of the particulars of holdings, provides for the insertion of the demand of the year, balance of former years and details of payment on account of current demand and arrear demand. This receipt the landlord is enjoined, under a penalty, to give the rayat on the occasion of each payment, and the annual statement at the end of every year. They are valuable evidence of the nature of holdings and rates of rent in rayats' hands.

25. It is said that the receipts and annual statements are not being given in all cases, and there may be false entries made in those given. The remedy is in the hands of those who administer the law ; and instead of these points being stated as true off-hand, a little inquiry to determine the facts may not be out of place. We may at once find, by reference to the records of civil and criminal courts, in how many cases receipts have been witheld, or in how many cases false entries have been made. The whole number of suits in Bengal and Behar under the head Rent law and under sub-head Damages for extortion or for withholding receipts, or on account of illegal restraint, or other cause, was 114 in 1889-90, while in 1886-87 it was 337—even in the latter case not a very large number, in all conscience.

26. The Behar Rent Commission, in place of launching the whole country on an expensive and harassing undertaking like this, proposed a speedier and less expensive remedy in order to meet the allegation that the Behar rayats have not in hand a trustworthy record of demands.

They suggested that the landlords should be bound to file in a public office accounts showing the amount of each rayat's rents and the area of his holding· These accounts, they said, might be verified and tested by a public official in the presence of the rayats concerned and a basis might thus be established on which subsequent enhancements or reductions of rent might be made, according as prices might rise or fall. If Government action is needed in the matter at all, the adoption of this suggestion, while serving all the purposes of a cadastral survey and record of rights, would be the least expensive, and, as re-valuations of estates for the purpose of road-cess are made from time to time, the opportunity might be taken of any such occasion to do what is thought needful. No additional expense would be needed, and all chance of useless friction would be avoided. If it were thought necessary, the returns filed on such occasions might be made by an executive order, to show the boundaries of each holding, and in case of dispute, the officer deputed to make the re-valuation might be empowered to settle disputes regarding boundaries, if any.

27. The third ground on which we supposed the Local Government could move the Government of India for sanction for a general survey and record of rights, would be the fact that there has been such a general increase of rents in this province since the passing of the Bengal Tenancy Act as to lead to the presumption that illegal enhancements have been made. We use the words "since the passing of the Bengal Tenancy Act" studiedly ; for all that the Revenue officers of the cadastral survey and record of rights can do, is to fix the "fair rents," and both under the law and the rules framed by the the Board of Revenue under the law and approved by Government, the existing rents are to be taken as "fair rents" unless prices have increased or fallen. With reference to the experimental tract, though, as we have seen, in view of the hopes raised in the rayats, the fixing of "fair rents" was applied for in the case of 7,520 out of 26,123 holdings, Mr. Finucane had to record as "fair" the existing rents. He says (para. 18 of the Report) : "In all cases in which fair rents had been settled, the existing rents were recorded as fair. The law

presumes that the existing rents are fair till the contrary is proved, and does not permit of their reduction except on the ground of a fall in the prices of staple food-crops since the rents were last fixed, or on the ground that the area of the holding is less than that for which the rayat has been paying rent. Neither of these grounds (which alone justify reduction in present rents in order to arrive at fair rents, as defined in the Tenancy Act) having been found to exist, it necessarily results that the existing rents cannot be reduced in order to arrive at the fair rent. On the other hand, landlords have not shown that prices have risen since the rents were last fixed, nor have they adduced evidence that the rayats are holding lands in excess of those for which they are paying rent, so that the result, so far as the procedings have gone, has been, that the existing rents have in every case been recorded as the fair rent." This is an important point, and though elsewhere he says (para. 22) : " It would be out of place to discuss here at any length the question whether the rents now being recorded as fair and equitable are in reality such. The Tenancy Act declares that existing rents must be presumed to be fair, and leaves, as has been already stated, no power to the settlement officers to reduce them, except where it is shown that the price of the produce has fallen since they were last fixed. Prices have not fallen in Behar in the short periods since rents were last fixed, and in this technical sense it may therefore be said that the rents which are being recorded are fair, but it is evident that it would be arguing in a circle thus to define the existing rent as the fair rent, and then to say it is fair because it exists. To record rents as fair in this manner can in no way constitute them fair and equitable according to the common interpretation of those terms. But though it would be premature, at the present stage of the operation, to discuss at length the question whether these existing rents, which are necessarily being recorded as fair and equitable, are in reality such in any true or solid sense of these words ; yet it may be here remarked that if, as the Government of India was satisfied in 1882, " the majority of rayat in Behar are rack-rented,' it follows that the character of these rents will not be altered by merely calling them fair."

The discussion appears to be a purely academic one. This, however, is enough to excite the present alarm in the zemindari body. The views of the head of the Department being thus pronounced, they apprehend that, rightly or wrongly, consciously or unconsciously, these views will be given effect to. But the law passed binds Mr. Finucane and binds the Government, and no sane Government will allow Mr. Finucane to give effect to his own views, in opposition to the law, and to confiscate the property of the zemindars. Mr. Finucane's experiment, however, showing that in all cases existing rents are fair rents as defined in the law, where is the rack-renting, and what necessity is there, from the known results of this experiment, to undertake a general survey and record of rights at an enormous expense?

28. The following figures will show that there has been no gen e-ral increase of rents in this province, so as to lead to the presumption that illegal enhancements have been resorted to —

	Total Road-cess in Behar in Rupees.	Total Public Works-cess in Behar in Rupees.
1885-86	14,87,233	14,72,912
1887-88	14,63,259	14,63,259
1888-89	14,33,353	14,23,353
1889-90	14,80,843	14,80,844

It will, perhaps, be said that the Road-cess and public-Work-cess are levied on a valuation roll made in 1882-83, but the affirm-ative of the proposition that rents have generally been increased in this province, so as to lead to the presumption that elligal en-nancements have been resorted to, has to be proved by those who would choose to rely on this as one of their grounds. From what we know—considering the attitude of courts, and the state of some of the rulings under which Abwabs, consolidated with the *Asal* jama years ago, have been eliminated from the present rents and contracts, not with rayats, but with ticcadars, modified, under the provisions of the Bengal Tenancy Act, we have reason to believe that the next re-valuation will reveal the fact that the general rent-roll of the province has suffered a considerable diminution since 1882-83.

29. In face of the state of the law adopted after 1882, the ques-tion whether the "majority of rayats in Behar are rackrented" comes, as we said, to have merely an academic character. The allegation had been made, and, when it was challenged, the only attempt made, previous to the passing of the Bengal Tenancy Act, to prove it, was to depute four officers to enquire into and ascertain the equitable rent rates in four selected areas. Two of them were appointed for Behar : Mr. Tobin for a selected tract in one of the South Gangetic

districts, and Mr. Finucane for a selected tract in one of the North
Gangetic districts. Mr. Tobin found that, instead of the rayats in
the district of Shahabad being rack-rented, they were prosperous
middlemen, receiving from the body of under-rayats five times as
mnch as they paid to their landlords.

On an examination of Mr. Finucane's Report a writer in the
Calcutta Review, in an article entitled "Is Behar Rack-rented ? An-
Enquiry into the Condition of the Behar Rayats," after closely examining Mr. Finucane's facts and figures, concluded thus : "To sum
up, we have shown that a variety of causes, foremost amongst them
competition and the prevalence of higher rents in the vicinity, have
conduced to bring up the rent rates in the tract examined by Mr.
Finucane : that these rent rates, compared with the rent rates pronounced to be low by a competent authority (Board of Revenue with
reference to Mr. Tobin's report) are not at all high ; that they are
not high with regard to the productiveness of the tract, when compared to the rent rate of the tract examined by Babu Parbati Charan
Rai. That, as a matter of fact, the incidence of rent in the district
of Mozafarpur, as found from the Road-cess returns, is not at all high.
That the valuation per square mile shows that the rent in Mozafarpur
is lower than the rents in several districts of Bengal. That Mr.
Finucane was not at all justified in throwing out of his calculations,
the prices of other valuable products and framing his tables on the
prices of cereals alone ; that even on that calculation it has not at all
been made out that the rents are high and are the result of illegal enhancement. That if private contracts were to be done away with and
only the method of Mr. Finucane adopted, in determining what is
equitable rate of rents, the rent rate, in tract examined by him, would
have to be raised all round, as the following table clearly shows, and
not to be reduced as he recommends :—

NAME OF TRACT EXAMINED.	Average rate per bigha in 1247 F., 1840 A.D.			Add 184 per cent. for increase in prices.			To al being new all-round rate.			Existing all-round rate per bigha.			Percentage of increase on existing rates that will have to be made.
	Rs.	A.	P.	Rs	A.	P.	Rs.	A.	P.	Rs.	A.	P.	
Tubka Khas ...	1	3	4	2	3	4	3	5	8	2	9	9	38
Tubka Magrebi ...	1	1	3	1	15	3	3	0	6	1	11	9	60
Tubka ...	1	9	0	2	13	0	4	6	0	3	5	11	30
Raqbabar. ...	1	14	0	3	6	0	5	2	0	2	4	8	128
Gangow	1	14	8	3	6	0	5	2	8	3	3	6	60

30. Under the fourth ground supposed though, along with other provinces, Behar has been, of late years, the scene of some serious rioting with reference to mosques and temples we are not aware of any agrarian disputes. We have been at some pains to examine the Administration Reports for a number of years, and the number of cases under the rent-law does not give much evidence of any such disputes. Excepting the suits for rent disputes under other heads are merely nominal ; and suits for rent and speedy disposals thereof, are the only points which the Bengal Tenancy Act did not properly pro. vide for.

31. Is, then, the exchequer of the Provincial Government in such a solvent condition, that it can apply its surplus revenue to an undertaking involving such a heavy expenditure ? And cannot such surplus revenue, if it exists, be better utilized for the good of the rayats ?

We have shown that the total outlay required even at the lowest figure of 9 annas per acre, would be $1\frac{1}{2}$ million, and not 88 lakhs, as is said to be the estimate of the Government of Bengal. But taking the result of similar operations elsewhere, we hold that the expenditure is likely to be 12 annas per acre, and not 9 annas, and the total outlay for 44,192 square miles of Behar will be 2 crores of rupees.

32. It will, perhaps, be replied that this expenditure is to be spread over a number of years ; but is the Government of Bengal, under its provincial contracts in any one year, so solvent, that it can spare a good round amount for a work of such questionable utility ? There are hundreds of other reforms which it has to postpone from year to year for want of funds. It has not yet been able to give us the proper contingent of Munsiffs to decide rent-suits. It has given us a sanitary primer ; but if, as, we believe, it cannot do for want of funds, the Bengal Government, as proprietor of lands, were to intro-duce, or assist the rayats in introducing, in all its khas mehal estates, those primary sanitary reforms which are absolutely needed for rural tracts, Bengal and Behar alike, how long could the neighbouring pro-prietors resist the influence of such good examples. Nowhere are " fads " so zealously protected and patronized as in India. One of these ' fads ' is the improvement of our agriculture. Year by year we have spent a good deal of money in maintaining a department which has no results to show, and which can, acccording to an authority whose opinions on the point ought to carry weight, have nothing to

show. Truth is at last, we are happy to say, being tardily recognized, and it was only the other day that Mr. Cotton, in England, said that it is not to improvement of agriculture, but to the development of our manufactures, that we must look to for the salvation of our poverty-stricken people. That poverty will soon reach its climactic point amongst our landless classes, the classes of Noniahs, Jolahas, &c,, who were once prosperous manufacturers and who have now to subsist by precarious day-labour. It is people of this class, and not yet the land-holding rayats, who go half starved from year's end to years's end. It is they who have to stint themselves in the matter of that necessary article of consumption the daily ration of salt.* But if we allow ourselves to go on with our " fads," and do not boldly recognize the fact that, to save people, they must have their manufactures restored, others, now better off than they, will be soon reduced to their position, by over-population, by our inexorable law of partition, and will soon come to share their penurious existence. Mr. Finucane's experimental survey and record of rights established the fact—a fact which was well known to all those acquainted with the economic condition of Behar—that the average total area held by a rayat, whether under the same or different landlords, was, as far as could be ascertained, about three acres. On the produce of these small holdings have to live five or six individuals (*vide* para. 18 and subsequent paras.), and as, every ten years, these small holdings will be divided into smaller and smaller portions, do what we may, in recognizing a peasant proprietorship, or in improving our present system of agriculture, the inevitable must certainly overtake us at last. Already the interest on capital ontlay which we pay from year to year out of the general revenue of this province for the Sone irrigation canals and similar works, is 21 lakhs ; the amount is increasing from year to year, as the canal revenue is diminishing. This sum represents 4 lakhs more than the land revenue of Shahabad, and is almost half the whole rental of that district. Is there any corresponding benefit ? In season of scarcity, when water is needed, the canal gives us no water. and the increased productiveness of the

---

* When this statement was first made by a witness before the excise Commission in a written statement, there appears to have been a stir, and one of the Commissioners was deputed all the way from Rajshahi to Bankipur to cross-examine him on the point. Now the published official Report shows that the average salt consumption in Behar is 9-seers per head, whereas it is 12-seers per head in Bengal.

soil is not such that it has in any way altered for the better the condition of the great mass of the people of the district, or enriched the general resources of Bengal and Behar. The zemindars of Behar have been abused in all quarters and pointed to as the cause of the poverty of the rayats in this province, and a Bengal Tenancy Act has been passed, confiscating half their rights, and yet what is the result ? Every year of scanty rains, or unseasonable rains causes distress amongst the great mass of landless people and alarm in our official body, and a cessation of rains, as was the case in 1874, is sure to bring on another famine. Then will our frantic and spasmodic effort to save people cost us again a crore-and-half, as the district of Dur-bhangha alone cost us in that year, chiefly to fatten contractors who would supply us with rotten rice, and underlings of sorts, and only a small part will be doled out in charitable centres to the famine-stricken people. One might almost be tempted to cry in agony of heart : " Let the poor wretches die, if you have only to save them for the purpose of living a few years of half-starved existence with increased burdens of taxation !"

33. It is time that, before we venture to spend two crores to give effect to another of our " fads," the truth that has been at least recognized, be given effect to. Let the Bengal Government convert Mr. Finucane's Department, partially, if not wholly, into a Bureau of Manufactures and Industries, and if it cannot, consistently with other interests, establish State manufactories on a large scale, let it spend the rents it gets as landlord in assisting its own rayats to set up manufactories for their special benefit. It had to take up the subject of high education, and though the time is not come, in our humble opinion, when it can gracefully retire without prejudice to such education, it might, in the same way, take up the subject of technical education, and retire from it when its aid is no longer wanted.

34. We do not assume, where nothing has been yet said on the matter, that it is intended to tax the landlords and tenants of Behar for the expenses of the proposed survey and record of rights. We have only a word to say in passing : Is there any difference between abwabs which zemindars impose on their rayats and those which the Government impose ? The burden is always the same, we suppose, and if the Government has saved rayats from illegal abwabs by the stringent provisions of the Bengal Tenancy Act, does it behove it to impose legalized abwabs on the rayats on its own behalf ? Did our

Knights of La Mancha save those whom they thought to be victims of zemindari oppression, to lash them to death in their own way

35. Then, lastly, it has to be shown that Government can maintain the large establishment needed for preserving and continuing the record out of its current revenue. In the course of conversation, a high official said the other day : "I do not see why there should be so much opposition, when what we aim at is *certainty* where there has been no *certainty*." He was told that "one of the reasons was, that this certainty cannot last long unless there is a proper arrangement for keeping up a Mutation Register under trustworthy officials."

36. The Secretary of State sanctioned the experiment on the understanding that, in the Patna Division, village accounts and accountants existed. The recent enquiry with reference to the amendment of the Patwari law proves that village accounts and accountants are as much wanting here as in Bengal Proper, and that the imperfect agency which exists up to date does not deserve to exist ; and accordingly the Secretary of State vetoed the proposal for the amendment of the Patwari law and the imposition of the Patwari cess in any shape or form. Since then, we believe, the system of village accounts and accountants supported by a Patwari cess in the North-West Provinces, which had been held up as a model for imitation in Bengal, has received its death-blow, a circumstance which should make the Bengal Government very chary of trying the North-West Provinces' system,—introducing official underlings and letting them loose in our villages. Mr. Finucane recommends, for wards' estates and khas mehals, the introduction of village agency, in the person of an official for every 10 square miles, on a salary of Rs. 20 per mensem, before whom, statements of changes are to be filed and by whom, on notice, objections are to be invited ; the said official, without coming to a decision, merely filing, as a contemporaneous record, both the statements of change and objection, if any. He further recommends the employment of a Deputy Collector for every 500 square miles. Probably, if a general survey and general record of rights were to be made, some such system would be suggested also for places surveyed. The whole establishment that would be needed on the above scale for 44,192 square miles of Behar would be roughly Rs. 88,384 for the officials on 20 rupees monthly, and about 25,000 rupees monthly for the Deputy Collectors, or say a total of Rs. 1,05,000, or an annual expenditure

of Rs 12,60,000 on these items alone. Then record-rooms would have to be made, establishments of other sorts provided for, and contingencies met.

37. A further question will be—whether a petty official on Rs. 20 a month, even for the limited duty which Mr. Finucane would assign him, can be relied on? We are afraid he will be no better than the Patwari, only, with his position recognized and a greater amount of salary given him, he will prove more extortionate. There is a saying current that, as soon as the Police Jamadar of old, whose salary used to be Rs. 7 a month, came to get Rs. 30 a month under the Constabulary system, he began to demand four goats from the village visited where he used to ask for, and have only one goat before, referring to the fact that his salary has been increased four-fold.

The preservation of records, the noting of contemporaneous changes, must, at least be entrusted to these men, and they will, we are afraid, find opportunities therein of aggrandising themselves, and not be such innocuous beings as Mr. Finucane expects. A little story appears *ápropos* :. Once an *Omedwar* went on worrying a Sahib, as Omedwars alone know how to do, to give him some kind of employ-ment. The Sahib, to get rid of the man asked him to employ himself in counting the waves of a neighbouring river. Armed with the Sahib's order in this behalf, he sat on the river bank and called upon all passing boats to stop and not interfere with his counting of the waves, till, to get rid of the annoyance, every passing boat settled on him a fine fee, and the *dustoori* for counting the waves came to be very profitable indeed to our Omedwar.

But what about the " certainty," if there is to be no decision on disputed points?

38. We have seen that the annual expenditure on one item alone will come up to Rs. 12,60,000, and that, taking into consi-deration all expenses, the annual expenditure for preserving and continuing the record cannot be less than Rs. 20 lakhs. Where is the money to come from? The landlords and tenants cannot be asked to pay. On a consideration of all matters, the Secretary of State is understood to have vetoed the imposition of a cess for the maintenance of the records in any shape or form, either in substitu-tion for, or in addition to, any existing cess for the maintenance of village accountants.—*Vide* para. 27 of Mr. Finucane's Report.

Is it proposed that this decision shall be reconsidered and revised? It will be an evil day both for landlords and tenants if additional cesses are to be imposed on them.

39. The present, again, is a season of scarcity. The *Hatia* did not bring that abundance of rain which was wanted, and the rains were otherwise unseasonable. By all accounts, only an eight annas crop is expected, and it is feared there will be some amount of distress, if not an actual famine.

40. It is an open secret that one of the members of the Board of Revenue, who knows Behar intimately, and some of the local officials, are opposed to the measure, and it is to be taken up only to give effect to the views of a few officials who think that the rayats will jump at the idea, and the rents be fixed for 15 years. In some part of the province rents have remained fixed for the last 60 years, and yet the halcyon days for rayats have not come. But, consistently with the provisons of the Act, we wonder how it is hoped that rents will remain fixed for 15 years simply through a record of rights being made.

41. The Secretary of State is said to have ruled, at the close of the year 1885-86, that the Experimental Survey should be abandoned·—*Vide* page 5, Bengal Administration Report, 1885-86.

We appeal to the Local Government to consider and to pause.

GURU PROSHAD SEN.

BANKIPUR,

22ud November 1891.

N. B.—Since this article was written, a Government Resolution, dated 9th November, on the Cadastral Survey and Record of Rights, has been published; but the arguments against the proceeding remain unaffected.

The landholders of Bengal have been greatly alarmed by vague and contradictory reports, touching the objects and intentions of Government in regard to the proposed Cadastral Survey. We are glad that the Government of Bengal has recorded a careful Resolution on the subject. It will clearly show the intentions of Government, and the land-owning classes will know exactly what position they should take in dealing with this important question.

The Bengal Tenancy Act (Sec. 101) provided that the Local Government may, in any case, with the previous sanction of the Governor-General in Council, make an order directing that a Survey be made, and a record of rights be prepared, in respect of the lands in a local area by a Revenue-officer. Soon after the Tenancy Act came into force a proposition was made for the survey of the Mozufferpore district as an experimental measure. Referring to this proposition the Secretary of State observed :—

"While fully admitting the advantages which would attend the establishment of village records and accounts, the formation of a record-of-rights, and the introduction of a field survey, I cannot avoid the apprehension that the difficulties of carrying out these measures in those parts of Bengal in which village accounts and accountants, if they ever existed, have long ago entirely disappeared, even from tradition and remembrance, may prove greater than you anticipate. Your present proposal, however, merely contemplates an experimental commencement of the work in the Patna Division of the Province of Behar, where the need for it is, you think, most pressing, and the conditions least unfavourable; and to this I will make no objection."

The survey was undertaken, and the results, in the opinion of the late Lieutenant-Governor, proved to be satisfactory. The Government of India concurred in Sir Steuart Bayley's view that it was desirable to extend the measure to other tracts. In reviewing the correspondence the Secretary of State observed that, even if the continuous maintenance of the village record could not be fully secured, still an accurate knowledge of existing facts would be of great advantage as affording a basis on which a better state of things might grow up under the Tenancy Act, and that a survey and record of rights ought to be attempted in other permanently settled tracts, where doubts prevailed as to existing tenures and rents. In September 1889, Sir Steuart

Bayley after considering the question in all its bearings, decided to resume the Mozufferpur experimental survey-settlement proceedings, and asked the Government of India to accord sanction under the Tenancy Act to a survey and settlement of rights of the Patna Division. Having regard, however, to the partial failure in the Patna Division of the autumn and winter harvests of 1888-89, and to the serious injuries caused by the floods of 1889 to the autumn crops in Champarun, Mozufferpur and Durbhunga, he proposed to postpone the commencement of the work until the effects of these calamities of season had disappeared. The Government of India stated in reply that no final decision could be given authorizing the survey until the question of cost and the share which it was proposed to accept on the part of Government was accurately determined. The question reserved has been determined, and the whole subject has again been recently laid before the Government of India, and proposals have been submitted for carrying out the survey and settlement of the four districts of the Patna Division which lie north of the river Ganges.

The Government of Bengal clearly represented the difficulty of the work in prospect, and the fact that the scheme would not in the commencement commend itself favourably to the landed interests concerned. But Sir Charles Elliott expressed his complete concurrence with the views expressed by his predecessor that the advantages which would accrue to the people from the survey and settlement proceedings would outweigh the inconveniences and difficulties that might arise. His Honour entirely agrees with all that has been said during the course of the discussion as to the advantage and, indeed, the absolute necessity, of such a survey-settlement if administration is to be conducted with complete and accurate knowledge of economic facts, if famine is to be successfully combated when it comes, and if the relations of landlords and tenants are to be put on a secure and definite basis by the authoritative registration of areas held and rents fixed. He regards such a measure as a necessary corollary to the Permanent Settlement and as the only way in which Government can give full effect to the principles laid down by the Bengal Tenancy Act as to the rights of the different classes of ryots by creating an accurate record of those rights, and establishing a system for registering them in future.

The proposed operations have now been sanctioned by the Government of India. Arrangements are being matured for making a commencement of the work this season. The field-to-field survey will be up in November next year. The reasons why it is in contemplation to confine the survey and settlement to the district of North Behar are that the evils arising from the uncertainties of tenures and want of a record of rights have been felt there more than elsewhere, on account of the poverty and density of the population

The objects of the cadastral survey and settlement of Behar, says the Resolution under notice, are to obtain an accurate record (1) of the area and situation of all villages and estates, of each tenure and of each ryot's holding within an estate, and (2) of the status of every one who has rights in the land and of the rent paid by each ryot and tenure-holder. In other words, the intention is to carry out accurately what every zemindar is understood to attempt to carry out more or less accurately, but 'often fails in doing.'

On every estate zemindari accounts are kept up, which correspond in all but accuracy to the *khasra* and *khatian* of the settlement, and it is incredible that the zemindars should really wish not to have the opportunity of making these accounts correct. The Lieutenant-Governor has recently ascertained by personal enquiry the value which gentlemen of such experience as Messrs. Burrows, Thomson and Mylne of Beehea in Shahabad attach to the information collected in the cadastral survey which was effected for the canal-irrigated villages in that district. His Highness the Maharaja of Tipperah is so convinced of the utility of a cadastral survey that he has recently made application to the Government to have such a survey carried out in all his estates which lie in British territory. It is within the knowledge of the Court of Wards and of Government that, in the zemindaries which have come under the temporary management of the Court, there is generally an ignorance on the part of the late proprietors' officials of the rights and interests appertaining to the estate which is altogether incompatible with successful administration. In one important estate still under the Court whole mehals had been lost sight of and had paid nothing to the proprietors for many years : in other estates, where survey-settlements had to be undertaken, it came to light that managers were ignorant whether the estates were compact or scattered, or where the lands were situated. It is a fact also, of which zemindars must be fully cognizant, that purchasers of estates are often unable to find out what are the boundaries of the property they have bought or to obtain any records showing who the ryots are, where their lands lie, or what their rents are. These are instances of the inconveniences and defects which would all be removed by a field-to-field survey and an accurate record of rights.

Referring to the gain to the ryot, His Honor says that the law has bestowed on him certain rights, and the Government has decided that it is the duty of the administration to provide him with the means of knowing precisely wherein they consist. This knowledge will benefit him in his dealings with his zemindar in any dispute as to the rent due to him, with indigo-planters when he wishes to lease his fields to them, and with the Opium Department officers when he applies for an advance for growing opium on his land. With regard to the cost of the proceedings the Gevernment of Bengal has come to the conclusion that the entire charge cannot be safely taken at less than eight annas an acre, though it is hoped that there will be some reduction in the expenditure when the operations are undertaken on a wider scale than they have hitherto been carried out anywhere.

" Of this estimated cost of 8 annas an acre, the Government of India has accepted the charge of one-eighth of the total expenditure as respecting the cost of traverse surveys. Of the rest the Lieutenant Governor has decided that half, or three-and-a-half annas an acre, should be paid by the zemindars, and the other half divided among the subordinate interests. Thus a ryot holding an area of 3 or 4 acres may have to pay 10½ or 14 annas, an amount which certainly cannot be considered excessive, since it ensures him security in the possession of those rights which the Tenancy Act has declared to belong to him. The lowest charge for a copy of an extract from the *jamabundi* exceeds one rupee, and His Honour understands that cultivators often pay even larger sums for documents or considerations of much less real value than the extracts from the *khasras* and *khatians* will be to them. The zemindars who own larger properties will necessarily have larger total sums, but not proportionately larger charges to pay : but in return, though no general increase in the rents of ryots can be contemplated, they will reap some return from the discovery of concealed holdings, and of tenures in which a large increase of area has taken place without any corresponding rise in rent, which will go some way towards compensating them for the outlay entailed upon them. Moreover, the survey itself will, it has been calculated, take about five years for two parties at the rate of 2,500 square miles a year, so that the total sum payable by the general body of zemindars each year will be distributed over a considerable period. In some cases no doubt, the aggregate amounts which will fall upon single zemindars in any one year will be large ; and to meet this diffi-culty the Government intends to facilitate payments by allowing them to be liquidated by instalments. Sir Charles Elliott has no doubt what-ever that in the end the zemindars will find the results well worth the money they will have, under the law to pay for the survey and settle-ment operations. He feels sure that the zemindars of the large estates in which such proceedings have recently been completed would agree in the view that they have received by an accurate and a well-ordered rent-roll which has been generally accompanied by a slight increase in rents, good value for their expenditure. It is the Lieutenant-Governor's in-tention to have published shortly an account of what the surveys and records of rights in those large estates have cost and the returns they have produced to the landlords, so that the zemindars of North Behar will be in a position to judge for themselves of the advantageous results which they may anticipate.

An assurance has been given that exsisting rights will in no way be touched.

We have also been assured that Government has not the remotest intention of undertaking the Survey in Bengal.

HINDOO PATRIOT, NOVEMBER 23, 1891.

THE Maharaja of Darbhanga made a telling speech at the Sonepur meeting. We publish his speech *in extenso* in another column. It will amply repay perusal. The Maharaja has clearly pointed out the evil consequences of the proposed Survey. He has formulated the grounds of objections. The objections lie in a nutshell. The heavy expense which the Survey will entail upon the landholders and the ryots, and the harassing litigation which it will create will be simply ruinous to the landowning classes. The Maharaja observes :

In Behar there will not only be the actual expenses incurred by Government in making the survey, but in addition there will be the crushing expenses of litigation to which the survey will give rise, and I need hardly say that both zemindars and ryots contemplate this litigation with horror. It is quite certain that the ryots cannot in the present state of the district afford to enter into litigation without impoverishing themselves, and it is equally certain they will litigate to the utmost, as shown by experience in other districts where cadastral surveys have been made. I am told that in the recent survey of a portion of the Purneah District over 2,400 cases were filed by the zemindars and ryots against the survey proceedings. Purneah, you all know, is the most thinly populated district of Behar. A great portion of the land is either a jungle or under water. In the densely-populated districts of Behar there will be infinitely more cases, and with appeals to higher courts which this litigation will involve it will be years before the settlement of a district is completed. I can imagine the confusion that will result while this litigation is pending, and cannot help thinking that the Lieutenant-Governor has not had his attention directed to this view of the subject. If we could have a cadastral survey effected without litigation and without harassment and expense to which this litigation will give rise, both zemindars and ryots would accept it with pleasure, but we zemmindars know that this is impossible. A cadastral survey with its record of rights means years of litigation, and this litigation will be equally ruinous to both zemindars and ryots.

Litigation and expense then are the two evils which will be inflicted upon the landholders by the Cadastral Survey. If they could be avoided by some magic influence, the measure could be tolerated, if not welcomed.

His Honor the Lieutenant-Governor, in replying to the address of the Tirhut Zemindars said that were he himself a landholder in the country, he would welcome a complete survey. It was very necessary that there should be some accurate record of the areas and situation of all the estates and of the character of the tenures and holdings in them. Put in an abstract form, the truth of such a proposition is incontrovertible. It is only when such a proposition is proposed to be carried out in practice that we realise its impractical character. The real question at issue is whether the advantages will outweigh the disadvantages: Opinion is at variance on this point. Government says that the measure will be beneficial to landholders, while the landholders affirm that it will be positively harmful to their interests, it will stir up litigation, create new claims, and revive the old. The harmony between the landlords and their tenants will be destroyed, and the ill-feeling which is sure to be created will be productive of incalculable mischief. Where then is the unmixed blessing which is promised ?

His Honor also told the Tirhut landholders that the cost was but a small matter when compared with the great advantages to be derived from the Survey. The landholders respectfully differ from His Honor with regard to the supposed advantages. An accurate survey and an accurate record of rights may be very good in their way. But considering· the vexation, the harassment, the discord, and ruinous expense, with which the Survey will be attended, the question is, will this ' accurate' Survey and record of rights be of the slightest benefit to either the landlords or tenants ? The 'accurate' Survey may be of use for statistical purposes, but landlords and tenants naturally fail to realise the benefit of *accurate* statistics when these are to be obtained by their impoverish-ment and ruin. His Honor said that he could give the zemindars the most positive assurance that every possible care would be taken to avoid all oppression, or fraud, or unnecesssry expense in carrying out the work. The assurance given by His Honor is of course of the highest value, and we are absolutely certain that His Honor will severely punish any breach of thé rule which he will lay down. But will all cases of fraud and oppression come to light, or to his notice ? Any one who knows anything of our administrative machinery is aware that cases of fraud and oppression, especially in relation to survey and settlement, can by no means be reached by legal processes. They are concocted in the dark, and the Head of the Admininstration will never be able to pry into the nefarious practices. These cases of fraud and oppression will defy detection.

Then His Honor speaks of unnecessary expense. Even the necessa-ry expense will be such as landlords and ryots will not be able to bear. Government estimates the cost at 8 annas per acre. But Government does not take into account the additional expense which the measure will entail upon the landholders and the ryots. The zemindars will have to entertain a large establishment to follow the Government Sur-veyors and Amins, to incur expense for providing supplies, and to bear other *et cetera* expenses which need not be mentioned. The ryots also will have to bear the same burden, though not to such an extent. They will also have to follow the settlement officers in person to the neglect of their proper work in the fields. This means utter ruin both to the landlords and themselves. It can easily be seen now how the estimated cost of 8 annas will swell into 8 Rs. per acre. We do not exaggerate, when we say that the cost will come to some 8 Rs., if we include the litigation expenses. Those that ever had the misfortune of going to litigation are well aware what a capacious stomach our courts and the court-followers and the litigants' *amlah* have when a case comes up to court for settlement. There will be an immense crop of litigation to the delight of the court-followers and the *amlah*. Witness the boundary cases in the survey settlement of the Banuli and Srinagar estates. We wish the settlement records of the Srinagar estate would be published They will clearly show that the apprehensions of the landholders that the survey-settlement operations will prove ruinous to the landholders and tenants are not groundless.

A correspondent asks us whether there are any means by which the threatened evil could be averted, and his estate saved. We may assure our correspondent that it is never too late to make a respectful representation to Government regarding the real state of affairs. If Government finds that the work has been undertaken on incorrect information, it will never shrink from reconsidering its position. What the landholders ought to do is that they should face the difficulty which has arisen, and represent to Government the real situation. Government, it should always be remembered, will never allow anything to be done which may have the effect of injuring in any the slightest degree " the just rights of single individual or of a class." We have the distinct assurance of His Honor the Lieutenant-Governor on this point, and there need be no apprehension that just rights will be touched.

The Committee of the British Indian Association have been engaged for some time in collecting information regarding the Survey. They applied for copies of correspondence on the subject, and represented to Government that the landlords have been greatly alarmed by the vague reports which have been circulated regarding the proposed survey. They respectfully wished to know the reasons which had induced the present Lieutenant-Governor to resume a survey which had been abandoned by his predecessor. They also submitted that a report had reached them that the provisions of the Tenancy Act relating to survey and settlement would be generally enforced throughout the permanently settled districts of Bengal, Behar and Orissa. In reply the Government has given to the Association a digest of the correspondence, and this digest has been embodied in the recent Resolution on Cadastral Survey.

In forwarding a copy of the Resolution to the Association, Government says : —" The Association will see from the sketch given of the proceedings up to the present time that the late Lieutenant-Governor did not abandon the project of survey, but only postponed it for causes which were avowedly temporary. They will also perceive that the Lieutenant-Governor does not intend to enter upon a survey and record-of-rights of the whole of the Lower Provinces, Bengal, as they appear from their letter under acknowledgment to apprehend." We see that it is not the intention of Government to extend the survey settlement operations to Bengal proper. This is so far satisfactory. But this does not in any manner take away in the slightest degree the grave responsibility which lies upon the British Indian Association, which represents the landed interests of Bengal, Behar and Orissa. The Association, is bound to guard the interests of the Behar landholders just as well as those of Bengal and Orissa. Most of the large landholders of Behar are members of the Association, and we are sure the Committee of the Association, in which the Behar Zemindars are strongly represented, will take such steps to avert the calamity as will prove efficacious. The Committee, we are assured, are keenly alive to the absolute necessity of taking prompt measures, and we earnestly hope that their efforts in remedying the impending evil will be successful.

ENGLISHMAN OF 3RD DECEMBER, 1891.

THE BENGAL CADASTRAL SURVEY.

TO THE EDITOR OF THE " ENGLISHMAN."

SIR,—As His Highness the Maharaja of Durbhunga said in his Sonepur speech, if a cadastral survey is undertaken, it will certainly not be at the request of either the zamindars or the ryots of Behar. But more than this. I find, as a matter of fact, that it will be in direct opposition to the deliberately expressed opinion of some of the most able and experienced officers under the Government of Bengal. It will be remembered that at the time of the discussion over the Bengal Tenancy Bill (now-Act VIII of 1885) all the District Officers were consulted, and I will quote some of the opinions then elicited from them with regard to the provisions of Chapter X. (provisions for cadastral survey and general record of rights) to prove the assertion that I have made above.

Mr. Beames, who was then Commissioner of the Bardwan Division, was of opinion that " to introduce the system into an old and permanently settled province will not only be very expensive but will stir up agitation and litigation on all sides. The officers whom I have consulted agree with me in thinking that the whole procedure is objectionable, and in hoping that the country is not about to be plunged into a state of confusion, unparalleled since the days of Native rule, merely for the purpose of endeavouring to arrive at a result which can never be attained."

Stronger language could not be used, I suppose, and the zemindars now oppose the proposal exactly on the same grounds as Mr. Beames, namely, on the ground of practical difficulties in the way of success. To a theoretical proposition like the one put by the Lieutenant-Governor of Bengal before the Tirhut landholders in reply to their address, that a complete survey and accurate record of rights would be a desirable result to attain, there can be only one answer, an answer in the affirmative; but that result can never be attained without sacrifices disproportionate to its value—without "plunging the country into a state of confusion unparalleled since the days of Native rule," as Mr. Beames expressively puts it, as his own and the opinion of the Collectors under him; and if the purchasers refuse to bargain for a boon at a price which they consider to be excessively high, Government, even though they may have the might, ought not to be guilty of the unwisdom, to say nothing of the impropriety, of forcing it down their throats.

Mr. Lowis, Commissioner of the Bhagulpur Division, and all the Collectors under him, objected to a cadastral survey, on the ground that the whole of its effect "will be lost unless arrangements are made for the mutation of names, &c., after the record is complete." Mr. Oldham, Deputy Commissioner of the Sonthal Pergunnahs, where a cadastral survey was made, acknowledged the difficulties of the operation and candidly confessed that it would be useful for a certain period, having proved so for nine years only in the Sonthal Pergunnahs. He would not attempt to keep up the record by entering mutations "in consideration of the vastness of the work."

An ounce of fact, it is said, is worth more than a ton of theories. Mr. Oldham spoke from personal experience of what actually happened in the Sonthal Pergunnahs where a cadastral survey was carried out. The effect of the survey was lost after the short period of nine years. No attempt was made to keep up the record owing to the vastness of the work, and, as a matter of fact we know that a fresh survey is being at the present moment carried on in some portions of that tract of the country. These are facts, and facts which constitute a terrible indictment against the wisdom of the present proposal.

A few considerations here suggest themselves to me. So far as it now appears from the Government Resolution and the public utterances of the Lieutenant-Governor, there is no indication that any endeavour will be made to keep the records up to date by mutation of names. On the contrary, the Secretary of State is said to have expressed the opinion that " even if the continuous maintenance of the village record cannot be fully secured, still an accurate knowledge of existing facts would be of great advantage," &c., &c. His Honor himself lays a great deal of stress in the Resolution on the necessity of such knowledge for administrative purposes. It then follows in the first place that Government will be a party benefited by the proposed cadastral survey, as it will afford them an " accurate knowledge of existing facts" for administrative purposes. And, in the second place, it follows, that the advantages offered to the zemindars are of secondary importance in actuating the Government to undertake the survey, as " the continuous maintenance of the village record cannot be fully secured." Under these circumstances it is only reasonable for the zemindars and the ryots to protest against being saddled with the cost of the survey. A better administration, as the result of a more accurate knowledge of existing facts, would equally benefit the classes interested in land as well as the landless classes, and it is but just that the cost ought to come from the general exchequer, and not from taxation on any particular class.

On the other hand, should an endeavour be made to maintain the records, to the cost of the survey—a " small matter," as the Lieutenant-Governor told the Tirhut landholders—will have to be added the annual cost of maintenance, which even the Lieutenant-Governor may not find in his heart to characterise as a " small matter," constituting, as it will, a crushing, permanent burden on the classes interested in land who have to pay in direct taxes in cesses alone double the amount of tax leviable on incomes other than those from land.

I propose to deal with other aspects of the question in a future letter.

M. NARAYAN.

Bankipur, November 26.

ENGLISHMAN OF 9TH DECEMBER 1891.

THE BENGAL CADASTRAL SURVEY.

TO THE EDITOR OF THE "ENGLISHMAN."

SIR,—Mr. Wilson, Collector of Midnapur, thus graphically pour-trayed the immense practical difficulties by the almost fabulous cost of the preservation by continuance of the record :—

"The proposed operations would be of no permanent value with-out the means of correcting the records and keeping them up to date, and I do not think it would be wise to enter upon a project, involving the expenditure of nearly four crores of rupees [the estimate here is for the whole of the territories under the Lieutenant-Governorship of Bengal, and is undoubtedly an under estimate] without considering how the record of rights is to be kept up, and what the annual cost of keeping it up would be. This is the more necessary, as to prevent the confusion which must result from the accumulation of arrears, the process of correction should follow closely on the preparation of the original record." Mr. Wilson then proceeded to point out that "the amount of work in respect of transfer and leases alone may be to some extent estimated by referring to the statistical returns of the Registra-tion Department, which show that 1,34,250 transfers and 19,519 were registered in the year 1882-83. If the survey of any district were complete it might be possible to require the survey numbers to be given in all leases and transfer deeds. The Registry Office could then furnish the Survey Office with the needful particulars regarding all registered transactions. This would be troublesome and expensive, and a considerable permanent staff would be required in the Survey Office. It must be remembered, however, that long before the survey and record of rights of any district was complete, and before, therefore, the mention of survey numbers in documents relating to land could be made compulsory, a considerable number of changes would have oc-curred, and consequently there would be much difficulty in bringing the entries up to date. With regard to the numerous transactions which are not registered, including enhancements, it will probably be suggested that the necessary information should be collected by means of patwaris. But the cost of this would be very great. If any reli-ance is to be placed on a patwari's papers, he must have a decent salary, and it can hardly be thought that Rs. 10 a month—the lowest pay of a mohurir—would be too large an amount to give in order to raise him above the temptations which surrounded him. Now, there are in Bengal 2,48,706 villages, and if the odd 48,706 be omitted as uninhabited, a patwari on Rs. 10 a month in each of the remaining 200,000 would cost in all Rs. 2,40,00,000 a year, or nearly two and-a-half crores of rupees. I take no account of the cost of the establishment which would be required in each district for the purpose of arranging and entering in the records the information supplied by patwaris, nor is it necessary to discuss here the percentage of dishonest or otherwise erroneous entries likely to be found in a patwari's papers. Who would bear the cost I know not, but whether the money is to come from Government or the zemindars, I would suggest that this large income, if really available from any source, should be devoted to the rapid construction of railways, canals and roads, as large public works of this class are, in my judgment, likely to be more useful than patwaris."

Lord Ulick Brown, Commissioner of the Rajshye Division, also had his attention drawn to this aspect of the question with the full concurrence of all the Collectors under him. He thus formulated his objections :—

" A record made in 1885 that A is an occupancy holder of holding B may be quite useless in 1888 owing to A leaving it, and to its being split into three holdings given to three non-occupancy ryots, or split into four bits, two of which are given to non-occupancy ryots and two to adjacent occupancy holdings, thus also affecting the record of this holding made in 1885. I do not think it would be possible by any legal provision to obtain correct information of the numerous changes in permanently settled estates, and if it were possible the business of recording changes would be so vast that it does not seem advisable to undertake it,...I think, therefore, that it is not worth while undertaking an operation of such magnitude in order to secure such limited advantages as could be expected from it, while much forgery and perjury would be inevitable."

Let alone the preservation and continuance of the record, even the accuracy of the entries made in it appeared to Mr. Wilson, whose opinion I have quoted in a preceding paragraph, as a matter difficult of attainment. It would thus seem that the temptation of an accurate record held out to the Tirhut landholders by Sir Charles Elliott and the expectations formed by him of great administrative advantages to follow the possession of such an "accurate" record by Government both resolve themselves into nothing.

Mr. Wilson thus points out how inaccuracies must necessarily creep in :—

"Every one concerned being hostile to the whole proceeding, no one would be very ready to give correct information. The general feeling in such cases is that if there must be a survey it is advisable to cripple its power of evil by supplying as many erroneous or distorted facts as may be. The statements of landords and tenants regarding rents and rights would not be found to agree, and it will not always be easy to decide which is right·····..., and I fear that when all is said and done any such general record will contain a very considerable percentage of erroneous entries."

The Commissioner of the Chittagong Division was equally pronounced in his opinion. Admitting the want of authoritative agricultural records in Bengal, he proceeded to say that "the work of effecting a remedy is truly a gigantic task, and if attempted on the proposed lines an impossible one." He apprehended that "almost every single entry" with regard to rent would lead to a "protracted dispute," and then went on to observe : "It would be possible to make out a record which will show only the status and position of the tenant, though even that would be a task of no mean magnitude ; but once we attempt to touch the question of rent we enter on an enquiry that covers the whole dispute which is at present agitating the agricultural community in Lower Bengal and putting such a strain on the relations existing between landlords and tenants. It may be necessary to enter on a work of such magnitude for the preservation of the public peace, but I do not consider that anything short of a grave crisis will be held to justify our taking in hand so intricate and delicate an undertaking."

I propose to conclude my remarks on this subject in a third letter.

Bankipur, November, 28.   M. NARAYAN.

ENGLISHMAN OF 10th DECEMBER 1891.
THE BENGAL CADASTRAL SURVEY.

TO THE EDITOR OF THE "ENGLISHMAN."

SIR,—I believe that "almost every single entry" in the record of rights will be disputed. The conclusion drawn from the results of the experiments already made, to the effect that there will be no increase in litigation, is absolutely worthless. In the first place the experiments have not as yet extended even to one complete district. In the second place, the public have yet but got an imperfect glimpse of the results of these experiments, and these results have yet to withstand t he test of public criticism. In the third place, they have to withstand the more important test of time—time alone can prove or disprove the capacity of these operations to increase or decrease litigation. In the fourth place, the reports which Government have received with regard to the results of these experiments are at best the *ex parte* statements of a Department which has to justify its existence by show of useful work, and is therefore vitally interested in showing the bright side of the picture only. It would, therefore, be but a common precaution to test these reports by the result of independent enquiries. And in the last place, we have the positive assurance of both the zamindars and the ryots that they are in the habit of litigating on much less provocation than that which will be afforded by a cadastral survey and general record of rights. Coming to some of these experiments in particular, the cases of the Banelli and Srinugger estates in the Purneah District are certainly not typical of all Behar. Purneah, as His Highness the Maharaja Bahadur of Durbhunga pointed out in his Sonepur speech, is the most thinly populated district in Behar, a great portion of the land is either jungle or under water, and there is not, therefore, that feverish anxiety in the minds of the zamindar or the ryots for the possession of every inch of land. If, therefore, there were 2,000 cases, instituted against the survey pro-ceedings, carried on in a portion of the Purneah district, we shall not be wide of the mark in estimating the number of cases at 24,000 or even 48,000 in such congested districts as Sarun and Shahabad, where land is so valuable, and the people are so litigious that they have been known to fight for even 1-20th part of a beegha up to the Privy Council.

I will conclude by quoting the opinion of Mr Cotton, then an officiating Commissioner, now one of the Secretaries to the Govern-ment of Bengal. Mr. Cotton was "constrained" to say, that he looked with "anxiety" on the provisions of the Bill which empowered the local Government to undertake a cadastral survey "in any case with the previous sanction of the Governor-General in Council." "The proposal to introduce a survey and record of right over the whole of

Bengal, wrote Mr. Cotton, " is by no means the panacea which some seem to consider it." He did not dwell so much on the difficulties of the proposal, but he objected to it " on the very ground on which it was generally supported." Mr. Cotton then went on in his own ex pressive and eloquent way to say : " It is well, no doubt, that an independent agricultural record should exist which neither zamindar nor zamindar's amla could transfer. [Para. 103 of Government of India's Despatch No. 6, dated 21st March, 1882.] Such record is very desirable on many grounds, but I see no reason for supposing that it will bring with it a general agricultural settlement or any material increase of rural prosperity. And a result has not ensued in those provinces in India in which a survey and record of rights has been accomplished. It is not fair to compare the North-West Provinces with Bengal, as other causes have led to the accumulation of wealth in our favoured province ; but I certainly do not find any evidence to show that the recordal of rights has led to the enrichment of the peasantry of Upper India.

And I am sure of this that in Bengal, where, owing partly to the accident of the Permanent Settlement, it has hitherto been the policy of Government to interfere as little as possible with the people, the attempt to make a survey and record of rights will give rise to great local opposition and to excessive litigation, by which many per- sons who are now well off will be impoverished. A survey and record of rights is necessary where disputes exist, where oppression prevails, and where the peasantry are poor and need protection. For this reason, the provisions of the Bill are likely to prove useful, if they are judi- ciously enforced. But over most part of Bengal it cannot be alleged that there are disputes, oppression or poverty ; to introduce a settle- ment of rents and record of rights in Bengal generally will merely excite disputes and kindle litigation. The normal relation of landlord and tenant in these provinces is one of compromise ; it is true that rights are unadjusted, the balance of rent is undetermined ; the current demand of rent is not fixed ; the area of cultivation is often unknown ; it is for the convenience of both parties that the claims of either are not put to the test, and yet it is not the case that the ordinary relations between landlord and tenant are unfriendly. The narrow induction drawn by local officials from occasional disturbances which come to their notice misleads them, and has misled Government into the delu- sion that general disaffection exists. The one or two cases of disturbance come prominently to notice, the thousands and thousands of instances in which order and contentment prevail pass by unobserved. But the existing state of things, which is satisfactory because it is in accordance with the custom of the country and not objected to by any, will certainly not continue after the appearance of the ' Revenue Officer' in the districts.

All that was elastic and unsettled will, under the new procedure, be stereotyped and fixed, and both parties will struggle with one another to the utmost in the Civil Courts in order that disputes may be decided which would never have arisen if the Surveyor's rod and the Settlement Officer's registers had not galvanised them into life. It is difficult to over-estimate the bitterness of feelings which a survey and record of rights will thus provoke. The evil, I think, will out-weigh any administrative advantages derived from it. I venture also to think that most persons who are competent from their experience and knowledge of these provinces to form an opinion on the subject will be found to agree with me in this deliberate conclusion, that a survey and record of rights, if it is calculated to settle disputes where they already exist, is equally calculated, where they do not, to call them into existence."

Sir Charles Elliott was pleased to tell the Tirhut landholders that the "high officers" with him, two of whom were named, "firmly be lieved that the survey was absolutely necessary and would prove most beneficial." The opinions of the "high officers" whom I have quoted above, the opinions of four or five Commissioners, endorsed probably by more than a dozen Collectors, are, I humbly beg to submit, entitled to as much respect as those of the two officers whom His Honor named.

M. NARAYAN.

Bankipur, November 26th.

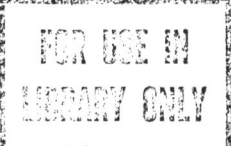

Lightning Source UK Ltd.
Milton Keynes UK
UKOW06f1932150816

280765UK00018B/350/P